# Experimental Psychopathology

## Recent Research and Theory

# CONTRIBUTORS

ABRAM AMSEL

JOSEPH V. BRADY

ROBERT S. DAVIDSON

JACK D. FINDLEY

W. HORSLEY GANTT

SUSAN A. GROSE

HARRY F. HARLOW

MARGARET K. HARLOW

ALAN HARRIS

J. ALAN HERD

R. T. KELLEHER

H. D. KIMMEL

FRANK A. LOGAN

JULES H. MASSERMAN

KENNETH B. MELVIN

W. H. MORSE

JACK SANDLER

JOSEPH B. SIDOWSKI

# Experimental Psychopathology
## Recent Research and Theory

Edited by

## H. D. Kimmel

Department of Psychology
University of South Florida
Tampa, Florida

 1971

ACADEMIC PRESS
New York and London

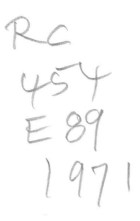

ACADEMIC PRESS, INC.
111 Fifth Avenue, New York, New York 10003

*United Kingdom Edition published by*
ACADEMIC PRESS, INC. (LONDON) LTD.
24/28 Oval Road, London NW1 7DD

LIBRARY OF CONGRESS CATALOG CARD NUMBER: 70-154383

PRINTED IN THE UNITED STATES OF AMERICA

# Contents

# LIST OF CONTRIBUTORS

Numbers in parentheses indicate the pages on which the authors' contributions begin

ABRAM AMSEL, Department of Psychology, University of Texas at Austin, Austin, Texas (51)

JOSEPH V. BRADY, Walter Reed Army Institute of Research, The Johns Hopkins University School of Medicine, Washington, D.C. (119)

ROBERT S. DAVIDSON, Psychological Research Laboratory, Veterans Administration Hospital, Miami, Florida (71)

JACK D. FINDLEY,* Walter Reed Army Institute of Research, The Johns Hopkins University School of Medicine, Washington, D.C. (119)

W. HORSLEY GANTT, The Johns Hopkins University and The Pavlovian Laboratory, Veterinary Administration Hospital, Perry Point, Maryland (33)

SUSAN A. GROSE, Department of Physiology, Psychiatry and Pharmacology, Harvard Medical School, Boston, Massachusetts, and New England Regional Primate Research Center, Southborough, Massachusetts (147)

HARRY F. HARLOW, The University of Wisconsin, Regional Primate Research Center, Madison, Wisconsin (203)

MARGARET K. HARLOW, Department of Educational Psychology and Primate Laboratory, Madison, Wisconsin (203)

ALAN HARRIS, Walter Reed Army Institute of Research, The Johns Hopkins University School of Medicine, Washington D. C. (119)

J. ALAN HERD, Department of Physiology, Harvard Medical School, Boston, Massachusetts (147)

R. T. KELLEHER, Department of Pharmacology, Harvard Medical School, Boston, Massachusetts (147)

H. D. KIMMEL, Department of Psychology, University of South Florida, Tampa, Florida (165)

FRANK A. LOGAN, Department of Psychology, University of New Mexico, Albuquerque, New Mexico (185)

JULES H. MASSERMAN, Department of Psychology, Northwestern University, Medical School, Evanston, Illinois (13)

KENNETH B. MELVIN, Department of Psychology, University of Alabama, University, Alabama (95)

W. H. MORSE, Departments of Physiology, Psychiatry and Pharmacology, Harvard Medical School, Boston, Massachusetts, and New England Regional Primate Research Center, Southborough, Massachusetts (147)

JACK SANDLER, University of South Florida, Tampa, Florida (71)

JOSEPH B. SIDOWSKI, University of South Florida, Tampa, Florida (231)

*Present address: Department of Psychiatry and Behavioral Sciences, The Johns Hopkins University School of Medicine, Baltimore, Maryland

# Preface

The field of experimental psychopathology has evolved from such diverse sources as Pavlovian conditioning laboratories, Skinnerian excursions into aversive stimulation, experimental psychiatry, and Spence–Brown–Miller motivation research with rats. This book is the first effort to bring under one rubric several of the most significant of these different but related research enterprises. The literature of experimental psychopathology is found mainly in a variety of specialized journals, but textbooks on abnormal psychology or psychopathology give very little treatment of the experimental phase of the subject.

This volume will be of interest to both scientists and clinicians who are concerned with the etiology and modification of abnormal behavior. Because its contents are broad in spectrum and highly current, anyone wishing to keep abreast of the present state of the art in experimental psychopathology will find areas of interest in this volume.

# Acknowledgments

The contributors to this volume first presented the major contents of their respective chapters in a weekly series of public lectures at the University of South Florida, during the spring of 1969. Thanks for the arrangements and for the necessary financial support are due to the Office of Academic Affairs of the University of South Florida, and especially to Vice President Alfred E. Lawton.

The editor also wishes to thank the contributors for their flexibility, speed, and cooperativeness in modifying and updating their oral presentations into highly readable and informative written chapters. Thanks are also due to the staff of Academic Press for their continuous assistance at all stages of this project. The editor, naturally, takes full responsibility for all of the written material not attributed explicitly to the authors, as well as for the overall organization and conception of the book.

# 1

# Introduction

As scientific disciplines, the study of abnormal behavior and the study of the stars and planets have some interesting similarities. Both have been the object of man's serious investigation and concern for more than two millenia. Both have suffered from a confused association with metaphysics and theology. And both have served as fertile soil in which highly imaginative and influential literatures have flowered. Yet, neither has been an *experimental* science for very long.

The transformation of speculative, naturalistic astronomy into a genuinely experimental discipline occurred, as is well known, at the moment that the first artificial satellite was lofted from earth by Soviet scientists. For the very first time in history, astronomers became able to employ the experimental principles of control and deliberate manipulation of critical variables, without which ability their predecessors had been limited to reliance solely upon patient, systematic observation and to the use of its sometimes misleading correlational consequences. It is little wonder that their theoretical wanderings sometimes imprisoned them in their own astral epicycles. Little wonder also that many contemporary men are still enchanted by astrology, that vestigial bridge between the mysteries of outer space and inner mind.[1]

Coincidentally, experimental psychopathology's sputnik also rose from Russian soil, although its first orbit was apparently almost entirely accidental. Two different investigators in Pavlov's classical salivary conditioning laboratory, Yerofeeva (1912, 1916) and Shenger-Krestovnikova (1921), serendipitously observed seemingly psychopathological behavior in their experimental animals following the use of novel conditioning procedures. The significance of Yerofeeva's important discovery escaped immediate attention ("The investigation of the higher nervous activity *under difficult conditions,* carried out in the course of M. N. Yerofeeva's experiments, unexpectedly resulted in the development for the first time of a chronic pathological state which, however, did not attract proper attention . . . . Possibly *on account of the special nature of the stimulus* used in these experiments, all these facts did not attract

[1] The coordinating principle here apparently being that, if nothing can be known for certain in either of two substantive fields, the unknowns of one can explain the unknowns of the other.

sufficient attention on our part") (Pavlov, 1927, p. 290, italics added). Shenger-Krestovnikova's famous circle–ellipse discrimination experiment, however, was a definite turning point. Where Yerofeeva had used an electric shock paired with food to generate pathology (in subsequent spatial generalization testing), Shenger-Krestovnikova found a neurotic-like breakdown without the use of any aversive stimulation whatever.

The two italicized phrases in the quotation from Pavlov, "under difficult conditions" and "on account of the special nature of the stimulus," have been selected for particular emphasis because they draw attention to what is probably the most important basic principle of experimental psychopathology, a principle which provides the common conceptual thread from which the experimental fabric of this book is woven. Put most simply, this principle is that normally adaptive behavioral processes provide the foundation upon which ultimately maladaptive patterns of behavior may be built, given an environment that is capriciously variable and often downright hostile.

What made Yerofeeva's experimental conditions "difficult," or the nature of the stimulus employed "special," was the inherently conflictful nature of the dog's appetitive reactions to food, on one hand, and its defensive reactions to shock, on the other. In this case the experimental environment placed simultaneous adaptive demands upon the animal with which its normal processes could not simultaneously cope. Parasympathetic and sympathetic reactions are mutually inhibitory.

Although Pavlov was unaware of it at the time, Shenger-Krestovnikova's experimental procedures were actually equally "difficult" and her stimuli just as "special." The behavioral adjustment required of the laboratory dog in an experiment in which food is repeatedly associated with a circle but is never presented with an ellipse is one which exists because of and depends upon the continued stability of this distinction. The very processes established during the initial discriminative conditioning phase of this experiment, the excitatory and inhibitory reaction tendencies, are responsible for the animal's breakdown when its environment subsequently changes (or is changed by the experimenter) capriciously. Experimental neurosis does not result from the procedure of presenting from the outset two highly similar stimuli while reinforcing only one, without any preliminary discrimination training on more highly dissimilar stimuli. Rather, the latter procedure will most often produce poor discrimination and, possibly, even poor conditioning.

The experimental programs described in this book exemplify the pervasiveness of this basic principle, since almost all of them utilize an explicit two-stage approach in which initially adaptive behavioral patterns are acquired and subsequently placed in confrontation with altered environmental demands. Masserman's "uncertainty" principle, described in Chapter 2, and Solomon's "unpredictability," considered in Chapter 9, both speak to its significance. In relation to this principle, the experimental strategy employed in much of the research that has been done in this field may be seen as involving the very elaborate and patient setting of a trap for the unsuspecting experimental subject. To set the trap the experimenter relies upon normal behavioral processes to establish initially adaptive tendencies. The trap is closed when the environment is changed by the experimenter. The latter stage may not always be temporally distinct from the former.

None of this would work, of course, if the adaptive mechanisms of the organisms under study did not have so fragile and critical a relationship with the environments in which they developed. Nor would the behavioral maladjustment which occurs outside of the laboratory be the enormous problem it is.

An interesting and illuminating example of one of nature's adaptive traps has been described and analyzed by Calhoun (1967). Every three to four years the Scandanavian lemming begins a fateful migration, first shown by scattered individuals and eventually by massive waves of up to a million or more, which takes these animals from their natural habitat in the upland plateaus down through the valleys and into the sea. The lemmings conclude their weeks-long trek by swimming as far into the ocean as they can before they all drown. As Calhoun has noted, "No clearer example of pathological behavior exists. All who exhibit it die" (1967, p. 3).

Obviously, a simple hereditary explanation is inadequate, since the individuals that survive are those least possessed by and capable of transmitting the aberrant tendency. According to Calhoun, the suicidal behavior is motivated originally by the lemming's aversion for overcrowded conditions. As the population grows without restriction, some individuals begin to move in the only feasible direction which results in less crowded conditions. Gradually, the lemming learns by differential reinforcement to move more and more in a relatively constant compass direction. As others do the same, the earlier movers must move farther on. The end state of this ecological trap is one in which mass panic takes the animals inexorably to their demise.

Calhoun has evaluated this conceptualization experimentally with mice as subjects. Forest and field mice maintain territorial ranges by emitting vocal signals which appear to be aversive to other individuals. The mouse tends to move toward the absence of signals and away from their presence. Using the ingenious device of removing all mice from a circular central area, he observed that the animals at the edge of the vacant circle began to move into it. Systematically removing all animals that entered the circle had the predicted effect of producing a population "implosion," as wave after wave of mice converged upon the continuously vacant center. The demonstration quite clearly supports the theoretical analysis which led to it.

The closely repeated observations of the phenomenon of experimental neurosis in Pavlov's laboratory, under two rather different procedural circumstances, had the historically significant effect of stimulating an abrupt shift in the focus of the great Russian's experimental program. The remainder of his scientific career was devoted to the study and explication of aberrant behavior in humans and animals. Furthermore, when the Russian findings became widely known through the translation of Pavlov's books, an entirely new approach to the scientific understanding of abnormal behavior was signalled. A genuinely *experimental* psychopathology became possible for the first time.

The significance of this change in direction may best be comprehended in relation to its two most important implications. First, the completely correlational method of behavioral analysis which was the empirical foundation of all earlier systematic efforts to understand psychological abnormality, including everything from Hippocrates' humors and Gall's prominences to the ingenious psychoanalytic theorizing of Freud,[2] could now be supplemented if not altogether supplanted by a direct experimental approach which was much less fraught with the dual dangers of loose conjecture and empirical untestability. Second, and historically of possibly greater significance, the continuity of animal morphology, physiology, and behavior, already beginning to assume a position on center stage in man's philosophical thinking, received a new extensive thrust from the early Pavlovian findings, since for the first time even such "uniquely human" phenomena as emotional breakdowns were seen to occur in subhuman animals.

The scientific advantages of manipulative experimentation over response-response correlational research in psychological science have been enumerated too many times in the past (Spence, 1956; Kimmel, 1970) to justify full repetition here. Perhaps the most effective illustration in practical terms of the basic conceptual limitation of correlationally supported arguments is to be found in the current unwillingness of many cigarette smokers to accept the conclusion of the Surgeon-General of the United States that heart disease and respiratory cancer are both made more likely as a result of the use of tobacco. To be sure, recent *experimental* demonstrations in subhuman subjects of the causative relationship between the inhalation of coal-tars and resins and the occurrence of neoplastic tumors will probably persuade even the most skeptical holdouts. Yet, until these studies have been thoroughly replicated and widely advertised, the inconclusiveness as regards cause and effect of statistically significant correlation coefficients has enabled even the mass of scientifically unsophisticated smokers to delay accepting the belief that their own use of cigarettes really may shorten their lives.[3] Correlational findings are apt to be as

---

[2] Varying degrees of armchair creativity are admittedly embraced within these extremes, although the absence of real experimentation remains the definitional *sine qua non* in all cases.

[3] This argument speaks only to the smoker's *acceptance* of the *conclusion* that there is a causal relationship between smoking and disease. There is little doubt that many who are persuaded of the conclusion will continue to smoke anyway.

much responsible for superstition as they are for enlightenment, as Skinner's pigeons and Malinowski's natives should have taught us.

The potential for spuriousness in observed correlations and the danger of superstitious behavior and belief which may result are demonstrated neatly in the results of an experiment by Timmons (1963). Human subjects were confronted with a four-button multiple choice apparatus and were instructed that nickels (money) could be earned by operating the apparatus. Unknown to the subjects was the fact that a contingent relationship with the reinforcement mechanism existed for only one of the four buttons, and this was on a response-contingent fixed interval schedule. Simply put, all the subject had to do to maximize his monetary gains was to operate the button in question, wait out the appropriate time interval, operate the button again, etc. Timmons was not surprised to find that none of the subjects adopted this most efficient mode of responding. Instead, each subject developed his own stereotyped ritual for operating *all four* of the buttons in complicated sequential patterns (e.g., A, B, C, D, D, C, B, A, A, A, B, B, C, C, D, D, etc.).[4] This outcome is, of course, the human analog of the key-pecking behavior of pigeons in fixed interval situations. Of more relevance to the present discussion was the additional finding that the subjects verbalized *beliefs*, when queried, which were in complete accord with their recorded motor patterns. They were quite convinced that the idiosyncratic response patterns they had used were both sufficient (which was obvious) *and* necessary for the production of the reinforcement.

The inability to effect direct manipulative control of independent variables, which is probably the most reasonable justification for using solely correlational methods, results in an unfortunate although understandable tendency to incline towards flexible theorizing regarding cause and effect relationships. The orientation of such theorizing is structural as opposed to functional (e.g., Guilford's (1961) work on the structure of intellect).

Corpulence and joviality, or leanness and morosity, may tend to coexist more often than chance would dictate, yet no contemporary psychologist would seriously argue that either causes the other. The observed covariation becomes, rather, a stimulus for speculation regarding the operation of other, possibly unidentified, variables. Or, simply a structural, descriptive model results. Even were it true that all observed correlations possess genuine reliability, such understanding as may be inferred from a reliable correlation depends too heavily upon the theoretical preconceptions and scientific style of the investigator. If a *manipulative* increase in variable A is followed consistently by an *observed* increase (or decrease) in variable B, however, and if a manipulative decrease in A precedes a decrease (or increase) in B, it may be possible to focus upon unidirectional theoretical constructions to summarize the relationship and

---

[4] This experimental production of superstitious, ritualistic behavior is, of course, also an illustration in microcosm of what "experimental psychopathology" is.

integrate it with connected ones. At least the theorizing is more likely to be closely tied to the particular variables in question.

Furthermore, straightforward empirical evaluation of the implications of theories arising from experimental as contrasted with correlational studies is usually more likely to be attained. This may be a trivial concomitant of the research style of experimenters as distinguished from correlators, or it may be inherent in the logic of the stimulus–response approach employed by the former. In either case, however, it is another benefit associated with manipulative experimental research as it is traditionally conducted.

The second implication of the discovery of experimental neurosis in Pavlov's laboratory was that it added confirmation and further heuristic stimulation to the already proclaimed continuity of animal physiology and psychology by showing that subhumans could display "human" kinds of behavioral abnormality. This implication was probably the more important of the two in question. The use of objective behavioral methods in the study of conditioning and learning had been developed by Thorndike and exploited by Watson into a full-blown behavioristic revolution which purged mentalism from, and enabled trans-species principles and theories to develop in, the areas of "normal" learning and motivation. Much in the same way, a completely experimental psychopathology may succeed in exorcizing the mentalistic ghosts still remaining in the closets of abnormal psychology. If the principles of conditioning and learning in fish, rats, and men cohere intelligently in systematic (normal) behavior theory, the same should, of course, be true for the principles governing "abnormal" behavior. To be sure, this argument probably implies that no real distinction between "normal" and "abnormal" need be made, although acceptance of this conclusion is not required for agreement with the less extreme assertion that systematic experimental research on the causes of pathological behavior in subhumans may teach us something about the etiology of abnormal human behavior. It is well known that epistemological difficulties attend any effort to establish an objective and unambiguous basis for distinguishing between "abnormal" and "normal" behavior. Normative approaches are incapable of dealing with asocial or antisocial behaviors of atypical individuals who otherwise appear to function effectively. Tissue-oriented distinctions make little behavioral sense and sometimes even fail to sort out organic conditions agreeably. Pain cannot be defined except subjectively and, even then, persistent approach to pain complicates its significance as a sign of pathology. In the face of this confusion, the editor leaves to the separate contributors the responsibility to adopt their own definitions of abnormality, or to avoid the issue entirely.

As it turns out, the methods most commonly used in experimental research on the genesis of pathological behavior generally require the use of subhuman experimental subjects. There are two obvious reasons for this state of affairs. First of all, the possibility that irreversible changes in behavior may be produced cannot entirely be dismissed in a subject-matter field as poorly understood as this. Although it is highly unlikely that the procedures most commonly employed in psychopathology research would have long-lasting maladaptive effects, the more dramatic and psychologically interesting the effects are, the more likely it is that they may be enduring. Second, the aversiveness and possible immediate danger of the actual experimental treatments often may make them inappropriate for use with human subjects on ordinary ethical and humanitarian grounds, even were the probability of irreversible, long-range, deleterious consequences reduced to zero.

It should be clear by now that the label "experimental psychopathology" is employed in this book in a somewhat more narrow way than is customary in the psychological literature.[5] Explicitly excluded from its current range of meaning is research of the survey, naturalistic, or correlational types, involving no deliberate manipulation of independent variables. Also excluded are experimental studies on psychotherapy, even though it is frequently the case that experimental programs in which the genesis of psychopathology is studied also may involve experimental efforts to alleviate the disturbance after it has been produced.

The decision to adopt this somewhat narrow approach to the definition of "experimental psychopathology" is not totally arbitrary, since the editor is of the opinion that the highly fertile field remaining to be tilled has suffered from imprecision in earlier, overinclusive definitions. Actually, a fairly literal reading of the two common English words, "experimental" and "psychopathology," is mainly involved. "Psychopathology" usually refers either to the *study* of abnormal behavior or to the abnormal behavior, itself. The only ambiguity potentially resulting from the combination of "experimental" and "psycho-pathology" stems from the fact that *either* the abnormal behavior in "psychopathology" *or* the study of it (i.e., the "ology") may be modified by the term "experimental." "Experimental psychopathology," thus, could mean either "the experimental study of pathological behavior (i.e., using the experimental method to study pathological behavior), or "the study of experimental pathological behavior" (i.e., the pathological behavior being studied is induced experimentally rather than developed naturally). The latter of these two possible meanings is employed in this book.

In the experimental study of psychopathology which has developed naturally, any differences between "normal" and "abnormal" subjects pre-exist the introduction of the independent variables under study. For example, subjects diagnosed as "schizophrenic" or "normal" may be observed under conditions of "imposed stress" and "no stress." It has been shown that certain chemical

[5]The present usage is even more narrow than the recent "comparative psycho-pathology" label employed by Zubin and Hunt (1967) as a title for the published proceedings of the 1965 meetings of the American Psychopathological Society.

by-products of adrenal cortex activity are present in increased amounts in the urine of the "normal" subjects following stress. This "normal" chemical consequence of exposure to stress is not found in the urine of the "schizophrenic" subjects. Even though the experimental manipulation of the presence or absence of stress is deliberate in this experiment, the necessity of diagnostic selection of "normal" and "schizophrenic" subjects keeps the principal independent variable, *the pathology,* from being experimentally defined. In "quasi-experimental" research of this type (Kimmel, 1970), the same limitations regarding making causal conclusions apply as restrict correlational research in general. Thus, we are no better able to comprehend the possible role of chemical factors in the *etiology* of schizophrenia because of this type of study than we would be without it.

A somewhat improved version of the foregoing experimental design (Dowis, 1964) permits nontraditional, *behavioral* distinctions to be made among clinically diagnosed groups in some baseline measure, prior to the introduction of either within-subject or between-subject independent variable manipulations. In Dowis' study, for example, three groups of human subjects, diagnosed as "normal," "psychoneurotic," or "schizophrenic," performed initially in a simple, two-choice button-pressing task with no external feedback. After the initial session, half of each group continued in the task with the addition of "evaluative" ("right" or "wrong") feedback following each response. The other half of each group received "nonevaluative" feedback (circles or triangles) in their second phase. Informational measures of sequential constraint (auto-correlational behavior) were employed to identify differences among the three diagnostic groups during the baseline, nonfeedback condition. Differences within subjects between the nonfeedback and feedback conditions were employed to evaluate the effects of presence of feedback. And, finally, differences between subjects established whether there were differential effects of the two types of feedback conditions.

Even with these conspicuous improvements in experimental design, however, the reliance upon natural developments to establish the major independent variable, pathology, limits this experiment to essentially descriptive, correlational speculations regarding the etiological history of psychopathology. What emerge are statements about the way schizophrenics, psychoneurotics, etc. behave in special situations and how their behavior changes when the situation changes. To be sure, this type of research is "experimental," and it *does* deal with pathological behavior. But, it is only when the history of the organism is capable of direct experimental manipulation, so as to produce pathological behavior, that "experimental psychopathology" becomes a full-fledged empirical discipline.

From an historical point of view, the fact that Pavlov used the term "experimental neurosis" to refer to the behavior observed by Yerofeeva and

Shenger-Krestovnikova suggests that the more generic "experimental psycho-pathology" be employed for experimental work in which abnormal behavior is the *product* of the various experimental manipulations and in which the basic purpose is to gain knowledge of the critical etiological variables governing the probability, extent, and qualitative nature of this product. The work represented in this book falls clearly under the rubric of this definition of "experimental psychopathology." Although not represented explicitly in the book, research on the psychopathological effects of various drugs (e.g., mescaline, lysergic acid, etc.), gross sensory deprivation (in both humans and subhumans), and early traumatic experience are also similarly categorizable.

Scientists who are engaged in research on experimental psychopathology would agree that one of the main purposes of their work is to discover and systematically explain the causes of psychopathological behavior in *humans* and, thereby, to permit its treatment and, possibly, even its prevention. The question is necessarily raised, however, whether we are really likely to understand a psychoneurotic or psychotic *person* better because of what we have learned in our laboratory research on rats, dogs, and monkeys. To some extent, the work described by the various contributors to this book provides a partial empirical answer to this question, insofar as the different contributors have succeeded in extending the implications of their laboratory results to human situations. It is of the utmost importance that the answer be obtained empirically, rather than deduced *a priori* from one or another theoretical conceptualization. The danger inherent in the latter approach is exemplified in an anecdote reported by one of the present contributors in an earlier publication describing his research on experimental neurosis in cats (Masserman, 1946). During a discussion period following a presentation of his findings to a group of psychiatrists and psychoanalysts, Masserman was asked how he could justify using the word "neurosis" to describe the aberrant behavior displayed by his experimental subjects, considering that neurosis "always" is the result of an unresolved oedipus conflict and none of the cats in the experiment had ever known their fathers!

The field of experimental psychopathology is still so young that it boasts of little more than a basic research strategy and a few landmark experimental discoveries at this point in its history. The earliest work done in Pavlov's laboratory has already been mentioned. Also worthy of historical notation are Watson and Raynor's work on experimentally induced phobic reactions, Maier's fixations in rats, Liddell's experimentally neurotic sheep, Gantt's dogs, Masserman's cats, and Brady's executive monkeys.

The present volume contains four major sections. In Part I, two of the earliest American researchers in the field of experimental psychopathology have written chapters which bring their work up-to-date and in which each presents his own systematic overview of the field as he now sees it. Part II contains three chapters describing significant behavioristic approaches to the development of pathological response tendencies. Part III has three contributions to the literature on experimentally induced maladaptive patterns of emotional (autonomic nervous system) reactions. And Part IV contains three chapters on experimental reseach dealing with the development of pathological social behaviors in rats and monkeys.

## REFERENCES

Calhoun, J. B. Ecological factors in the development of behavioral anomalies. In J. Zubin and H. F. Hunt (Eds.), *Comparative psychopathology, animal and human.* New York: Grune and Stratton, 1967.

Dowis, J. L. *The effects of evaluative and non-evaluative feedback on sequential behavior in psychiatric illness.* Unpublished Ph.D. Dissertation, Univer. of Florida, 1964.

Guilford, J. P. Factorial angles to psychology. *Psychological Review,* 1961, **68**, 1-20.

Kimmel, H. D. *Experimental principles and design in psychology.* New York: Ronald Press, 1970.

Masserman, J. H. *Principles of dynamic psychiatry.* Philadelphia, Pennsylvania: Saunders, 1946.

Pavlov, I. P. *Conditioned reflexes.* (Tr. by G. V. Anrep). London: Oxford Univ. Press, 1927.

Shenger-Krestovnikova, N. R. Contributions to the question of differentiation of visual stimuli and the limits of differentiation by the visual analyzer of the dog. *Bulletin of the Lesgaft Institute of Petrograd,* 1921, **3**, 1-43.

Spence, K. W. *Behavior theory and conditioning.* New Haven: Yale Univ. Press, 1956.

Timmons, E. O. *Implications of awareness-applied areas.* Unpublished symposium paper (Southeastern Psychological Association), Miami, Florida, April, 1963.

Yerofeeva, M. N. Electrical stimulation of the skin of the dog as a conditioned salivary stimulus. Thesis, St. Petersburg, 1912.

Yerofeeva, M. N. Contribution to the study of destructive conditioned reflexes. *Comptes rendus de la societé biologique,* 1916, **79**, 239-240.

Zubin, J., & Hunt, H. F. *Comparative psychopathology, animal and human.* New York: Grune and Stratton, 1967.

# PART 1

The first post-Pavlovian generation of researchers on experimental psychopathology boasts two scientists-emeritus, Jules H. Masserman and W. Horsley Gantt. It is most fitting that a book on this subject begin with their work, since between them is shared the joint distinction of priority and persistence in the creation of the conceptual and empirical foundations upon which the field has been built.

Masserman was trained in psychiatry and psychoanalysis. Probably most responsible for the experimental direction his work early took was his firm foundation in the dynamic psychobiological approach of Adolph Meyer, one of his teachers. His book, *Principles of dynamic psychiatry,*[1] in which he first systematically described and analyzed his pioneer experiments on experimental neurosis in cats, was profoundly influential in establishing that the Pavlovian phenomenon could be induced by instrumental conditioning methods quite different from those emphasized by the great Russian and also that experimental psychotherapy was an equally valid scientific enterprise. Masserman's present contribution describes some of his more recent work using monkeys as subjects and greatly broadens Masserman's earlier basic conceptual scheme. The principal shift has been from emphasis on the notion that the organism's adaptive capacity may be unfairly tested by certain conflictful situations, resulting in neurotic breakdown, to an emphasis on the broader question of the consequences of the organism's inability to predict and control critical events in its environment.

W. Horsley Gantt first met Pavlov when he visited the Soviet Union as a member of a medical relief team following the Russian famine of 1922. He, too, had originally been trained in medicine and psychiatry. He was so impressed with Pavlov and his work that he arranged to return to Russia to learn more of it, although the second trip could not be accomplished until 1929. No single individual has been more closely identified with research on experimental neurosis in the 40 years since. In his contribution to this volume, Gantt reviews the development of experimental neurosis in relation to his theoretical concepts of *autokinesis* and *schizokinesis,* and enlarges upon the Pavlovian notion of *effect of person* in the etiology of pathology.

---

[1] J. H. Masserman. *Principles of dynamic psychiatry.* Philadelphia: Saunders, 1946.

# 2

# The Principle
# of Uncertainty
# in Neurotigenesis

JULES H. MASSERMAN

Northwestern University
Medical School

## I. INTRODUCTION

In the musical form called Theme with Variations, the principal motif is announced at the opening, re-examined in various aspects throughout the composition, and recapitulated at the end. The theme of this essay is in its title, transposable into a minor key question as follows: Are aberrations of behavior induced by conflicts of motivation or adaptation, or does the underlying neurotigenic anxiety arise from the organism's apprehension that impending events may exceed its powers of prediction and control?

Before we can parse the adjective "neurotigenic," it must be confessed that after diverse trials, we are reduced to defining the root term "neuroses" more broadly as those deviations of conduct sufficiently troublesome to the contingent culture to require service (from the Greek *therapeien*) by variously designated officers of the society affected. After being duly commissioned as one such officer called a psychiatrist, some 40 years ago, the author began re-examining the multiplex and frequently contradictory theories of neurotigenesis that he had been taught. As in other disciplines, the historical, comparative, and experimental approaches were useful, provided one had always at hand William of Occam's famous razor, *"Entia non sunt multiplicanda praeter necessitatem,"* and Albert Einstein's dictum[1] that a scientific proposition should be as simply stated and as broadly applicable as possible. To expand our opening theme, then: Doubts and trepidations about our capacities to predict and cope

---

[1] The grand aim of all science is to cover the greatest number of empirical facts by logical deductions from the smallest number of hypotheses or axioms.

with impending and important events induce the internal physiologic signals we interpret as "anxiety," and variably actuate the symbolically evasive (phobic), hopefully repetitive (compulsive, ritualistic), regressive-dependent (depressive), reactively overassertive (paranoid), dysaffective and dereistic (schizoid), and other individualized attempts at mastery or denial which, depending on the extent and duration of their deviation from current cultural norms, are then labeled "idiosyncratic," "neurotic," "sociopathic," or "psychotic." Let us glance briefly at the evidence for this more comprehensive generalization.

*Historical*: Hippocrates classified human *temperaments* according to predominant "humors": i.e., an excess of black bile made one *melancholic*; of yellow bile, *choleric*; of phlegm, *phlegmatic*; and of blood, *sanguine*; regrettably, however, no one could quite foretell when anyone else would become "temperamental" or be "in a bad humor." Two millennia later, Wilks' taxonomy of abnormality reverted to Plato's simpler dichotomy of *imbecility* and *madness*; according to Wilks, *stupidity* and *morosity* were the only forms of disorder, but again in impalpable admixtures. In the eighteenth century, Cullen coined the unfortunate term *neurosis* to mean the behavioral manifestations of putative diseases of the central nervous system, whereupon Feuchtersleben promptly confounded this usage by terming the "disease itself" a *neurosis* and its highly variable symptoms a *psychosis*. Kahlbaum, Kraepelin, and Bleuler then attributed most behavior disorders to uncontrollable genetic factors, thus further adding the dread of futility to the quandaries of therapy.

Sigmund Freud, in all earnestness, tried to clarify some of the issues by differentiating "actual neuroses," supposedly due to physically debilitating sexual excesses, from "psychoneuroses" caused by recent sexual traumata. When this explanation proved insufficient, he attributed his patients' sexual sensitivities to their having witnessed parental intercourse in the "primal scene," thereby giving rise to an Oedipus complex and the persistent incubus of a "fear of castration." When this, too, proved unverifiable, he resorted to the postulate that illusory "screen memories" of the horrendous event could be equally devastating; and finally, when the hedonistic aspects of the libido theory again proved inadequate, he coupled self-preservation and procreation under the "life-instinct Eros," and counterposed Eros against "Thanatos"—composed of inscrutably repetitive-compulsive instincts toward dissolution and death. It will be of absorbing interest to cultural historians to speculate why these simplistic formulations intrigued two generations of intelligentsia much as, for that matter, Gall's phrenology and Mesmer's "animal magnetism" had done previously. One factor may be that Freud based his inferences on the transactional myths obligingly tendered him by his resignedly compliant or subtly mocking patients, and then correlated these with the supposedly universal Hellenic legends of Narcissus, Electra, Oedipus *et al*. Since, as Freud frankly proposed to Einstein, *all* science is an ever-contingent myth, this is in no sense a pejorative statement.

Indeed, I consider myself a card-carrying analyst,[2] renegade only in the sense that I am inclined to interpret man's myths, both individual and cultural, as expressing much deeper wisdoms concerning his doubts and tribulations than those usually associated with their eponyms. For example: Was Narcissus "in love with himself," as Freud would have it, or did he become so enamored of his vaguely reflected *image* that his friend Almeinas and his mistress Echo forsook him? Again, whether or not mourning became the tragic Electra, her mourning certainly became fatal to her mother Clytemnestra, her mother's lover Aegisthos, and nearly so to her brother Orestes and practically everyone else involved. But perhaps the most inclusive and poignant dramatizations of man's eternal uncertainties are epitomized in Sophocles' trilogy on Oedipus—a succession of myths which, far beyond epitomizing merely a middle-class Viennese son's supposed desire for coitus with his mother countered by Freudian fear of his father's terrible swift sword, deals much more deeply with nearly all human travail and triumph from childhood survival to the ultimate denial of death. Let us review the content of these poignant parables, the significance of which is much more complex than implied by Ferenczi's use of that term:

Laius, King of Thebes, is warned by an oracle that his son would slay him—as indeed all children inevitably displace their elders. Torn by doubt and fear, Laius avoids the onus of direct infanticide by pinning together the ankles of the newborn Oedipus ("swollen feet") leaving him in a basket—there being no Nilotic bulrushes about—on Mount Cathaeron. However, Oedipus is found by a kindly Corinthian shepherd and adopted by Polybus, King of Corinth—as indeed our own rejected children are partially rescued by baby-sitters, nursery teachers, pedagogues and other surrogates. But Oedipus is never certain that he is "really" the true Prince of Corinth, cannot get satisfactory assurances from King Polybus or Queen Merope (for that matter, who *can* be absolutely sure of his paternity) and is further perplexed when he learns at Delphi that he must kill his father and marry his mother. Trying to escape his fate (as who does not?) he vows never to see Polybus or Merope again, and leaves Corinth to wander in search of what Erik Erikson would call his "true identity." At a crossroads outside Thebes an old man blocks his right-of-way and is killed in the ensuing battle—(as all oldsters who dare too long to challenge imperious youth will be disposed of in their turn). To display his intellectual as well as physical vitality, Oedipus then also conquers a Sphinx whose "riddle" (the old nursery puzzle about the quadri-, bi-, and tripedal locomotion of aging man) he easily solves, and thereby emancipates the Thebans from years of sphincteric terror. For reward he is given the vacant throne of Thebes and marries the widowed Queen Iocaste.

And yet, nagging doubts remain (who is free of them?) and Oedipus, after more years of restless searching, learns from the shepherd who rescued him the awful truth that he had indeed killed his father and cohabited incestuously with his mother—"awful" of course only

[2] Provided psychoanalysis is redefined in more modern terms as (a) research into the motivations and vicissitudes of human behavior through an intensive study of verbal and other transactions between patient and analyst, (b) a continuously contingent and modifiable theoretical structure, leading to (c) a dynamic approach to the rationale and technique of therapy.

because he fears that others regard it so. He blinds (not castrates) himself in expiation and thereby becomes a pathetic rather than reprehensible figure, curses his own unwanted sons, Eteocles and Polynices, and then pre-empts the services of his daughters, Antigone and Ismene, in his further wanderings throughout Hellas—as all aging parents since Agamemnon sacrificed Iphegenia try to do. Finally, at the Grave of Colonus outside Athens he defies the Fates and becomes a demi-god—thus acquiring the archangelic status we all believe we deserve.

There are, of course, many variations of these myths, not only in Greek but in Hungarian, Rumanian, Finnish and even Lapland folklore. For example, Homer has Iocaste commit suicide, after which a more rational Oedipus completes his reign in relative peace. But whatever the versions, the myths are never naively monothetic; instead they portray almost any nuance of the imperative, ceaseless seekings for order and certainty that imbue the human condition and the temporary triumphs, tantalizing terrors, and terminal tragedies that are inevitably man's fate unless he can wishfully believe himself superhuman.

Since the "Oedipus complex" is thus all-inclusive, the "libidinous drives" of the "pre-Oedipal phases" also lose their supposed specificity except in the sense that all human longings and transactions remain charged ("cathected" in analytic patois) with uncertainty. Thus "anal aggression" may meet with counterreactive hostility; "oral dependencies" are always precarious, and even "primal narcissism" itself, despite wishful philosophies or theologies to the contrary, is ever on the brink of existential obliteration. In essence, then, no one is ever quite sure of his continued health, or of the reliability of his friends or, for that matter, the verity of his beliefs, and the intensities of his anxieties are in direct proportion to his uncertainties in any or all of these spheres.

## II. COMPARATIVE APPROACHES

As was true for the foregoing tachistoscopic review of various concepts of neurotigenesis, we can here glance only tangentially at the corresponding thesis that, despite their seeming diversity, all of the successful methods employed to alleviate what we have called our ultimate or *Ur*-anxieties in all times, places, and cultures likewise have but three dynamic vectors in common: to relieve man's concern about his physical prowess, to render his ethnocultural adaptations less precarious, and to foster his theophilosophic serenity. To bring this home to psychoanalytic trainees or other neophytes, one might propose some polemic postulate such as:

*Resolved, that cerebral electroshock and classical analytic techniques are essentially more alike than different in their therapeutic actions and effects.* This usually evokes a storm of protest that any analyst or neuropsychiatrist should know that the two methods *are manifestly and incomparably different inasmuch as*[3]

"EST is enforced ... physical, ... impersonal, ... stereotyped, ... rigidly conducted, ... suppressive, ... antimnemonic (and) intellectually impairing," *whereas in diametric contrast*, "psychoanalysis is voluntary, ... dynamic, ... exquisitely interpersonal, ... flexible, ... evocative, ... restorative of memory (and) designed to explore the Unconscious so as to develop to the full the patient's cognitive and adaptive capacities through '*insight*.' " At this juncture it may be pointed out that the last catechism inadmissibly begs the question since, in the historical and comparative contexts in which the problem was posed, "insight" itself could be operationally defined only as that temporarily ecstatic state in which patient and therapist transiently share approximately the same illusions as to the cause and cure of each other's difficulties. With such additional goads, the student begins to explore subtler dimensions of therapeutically significant *similarities* between electroshock and analysis, and comes up with the following:

*Physical parameters*: Both EST and psychoanalysis offer an interim clinical escape from mundane concerns about external reality on a sensorially isolated bed or couch (Greek: *klinikos*) presided over by a certified and trusted parental surrogate for about the same total number of recumbent hours. Both methods also serve to disorganize current percepts and patterns of deviant behavior: EST by direct cerebral diaschises followed by at least partial synaptic reorganization; analysis by semantic and symbolic dissociations and subsequent alteration of concept and response.

*Interpersonal influences*: In each case the patient, under more or less subtle or overt pressure, selects the physician and the method of therapy he regards as most likely to improve his individual and social well-being. Reciprocally, the patient is accepted as "ill" and in need of help by a dedicated therapist who is convinced of the special validity of his own theories and the efficacy of his techniques-and thus rounds out a *folie à deux* that is nevertheless often operationally effective.

*Social parameters*: Both methods entail covert physical, economic, social and other sanctions that progressively resolve the patient's ambivalences and indecisions: in EST, persistence of disapproved conduct on the part of the patient subjects him to more incarceration, more quasi-lethal experiences, more postictal headaches, continued exclusion of visitors and other penalties; in analysis, excessively mortgaged time and expense, more patronizing, depreciating and disillusioning "interpretations" given without privilege of really effective repartee, the induction of a discomfiting "transference neurosis" (which Freud himself deplored as "an artifact of poor technique") plus the everpresent Kafka-esque threat of having an "unanalyzable character disorder" i.e., being labeled by the therapist as incurably obnoxious. Conversely, there are highly desirable rewards for changes in behavior more in accord with the therapist's standards as eventually sensed by the patient (the "patient compliance" of Ehrenwald): e.g., after "successful" EST, expanding hospital privileges, escape from eventually resented institutionalization, and restored familial and social status; or, after analysis—at least until recently—an assumption of cryptic wisdom privy only to the initiate, acceptance in the sophisticated elite of the "thoroughly analyzed" in the suburban cocktail circuit and, for institute trainees, official admission to and referrals from the local psychoanalytic society, which until recently guaranteed economic plenty, high social status, and serene metapsychologic superiority.

[3] Adapted from an address by the senior author to the Australia–New Zealand Academy of Psychiatry, September 16, 1968.

*Mystical*: In the latter sense, patient and therapist in both methods join in an essentially worshipful belief either that Bini and Cerletti on the one hand or Freud on the other brought providentially inspired salvation to ailing mortals, attainable through somewhat differently prescribed rituals of suffering, expiation, enlightenment and reacquisition of metaphysical grace. Any agnostic who, at national meetings, has attended the Section on Electro-Convulsive Therapy or—usually at another hotel at a discretely noncommunicative distance—a Seminar of Psychoanalytic Theory and Therapy, will have experienced the unmistakable aura of sacerdotal devotion as well as the purportedly scientific import of both proceedings.

Similar whimsical parallels can, of course, be constructed, say, between vitamin therapy and "nondirective counseling," *Dauerschlaff* and psychodrama, or colonic lavage and Christian Science, even though each procedure has its special dynamics and clinical applicabilities. Nevertheless, within the bounds of reductionist sophistry, objective analyses of the therapeutically operational factors in each method may help clarify the common vectors of the resolution of doubts and a restoration of confidence, however temporarily or lastingly effective, in the outcome of decisive action.

## III. EXPERIMENTAL AND CLINICAL CORRELATES

Since this aspect of biodynamics has been the author's especial concern for a third of a century, permit me, first, a comment on the relevance of animal research to psychiatric theory and therapy; next a statement of four testable propositions as to normal and abnormal behavior; and third, brief descriptions of relevant laboratory observations and their possible clinical analogs.

Two preliminary questions may still sometimes arise at this juncture: "Are animal experiments *really* (sic) applicable to the subjective and social complexities of human behavior?" Or, in a more subtly patronizing vein: "Must we not be careful about *anthropomorphizing* animal data and be on guard against drawing false clinical inferences?" Such questions—Darwin, Pavlov, Simpson, Tinbergen, Harlow and others be thanked—are now seriously raised far less frequently than formerly, but in briefest riposte may be respectively considered thus:

*Neurophysiologically*, just as the human central nervous system, although manifestly more highly developed in some respects, is nevertheless of the *same basic design* as that of other chordates, so also is human conduct more responsive to complex communicative and social influences—and thereby more contingent and versatile *but not different in basic adaptational patterns*—than the behavior of man's somewhat less pretentious, preemptive, pompous, and pugnacious fellow-creatures.

*Epistemologically*, no "datum," whether labeled "material," "experimental," "intuitive," or whatever, is ever really "given" in pristine purity by a gracious cosmos; instead, since "data" can never be more than man's incomplete, exceedingly fallible, and artificially categorized perceptions of his supposed universe, terms such as "real," "objective," "subjective," "anthropomorphic," etc. become tautologic shibboleths, meaningless to the modern logical-positivist rationale of science. Man may proudly claim a sole right to neuroses; nevertheless, studies in animals are disconcertingly reminiscent not only of the development of individual and social conduct in man, but significant to the therapy of his neurotic and psychotic deviations. Since "science," then, is but a testing and refinement of contingent premises, can such postulates be formulated for the most complicated field of all: animal behavior?

## A. Biodynamic Theses

We have essayed to test in our own work the following four relatively simple and parsimonious hypotheses, respectively applicable to motivation, learning, adaptability, and neurotigenesis, and operative in both animal and human conduct:

1. *Motivation*: The actions of all organisms are directed toward satisfying physiologic needs, and therefore vary with their intensity, duration, and balance.

2. *Perception and response*: In seeking these fulfillments, organisms conceive of and interact with their milieu not in terms of an absolute "external reality," but in accordance with their genetic capacities, rates of maturation, and unique experience.

3. *Range of normal adaptation*: To maintain adequate levels of satisfaction, higher animals develop a broad range of adaptive techniques by employing versatile methods of coping with difficulties or by modifying or changing goals as necessary.

4. *Neurotigenesis*: In its original formulation, this hypothesis held that when physical inadequacies, environmental stresses, or motivational conflicts exceed an organism's innate or acquired capacities for adaptation, internal tensions (anxiety) mount, neurophysiologic (psychosomatic) dysfunctions occur, and the organism develops overgeneralized patterns of avoidance (phobias), stereotyped behavior (obsessions and compulsions), aberrant conspecific and extraspecific transactions (social deviations), and regressive, hyperactive or hostile, or bizarrely "dereistic" (hallucinatory, delusional) responses analogous to those in human neuroses and psychoses. We would now add that the various forms of "conflict," whether postulated as an impasse among counterposed attractions and aversions, or between mutually exclusive attractions or equally balanced fears, may be subsumed under a broader etiologic rubric: namely, that in each instance the organism apprehends a failure to predict and control events important to its welfare.

These "biodynamic principles," always subject to modification by further data, have emerged from the work conducted by my associates and myself during the past three decades. Below is a brief review of our principal observations.

## B. Ontological Studies

*Phases of development*: Our records and films of individual animals of various species from infancy to adulthood have confirmed the thesis that their young, as Piaget and others have shown for the human, normally evolve through an orderly succession of stages during which sensory modalities are distinguished and resynthesized, *individualized* concepts of the environment are developed, manipulative skills are refined, early dependencies on parental care are relinquished in favor of exploration and mastery, and peer, sexual, and hierarchic relationships are evolved. Infants given a stimulating early milieu, opportunities for continuously nutritive and protective contacts with parents or their surrogates, and later with peers, manifest progressive self-confidence, acquire motor and social skills, and develop "group acculturations" insofar as, by trial and error, their adaptations become experientially (*ex-perio*, that which pierces through), more competent and secure. These expansions of the organism's concepts of physical and social "realities" also render its choices more perplexing and fallible and thereby potentially neurotigenic.

*Learning and symbolism*: During this development, animal young show patterns of dependency, exploration, play, fetishism (i.e., continued attachment to objects such as rubber gloves used in early feedings), "tantrumy" rebelliousness, gradually more effective adaptations, and other characteristics significantly parallel to those in human children. In this process, the parents or surrogates involved, even when the latter are not of the animal's species, impart their own traits to the adopted young. For example, a rhesus monkey raised from birth in an assistant's home learned to respond sensitively and adequately to many intonations of language and patterns of human action, but never acquired some of the aversions (e.g., a fear of snakes) supposedly "innate" in rhesus monkeys raised by their own mothers.

*Early deprivations*: In contrast, young animals prevented from developing adaptive capacities by prolonged periods of solitary confinement, even though otherwise physically well cared for, do not develop normal initiative, physical stamina, or adequate social relationships.

*Character deviance*: Unusual early experiences may engram peculiar characteristics which persist through adulthood. For example, if a young animal is taught to work a switch and thus subject itself to increasingly intense but tolerable electric shocks as a necessary preliminary to securing food, for the rest of its life it may, apparently to avoid the uncertainty of other choices, continue to seek modalities for eliciting such shocks even in the absence of any other immediate reward, and may thus appear to be inexplicably "masochistic" to an observer unacquainted with its unique experiences.

*Neonatal brain injuries*: A remarkable finding was that adequate care and training could in large part compensate for extensive brain damage in the newborn. Monkeys subjected to the removal of both temporal or parietal cortices at birth but given a protecting and nonconflictful home emvironment thereafter suffered minor kinesthetic and adaptive impairments which could be revealed only by elaborate tests (e.g., variable oddity selections) or during periods of sensory deprivation, but developed otherwise adequate individual and social adjustments. On the other hand, in the absence of such special care and training, bilateral lesions in the thalami, amygdalae, or in cerebral areas 13, 23, and 24 impaired adaptive capacities more seriously in young than in adult animals, and did not ameliorate experimentally induced neurotic behavior as effectively as in the case of adults.

*Early "psychological" traumata*: These were even more devastating: if the young animal was subjected to unpredictable or exceedingly severe conflicts among counterposed desires and aversions, or between mutually exclusive satisfactions that presented dilemmas as to which, both, or neither reward would be available, the animal developed deeply ingrained inhibitions, fears, rituals, somatic disorders, social maladjustments and other aberrations of behavior which became highly elaborate and more difficult to treat than those originating in adulthood as described below. A confusion of cues produced similar effects.

## C. Social Relationships

Animal societies in the laboratory as well as in the feral state organize themselves in hierarchies of relatively dominant and submissive members, with leadership and privileges generally preempted not by size or strength alone but in accordance with special aptitudes and "personality" skills. However, these relationships could be modified in the following significant ways:

## D. Parasitism, Industrial Strife, and Technological Solutions

Cats or monkeys could be trained to operate a switch mechanism that dropped a reward of food into a distant food box. When two conspecific animals so trained were placed together, in most pairs each would for a time alternate in working the switch while the other fed; soon, however, one would begin remaining near the food box in an attempt to subsist solely on its partner's labors. This usually occasioned a sit-down strike on the part of the worker whose rewards had been preempted, but eventually a fairly stable worker-parasite "industrial" relationship would be established in which the former operated the feeder energetically and sufficiently often to provide enough pellets for both.

Significantly, two such workers among fourteen pairs proved to be adequately "intelligent" (i.e., possessed of unusually high perceptive–manipulative capacities) to jam the switch so that the feeder mechanism operated continuously, thus solving a social problem by a form of technological automation.

*"Altruism"*: Some monkeys continued to starve for many hours—though never more than a day or so—rather than pull a lever to secure readily available food if they perceived that this also subjected another monkey to an electric shock. Such "succoring" behavior was apparently less dependent upon the relative age, size or sex of the two animals than on (a) their individual "character," (i.e., relatively constant patterns of conceptualization and response) and (b) whether or not they had been "well-adjusted" cagemates (i.e., had developed mutually predictable and favorable interactions).

*Aggression*: Conversely, actual fighting between members of the same species to establish various relationships was minimal; primacy and dexterity manifested by only occasional gestures of preemption were nearly always sufficient to establish dominance and privileges. Indeed, physical combat appeared only under the following special circumstances:

(a) When an animal that had attained a high position in its own group was transferred to one in which it came into direct conflict with new rivals themselves accustomed to dominance, and thereby had to adapt to unaccustomed challenges.

(b) Similarly, when a dominant animal was subjected to an unexpected territorial rebellion by an alliance of subdominants.

(c) When a female with increased status derived from mating with a dominant male thereafter turned on members of her group that had previously oppressed her.

(d) When a dominant animal, by being made experimentally neurotic, fell to a low position in its own group and thereafter expressed its frustrations by physical attacks on both inanimate and living objects in its environment.


### E. Experimental Neuroses and Psychoses

*Methods of induction*: As stated in the earlier versions of the fourth biodynamic principle, marked and persistent deviations of behavior could be induced by stressing the animal between mutually incompatible attractions and aversions: as, for instance, subjecting a cat to an *unpredictable* electric shock during conditioned feeding, or requiring a monkey to secure food from a box in which, on several occasions, he had *unexpectedly* been confronted with a toy snake—an object as representationally dangerous to the monkey as a live one, harmless or not, would be. Yet counter to early Freudian doctrines of neurotigenesis, either actual or anticipated fear of injury need not be involved at all, since later experiments demonstrated that equally serious and lasting neurotigenic effects could be induced by facing the animal with difficult choices among mutually exclusive satisfaction—situations that parallel the disruptive effects of prolonged hesitations among equally attractive alternatives in human affairs.

More recently, we have employed variably delayed auditory feedback of the animal's own vocalizations as another method of rendering its physical milieu unpredictable and thereby anxiety-provoking and neurotigenic. Four rhesus macaque monkeys, born in the laboratory in 1965, were separated from their mothers shortly after birth and subjected to social deprivation and relatively impersonal caretaking. The infants soon developed exaggerated oral patterns, rigid posturing, curling or repeated circling movements, head-clasping, and body-clutching. Three more animals, born and isolated the following year, showed similar effects.

Twenty-two months after the birth of the first infant, the seven monkeys were placed together in a large pen, but continued their stereotyped pacing and rocking, cataleptic posturing, digital sucking, and social withdrawal. They thus differed markedly from seven control monkeys, which, in a concurrently formed group, displayed normal patterns of play, threat, grooming, and dominance. Behavioral checklists were kept daily on the two groups.

Four months after the animals were group-housed, training trials began. The experimental chamber was a sound-deadened enclosure containing a primate restraining chair equipped with five white "clearance" lamps and a green "reward" lamp, a food tube and holder, and a feeder. The animals were transported individually to the laboratory, installed in the chair and put through an operant conditioning procedure. The experimenter observed from an adjoining booth. The animals' task was to vocalize for a prescribed period of time to illuminate the lamps sequentially for a banana pellet available only to their tongue. Early in training, the subjects were given five "free" lights and required to vocalize for the sixth. Each time they met a criterion of 24 completed vocalizations in a 10-min. experimental session, the number of free lights was reduced by one. At first, the animals were trained to sustain their responses for from .3 to .5 sec., but later the better performers were extended to as much as 1.5 sec.

Six isolates and five normals so trained were then put on a restricted food schedule, assigned the starting lamp on which they gave the steadiest performance in training, and adapted to padded earphones and simultaneous feedback. In the tests, which were started when the animals' weight and vocal output stabilized, a counterbalancing procedure was used; all the animals were subjected to a feedback of their voice delayed by a quarter of a second before and after a simultaneous feedback series.

Delay was then introduced. Initial reaction to the delay was a slowdown in responding by both groups—fewer vocalizations started and completed, and less time spent vocalizing. The accompanying "anxiety" is shown in Figure 1.

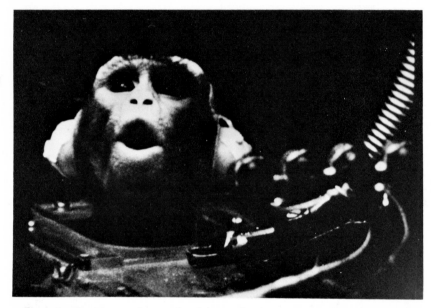

**Figure 1.** Anxiety reaction produced in monkey by delayed auditory feedback of its own vocal productions.

The animals adjusted, however, and by the 5th delay session their vocal output returned to and then exceeded the levels achieved in the simultaneous feedback sessions. When the "normal" or synchronous feedback condition was reintroduced, vocal behavior was again disrupted, indicating that any change in the accustomed temporal sequences was disorganizing for the animals. These data are summarized in Table I.

The taped vocalizations were classifed, tabulated, and rated for equivalence to human stuttering, stammering, slurring, and other sounds. Some qualitative differences under the two feedback conditions were noted, as well as similarities to speech defects in the human.

Finally, we have used experimental techniques that even more specifically demonstrate the devastating effects of sequential or temporal uncertainty; for example, if a monkey is taught to work a series of five switches and a final lever in a given order to secure food or avoid shock, and is then faced with bewildering variations in the required sequence and timing of the switches and lever, shown in Figure 2, it becomes highly disturbed, refuses to feed or escape, attacks the apparatus and develops other striking aberrations of behavior.

TABLE I   Number of Responses under Normal and Delayed Auditory Feedback[a]

| Measure | Group | 1-5 Simult. | 6-10 Delay (.25 sec.) | 11-15 Delay (.25 sec.) | 16-20 Simult. |
|---|---|---|---|---|---|
| Voc. started | Isolates | 4342 | 3582 | 4404 | 3940 |
| (.08-sec. units) | Normals | 3979 | 3414 | 4047 | 3635 |
| Voc. time on | Isolates | 1870 | 1471 | 1807 | 1575 |
| (.2-sec. units) | Normals | 1945 | 1607 | 1965 | 1769 |
| Voc. completed | Isolates | 1120 | 867 | 1018 | 930 |
| (.3-sec. units) | Normals | 1352 | 1022 | 1200 | 1115 |

[a] Isolates, $n = 6$; normals, $n = 5$

Figure 2.   Emotional reaction of monkey following unpredictable variations in sequence and timing requirements during multiple-choice responding.

These adverse reactions are minimized if, during the experiment, the confused and thereby disorganized animal is permitted to profit by the example of a monkeylike automaton in an adjoining compartment programmed to work the final lever in proper order and time (Figure 3).

Any of these stresses, when they exceeded the animal's adaptive capacities

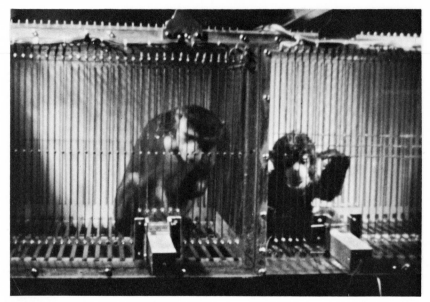

**Figure 3.** Attenuation of disturbed reactions to sequential/temporal uncertainty when animal is able to observe monkeylike automaton in adjoining compartment (toy monkey on right).

induced physiologic and mimetic manifestations of anxiety, spreading inhibitions, generalizing phobias, stereotyped rituals, "psychosomatic" dysfunctions, impaired social interaction, addiction to alcohol and other drugs (v.i.), regressions to immature patterns of behavior, and other marked and persistent deviations of conduct.[4]

*Constitutional influences*: Animals closest to man showed symptoms most nearly resembling those in human neuroses and psychoses, but in each case the syndromes induced depended less on the nature of the conflict—which could be held constant—than on the constitutional predisposition of the animal. For example, under similar stresses, spider monkeys reverted to infantile dependencies or catatonic immobility, cebus monkeys developed various "psychosomatic" disturbances including functional paralyses, whereas vervets became diffusely aggressive, persisted in bizarre sexual patterns, or preferred hallucinatory satisfactions such as chewing and swallowing purely imaginary meals while avoiding real food to the point of self-starvation.

---

[4] The experimental techniques and results here described have been recorded in a succession of motion picture films distributed by the Psychological Cinema Register, Pennsylvania State University, Audiovisual Services, University Park, Pennsylvania. The latest of these illustrates its title: "The Neurotigenic Effects of Manipulative Unpredictability."

## F. Factors That Accentuated Neurotic Symptomatology

Experimentally, these were precisely those that also exacerbated the loss of control over, or prevented escape from the stressful situation: i.e., increase in either hunger or fear or forced transgression of the phobic, compulsive, or regressive patterns described above. Under such circumstances anxiety mounted to panic, inhibitions became paralyzing, and psychosomatic disturbances grew serious enough to threaten the life of the animal.

## G. Procedures That Ameliorated Neurotic Aberrations

It would be inaccurate, of course, to state that the choice of methods selected for investigation was not influenced by the author's psychiatric and psychoanalytic training, since certain preferences, consciously or not, undoubtedly remained operative. Nevertheless, various techniques of "therapy" were investigated as objectively as possible, of which the following, with brief mention of their possible clinical parallels, were found most effective:

1. *Satiation of one of the conflictful needs*: If a neurotic animal with marked inhibitions of feeding and spreading symbolic aversions were tube-fed, its neurotic symptoms were temporarily relieved, only to recur when the necessity and the fear of spontaneous feeding returned simultaneously.

To cite a single clinical comparison: sexual intercourse may relieve repressed desire temporarily but does not usually dispel symbolically elaborated conflicts and may, indeed, exacerbate them. It will be recalled that such observations forced Freud to abandon his early attribution of the neuroses to quasi-physiologic "toxic accumulations" of "repressed libido."

2. *Prolonged rest away from the neurotigenic situation*: This blunted the other horn of the dilemma by removing the animal from the original environs of conflict. It is significant that this form of relief was minimal in monkeys in whom, as in the case of man, neurotic reactions quickly became generalized; moreover, animals which were returned to the laboratory even after a year of relatively peaceful sojourn elsewhere soon redeveloped their neurotic patterns, even though the original traumata were not repeated.

Clinically, "rest cures" and vacations away from disturbing situations may alleviate acute symptoms, but do not necessarily dispel the underlying and potentially disruptive tensions. Soldiers with "combat neuroses" may feel relieved when removed from immediate danger, but unless the impasse between selfpreservation versus military duty is effectively resolved, exposure to any situation reminiscent of this conflict almost inevitably spells the reappearance of neurotic reactions.

3. *Forced solution*: When hunger was maximal (from one to three days of

starvation), food was made particularly attractive and openly available and no escape from the temptation was possible, some neurotic animals broke through their feeding or other inhibitions, began eating spontaneously, and showed gradual relief from the various neurotic symptoms originally engendered by the hunger-fear conflict. On the other hand, animals with lesser readaptive capacities, when placed in similar situations calculated to break the motivational impasse, reacted instead with an exacerbation of phobias, somatic dysfunctions, destructive aggressivity, or a retreat into a quasi-cataleptic stupor.

Thus also, actively directing patients paralyzed by indecision and anxiety into some decisive course of action is occasionally necessary and effective, but may likewise present the danger of further bewilderment, panic, or even psychotic reactions if the predictive and adaptive capacities in space, time, and modality are seriously exceeded.

4. *Spontaneous re-exploration and solution*: Animals which had been trained merely to respond to an automatic food signal and which were then subjected to a counterpoised fear of feeding remained neurotic indefinitely since, without special help, they had no way of reexploring the traumatic situation. Markedly different, however, was the case of animals that had been taught to manipulate various devices that actuated the signals and feeder, because in this way they could exert at least partial control over their environment. This stood them in crucial stead even after they were made neurotic inasmuch as when their hunger increased, they gradually made hesitant but spontaneous attempts to reexplore the operation of the switches, signals and food boxes, and grew bolder and more successful as food began to reappear. If the fear-engendering situations were prematurely repeated, their effects were even more traumatizing, but if each animal's efforts were again rewarded with food as in its preneurotic experiences, it eventually became, to all appearances, as confident and effective in its behavior as ever.

This, perhaps, is a paradigm of how most conflicts—and "larval neuroses"—are resolved in most instances by spontaneous reexploration of the problem situation, leading to the immensely reassuring discovery that something temporarily feared either does not recur or may be mastered if it does. Pertinent also is the necessity all of us feel for acquiring a large variety of techniques to control our environment, not only for normal living but also as a means of trial reentry after retreat or flight. Explicitly, we invoke this principle in preparing our children for a wide range of contingencies; pragmatically we employ "occupational therapy" or "job training" in our correctional institutions and hospitals to give our patients the skills, whether major or minor, which they can later utilize to meet social challenges in the world outside. Implicitly also, a comparable process is at work in psychoanalysis as the analysand, in a protective, permissive situation, re-explores his conflictful and deeply repressed interpersonal desires and fantasies both verbally and through his transference relationship *(vide infra)*, finds himself not punished or rejected as he had, consciously or not, feared he might be and thus, gaining confidence and aplomb, retransfers and "works through" his relationships with things and people in the real world *everywhere* around him.

5. *"Transference" therapy*: This leads to the question: what about animals that had been trained to respond only to external signals and had not been taught manipulative or social skills; or if so taught, were later rendered too inhibited to use them? In such cases, it was found possible to alleviate the neurotic behavior through the more direct influence of the experimenter, who could assume the role of a reorientative trainer or "therapist." Dynamically, this influence itself was derived from the circumstance that the animal had been raised in a provident, kindly manner either in the laboratory by the experimenter himself, or elsewhere by someone who also liked animals. Indeed, if the latter were not the case, when the animal came to the laboratory the first requirement was to dispel its mistrust of human beings and to cultivate its confidence; in effect, to convert an initial "negative transference" into a "positive" one.[5] If, then, the animal's expectancy with regard to the experimenter, based on its experience with him or *his surrogates*, became predominantly favorable (positive transference), that expectancy could be utilized "therapeutically" for retraining and rehabilitation, however minimal the initial steps. For example, even the most "neurotic" animal, huddled in cataleptic rigidity in a dark corner, might be led by gentle petting and coaxing to take food from the experimenter's hand. Once this initial receptivity was established, the animal might be induced to eat from the floor of the apparatus if the experimenter remained near the cage; later, it sufficed that the "therapist" was merely in the room. At any stage of this retraining the premature repetition even of a faint feeding signal could precipitate the conflict and disrupt the animal's recovery, perhaps irrevocably. However, if the experimenter exercised gentleness and patience and did not at any time exceed the gradually regained tolerance and capacities of the animal, he could eventually induce it in successive stages to open the food box, to begin again to respond to signals and manipulative switches, and to reassert its former skills and patterns of self-sustenance. The retraining could then be continued to include acceptance of

[5] Whenever possible, all experimenters dissociated themselves (though such disassociation was rarely complete in the case of dependent dogs or the highly perceptive monkeys) from the animal's traumatizing experience by having the latter administered either by remote control or by an automatic electrical governor on the apparatus. Significantly, some experimenters were not able to secure this favorable relationship in normal animals, and were correspondingly unsuccessful in helping neurotic ones. In our laboratory, this was particularly true of an assistant who had himself been raised in an oriental country where cats and dogs were kept as guards or as scavengers, sometimes eaten, but almost never liked, respected, and protected.

previously traumatic stimuli, so that eventually the animals would welcome even an airblast or electric shock (though not the toy snake) as itself a harbinger of food or other rewards. After such patterns were in their turn reestablished, the therapist could complete the process by gradually withdrawing from the situation as the animal reasserted its self-sufficiency, until finally his personal ministrations or presence was no longer necessary.

To claim sweeping identities between the mechanics of these experiments and the almost incomparably more complex dynamics of clinical psychotherapy and psychoanalysis would be an obvious oversimplification; however, certain parallels need not be overlooked. The psychotherapist, too, is preconceived as a parental or helpful surrogate, else his aid would not be sought at all. Wishfully endowed by the patient with anticipatory concern and competence (though often this is explicitly denied), the properly trained and experienced therapist gently but effectively approaches the patient in his neurotic retreat, fills his needs personally in so far as practicable, permits him to reexplore, retest, and reevaluate experiential symbols and their disruptive conflicts, first in the protected therapeutic situation, then gradually—and never more rapidly than the patient's anxiety permits—in the outside world, and finally fosters and redirects his personal relationships onto people and activities that can play a favorable and permanent role in the patient's future. This done, the therapist may relinquish his Vergilian role of guide and mentor as the patient takes his place once more in the world and no longer needs the therapist personally except, perhaps, as another friend among a new-found many. Words, of course, are facile but sometimes deceptive instruments of communication, and abbreviations of statement should not contain abrogations of fact; neverthelss, perhaps it will be seen that, in a field more plagued by over-obfuscation than by over-simplification, these comparisons and parallelisms are more than merely rhetorical.

6. *"Social" therapy*: In some animals, the effectiveness of a sixth method dubbed, debatably but conveniently, "social" therapy or "therapy by example" indicated that one factor in the process of so-called "transference" therapy was the relatively impersonal one of making the solution of a motivational or adaptational impasse seem easier or at least possible. In this procedure, the neurotic animal was simply placed with a well-trained normal one and permitted to watch the latter work the switches and signals and then feed unharmed. After from one to several days of such observation, about half the neurotic animals would begin to approach the food box, cower less at the signals, tentatively try the switches, and finally "emulate" the normal animal in resuming effective feeding patterns. Once the conflict was thus resolved, its other neurotic expressions were also in large part—but never completely—mitigated, and the animal, aside from minor residuals such as slight furtiveness, restlessness, or tension, appeared to be recovered.

Though the method was simple and certainly took the least effort on the part of the experimenter, it seems most difficult to formulate theoretically, especially since the convenient fiction of a postulated "interanimal relationship" or "identification" was dispelled when, in a control series of experiments, the neurotic animal could also be induced to resume feeding when an appropriately furred, scented, and activated automaton mechanically "answered" the signals, opened the food box, revealed the presence of tempting pellets, and otherwise changed the neurotic animal's external and internal milieu.

Perhaps, as implied previously, this is the solipsistic nidus of all "interpersonal relationships." But whatever the dynamics, we utilize such influences empirically in our clinical work. To cite one instance, we place a neurotic child in a foster home or a special school in the hope that our young patient may be favorably influenced by the "example" of normal children being duly rewarded for patterns of behavior we wish our patient to acquire.

7. *Employing electroshock or other methods of producing cerebral anoxia and diaschisis* to disintegrate the neural basis of conflictful conceptualizations and their undesirable effects on behavior—a method that may be utilized in humans, although never without some impairment, however subtle, of future capacities.

8. *Performing various brain operations* to induce similar neuropsychologic disorganization; in monkeys, lesions corresponding to cortical areas 12, 23, and 24 were, as noted, most suitable for this purpose. However, our work in this field indicated that the after-effects of any brain operation depended not only on its site and extent but also on the preceding experiences and characteristics of the operated subject. For example, bilateral lesions of the dorsomedial thalamic nucleus impaired the learning capacities of a normal animal but left it gentle and tractable; in contrast, the same operation rendered a neurotic animal irritable and vicious.

9. Finally, *various drugs could also be used for the temporary disorganization of disturbing perceptions and conflictful reactions,* thus facilitating other methods of therapy. Additional pharmacologic observations were as follows:

(a) Effectiveness: Most of the commercially promoted "ataractics" (meprobamates and phenothiazines) were less generally effective than drugs long tested in clinical therapy; e.g., alcohol, paraldehyde, and the barbiturates and bromides.

(b) Preventive Action: Such drugs, if administered in mildy obtunding doses *before* subjecting an animal to stress or conflict, would also partially prevent the after-effect of an otherwise traumatic experience. By analogy, humans, too, are apt to take an alcoholic "bracer" or a trusted "tranquillizer" to narrow the conceptual field of threatening possibilities before asking for a raise, proposing marriage, or contemplating some other potentially hazardous undertaking.

(c) Addiction: However, a neurotic animal permitted to experience the relief from inhibition produced by alcohol would then prefer alcohol to nonalcoholic food and drink, and thus develop a "dipsomania" which would persist until its underlying neurosis was relieved by other means. In man, similar psychopharmacologic effects of addictive drugs are demonstrably operative but are, of course, complicated by highly individualized ethnic and culturally symbolic influences.

## IV. HUMAN CORRELATES

These observations, then, added to those of Sechenov, Pavlov, Gantt, Delgado, Skinner, Mirsky, Brady and many others cited in previous reviews of the literature, may have helped to clarify basic issues relevant to both "normal" and "deviant" behavior; however, since man's perceptive, mnemonic, symbolic and adaptive capacities are undeniably much (though not by necessity "infinitely" or "by quantum jumps") more complex than those of any other animal, it is obvious that ethologic or experimental studies alone cannot furnish data that completely "explain" human conduct. Comparatively speaking, man seems to differ from all other animals in having developed three ultimate (Ur—) axioms, beliefs, assumptions, aspirations, categorical imperatives—no term quite expresses their ubiquitous dynamics—that are indeed uniquely immanent in human motivations and transactions. We may, in briefest form, describe them as follows:

First, an urgent seeking for the knowledge and technology with which to control the material universe and eventually conquer disease and death.

Second, a persistent need for human relationships that, despite debacles of distrust, have led from the primal mother–child dyad through loyalties to the family, clan, tribe, state and nation, to a growing imperative toward the brotherhood of man.

And finally, an existential faith that man's being has an enduring dignity and significance in some universal teleologic, theologic or eschatologic system that extends beyond the here-and-now into eternity.[6]

*Coda in harmonic minor*: To repeat our opening theme, then, unpredictability may give existence its zest, but also imbues it with an anxiety that can best be ameliorated by rendering life, friends, and future more nearly certain.

---

[6] In this triplicate context, the experimental analogs of our techniques of therapy may be correspondingly regrouped as follows: *Physical*: Gratification of somatic needs, relief of stress, pressure to adapt, reassertion of skills, and the use of drugs, electroshock or other cerebral alternatives (experimental methods 1, 2, 3, 4, 7, 8 and 9). *Social*: Dyadic retraining or conspecific group rehabilitation (experimental methods 5 and 6). *Meta-physical–Existential*: Implicit in a primal joy in life, and some animals' faith in, and devotion to, their glorified human master.

# 3

## Experimental Basis for Neurotic Behavior[1]

### W. HORSLEY GANTT

The Johns Hopkins University and
The Pavlovian Laboratory, VA Hospital
Perry Point, Maryland

## I. INTRODUCTION

Concerning the human being, the psychiatric criteria accepted for neurotic behavior are those subjective feelings that either impair the function of the individual as judged by others or that disturb his own mental performance. Regarding psychosis, the practical use of the word depends upon (1) the mental inability of the subject to care for himself in his social surroundings, or (2) his serious inability to interact normally with the people around him. These are not rigid definitions; they do not ordinarily include criminals or organic defectives.

Since in the majority of psychopathologies there is lacking a known and recognizable cause as well as the objective type of test generally used in medicine, we have as yet no better criteria for classifying neuroses and psychoses than the above practical ones. As regards the minor neuroses, one has to remember that what is abnormal behavior in one culture may not be abnormal in another. Jeanne d'Arc was considered a witch in her time; she might have been a heroine in ours. Psychiatrists are still confused as to whether to affix a psychiatric diagnosis on Hitler, Stalin, or Sirhan. These examples bear witness to the lack of criteria in psychiatric diagnoses and how much they relate to changing cultures rather than to reliable disease entities.

In the human, the definitions are made chiefly on the above criteria; in the

---

[1] This is the title of a book that I wrote in 1944 summarizing my experimental work and concepts at that time. This chapter in the present volume reflects an updating of my material to include additional concepts based on newer experimental work as of 1969.

study of animals, where we cannot get subjective reports, the judgment concerning the existence of a neurotic or a psychotic state is made chiefly on the basis of the external behavior and the measurement of autonomic functions. Abnormal states have been studied in great detail in the dog; here we see conditions ranging from those comparable to mild anxiety (tachycardia, accelerated respiration, etc.), to manic and depressive states, including immobility comparable to catatonia, and even depression leading to death.

## II. CAUSES OF HUMAN PSYCHOSIS

Some of the causes of human psychosis are easily detected while others remain obscure. Among the former are organic deficits, such as in microcephaly and idiocy, the prolonged action of harmful chemicals, e.g., Korsakov's psychosis (alcohol), plumbism (lead), and the results of infections, e.g., general paresis (syphilis), and encephalitis, also vitamin deficiencies (pellagra, beri-beri).

Besides these established causes, whether there is a biochemical basis for schizophrenia has not yet been settled. Some workers, such as Heath (1954) and a number of Russians, claim that schizophrenia depends upon chemical changes in the blood. Although as Wolf, Thomas, and others have shown, there are blood changes, e.g., increase of cholesterol level under conditions of stress, it has not yet been established whether the composition of the blood is a cause of the psychosis or whether it is a result, or indeed whether it may not arise from some cause accompanying but not intrinscially related to the psychosis.

Even if there were an abnormal biochemical condition in the blood of schizophrenics, one faces the problem as to whether the chemicals are the cause or the result of the psychosis.

Abnormal behavior has been ascribed by a foremost neuroanatomist to the lack of inhibitory structures in the brain. Oscar Vogt, when in his advanced eighties, told me in 1957 that he had discovered in murderers and some other criminals a lack of an "inhibitory strip" in the parietal lobe, cells which he considered responsible for the function of inhibition on this higher level of behavior. Chromosomal abnormalities also are alleged to be related to abnormal behavior.

Thus, one sees that behavior can be related to anatomical, structural, and chemical causes. Where these causes are not detectable in ordinary behavior, we have to study them as they are produced by contacts between the individual and his experience with the external environment.

### A. Genetic Factors

A contribution to the analysis of genetic types has been made by Murphree and Peters (1967). They have been able to breed dogs with very abnormal behavior patterns not only in the gross behavior but in the cardiovascular reactions (see *effect of person*). This is a factor of supreme importance in the genesis of neurotic disturbances. But the study of human genetics, except for the prevention of a few organic diseases such as hemophilia, is almost hopeless since in the field of behavior we cannot unite on what kind of human we want.

## B. Types

Many scientists have considered that there are genetic and constitutional "types" which determine the form of the psychosis. Among these are Kraepalin, Kretschmer, and, more recently, Sheldon and Stockard. Pavlov, attempting to explain why some of his dogs and not others were susceptible to external stress, reverted to the Hippocratic classification and put his dogs into the traditional phlegmatic, sanguine (both normal), manic, and melancholic (both pathological) types. This classification, since Pavlov, has been modified by Krassutski and others in Russia (1928).

Abnormal behavior may ensue from either the lack of the stimulus of other living beings, as in isolation, or it may occur where there is excessive stimulation from too many living beings and the want of rest. The balance between this want of the presence of other living organisms and the pressure of too many is partly based upon what is normal for that particular species; some animals are solitary, others gregarious. This is an important question needing elucidation, especially in our present human era of increasing populations and urbanization.

No satisfactory system of classifying types has been evolved, though many have been suggested. The fallibility of all the systems described is that they are descriptive names for what occurs *after* the appearance of the pathological state, but there have been no reliable ways of predicting that the subject will show pathological behavior *before* it has actually appeared.

This means that we do not know how to test an individual that is behaving normally to reveal that under some circumstances he will now or in the future develop a pathological behavioral state. Since the ultimate province of science is to predict rather than to name, one should be able to foretell whether any event will occur and what its contingent circumstances are.

Pavlov also noted that there are stages in the development of neurotic states, as seen in the balance of the conditional reflexes. He described these phases as paradoxical, ultraparadoxical, and inhibitory.

It was Pavlov's opinion that inhibition was a protective function, saving the individual from damaging overreactivity. He saw the nervous system as acting in a sort of feedback, governing way to preserve itself by inhibiting further activity. And in catatonia and some schizophrenics, inhibition, chiefly regarding people, is a marked feature of the disease.

From my work it would appear that one can foretell to some extent whether an individual will display neurotic symptoms by exposing him to a mild stress situation, and measuring his reaction. The effect is assessed chiefly through the changes in the components of the formed conditional reflexes (cardiac, respiratory, motor, secretory, sexual, GSR) to the previously formed conditional reflexes.

From such a simple test using the conditional reflexes it seems that one may find out partially which individuals are susceptible to breakdown and which are resistant. This results in two main categories—weak and strong. One may further detect in which direction the breakdown will occur, whether toward an inhibitory or toward an excitatory state (Gantt, 1942; 1943).

How the animal breaks down seems to depend upon some innate constitutional factor rather than upon the kind of stress situation imposed. Thus, regardless of how one produces the stress, whether differentiation in the food or in the pain area, a certain animal will inevitably become manic, while to the same external stress another animal will become depressed and melancholic. This was seen in Pavlov's dogs subjected to the emotional disturbance of a flood, and in my own dogs which underwent the emotional trauma of overcrowding, exposure to many new and unknown dogs, severe emotional conflicts and fights. Some weathered the intense event with little disturbance, others became hyperactive or manic and others depressive. With some dogs the event resulted in a disturbance of only a short duration, in others of very much longer duration. The same external procedure may in one animal produce anxiety and mania and in another melancholia and even death, as seen in our dogs, especially Nick and V3 (Gantt, 1944; 1952b; Newton and Gantt, 1968).

## C. Environmental Causes

In Pavlov's description of experimental neurosis, a term which he used for any pathological nervous state in his dogs which was produced in the laboratory, he thought that the disturbance was due chiefly to what he called a conflict between excitation and inhibition. His first observations were made about 1921 when he was studying the ability of the dog to discriminate between two highly similar visual forms, one of which was followed by food and the other not. When the dog was confronted with such difficult differentiations his behavior became disturbed in different degrees.

As we look at difficult differentiation between two visual stimuli from a human point of view, logically it is hard to see why such an apparently innocuous confrontation should disturb the dog so seriously. Why does he not simply neglect the signal which he cannot discriminate? Such questions are difficult to answer logically because the nervous system and the living organism do not always work according to what appears as logic.

However, there is a great deal of evidence that a preponderance of human difficulties depend upon the inability of the individual to marshal the process of inhibition so that it does not conflict with a closely related process of excitation. Many examples can be found (Gantt, 1968).

In addition to the conflict between learned excitation and its related inhibition, there are other causes of neuroses found in dogs. One of these is what can be classified as emotional traumata, a term which lacks precision. Among these as mentioned above, are severe fights among the dogs, markedly disturbed relationships such as overcrowding, separation from habitual mates, etc. These factors involving other individuals seem to be more potent than simply infliction of pain or deprivation of food.

The application of the simple principles seen in the laboratory to the human is greatly complicated by the tremendous ability of the human for generalization. While in the dog we see the generalization of a positive conditional reflex to a tone of 260 to all related tones, also places and other elements of the environment, in the human being we see a greatly increased generalization which is represented in the mediating function of language. On this function is directed a great part of the tragedies as well as the triumphs in the human—his bestial wars, his sadisms, his cruel annihilations of those holding different opinions, as well as his stupendous achievements in mathematics, science, and engineering leading to his exploration of space. Although the functions of induction, differentiation, schizokinesis, autokinesis, and effect of person are common throughout a wide range of the animal kingdom, the function of language and its elaborations occur only in the human.

Concerning overcrowding, recent evidence shows that there is an optimal organism/space arrangement for different species depending upon what the species has been adapted to. Some, as the dog and the honey bee, require the presence of either the human or its own kind to survive. What this optimum is for the human has not yet been determined. But it is known that either a strange environment, or too few or too many others in it can result in death. I have seen dogs that succumbed apparently from a want of the past companionship of their human friends.

Other factors in the development of neurotic states will be described under the terms Schizokinesis and Autokinesis.

## D. Measures of Disturbed Behavior

As mentioned above, in the animal we do not have access to subjective states as they are reported through language to us by another human being. We must depend entirely upon measures that are independent of language. First among these objective signs is the general behavior. If we have known the particular dog previously, a deviation from its usual general behavior would signify a disturbance. As the dog is familiar to the human, we can easily detect disturbances of general behavior. For example, depression is shown by the dog's retreating to a corner, tucking his tail, unresponsiveness, or refusal of food in the presence of a human (Gantt, 1944). What corresponds to anxiety with the human being is shown in the dog by exaggerated muscular activity (daily running), inability to remain quiet, increased respiratory rate, and tachycardia. This overactivity leads to what is comparable to a manic state; extreme restlessness and markedly exaggerated autonomic symptoms (cardiac, respiratory, genito-urinary).

Other autonomic systems may be involved; the sexual reflexes are among the most delicate barometers of a disturbance of behavior. In order to evaluate a disturbance of the sexual system it is necessary to have some measure of the sexual reflexes in the individual dog. In the male dog we have used the elicitation of sexual erection and ejaculation by stimulation of the external genitalia, either faradic or manual. We measure the following items: latent period and duration of erection, amount of ejaculation, and sperm count. Knowing what these items usually are in the individual, a deviation is evidence of a disturbance of behavior. We often find a sexual deviation before a deviation in any other autonomic function we have measured. We have seen that even one or two difficult differentiations, e.g., between an excitatory and an inhibitory tone based on food, results in a failure to obtain sexual reflexes for as long as a week. At present we have devised no corresponding sexual measures for the female (Gantt, 1949).

When dogs become markedly disturbed, the form of the disturbance depends upon the particular dog. In some there is a wide extension of a manic type to various physiological systems: refusal of food even after 24 or 48 hours starvation in the environment where the disturbance was produced, sexual erection in this environment, marked tachycardia, failure to give any of the conditional reflexes formed in the laboratory as well as great changes in the unconditional reflexes (food, sexual, pain), and, in the other direction, immobility, complete lack of sexual reflexes with catatoniclike states and great cardiovascular changes to the presence of a human being (Murphree, Peters, and Dykman, 1967).

In one dog, catatonia was regularly produced by the presence of any person, and the fluctuations in heart rate varied from 160 to 20 in the presence of a person and of blood pressure from 150 when alone to 80 in the presence of a person (Newton and Gantt, 1968).

## III. PRINCIPLES OF NEUROTIC DEVELOPMENT

In the studies of the dog over its life span we see several principles that we could not see if the animal were observed for only a few months. This is made possible by a careful study of several physiological systems, both for the unconditional reflexes as well as for the corresponding conditional reflexes. The physiological systems which we have studied most intensively have been the gross motor, the salivary, the cardiovascular, the respiratory, the sexual, and the urinary. Other functions which are easily measured are the vestibular and some hormonal systems. In order to perform these investigations we must have the individual under observation for long periods of its life (Alpern, Finkelstein, and Gantt, 1943).

## A. Effect of Person

We have investigated especially the *effect of person*. By this I mean the influence of one individual on another, not necessarily the human. There are many instances of the profound effect of this throughout the animal kingdom, an influence which may be great enough to lead to death without any infliction of physical injury. This effect of person may take two forms: (1) He may act as a signal for some past experience in the same way as any other conditional signal acts. Thus, the person who has mistreated a child or dog may elicit anxiety, fear, or aggression. This is the more evident effect of person. (2) There is another less understood, obscure influence of one individual upon another. Without knowing its mechanism we see the profound effect. Whether it depends upon some undiscovered information–transmission relationships remain to be seen. Here is a vast field for investigation, but adequate methods are presently lacking.

We have previously described the many ways in which Pavlov noted the profound effect the person had on his dogs. For this reason, he built the soundproof "cameras," designed to eliminate the effect of person as well as other extraneous stimuli. Pavlov found that when he reintroduced the person, there was a pronounced effect, especially on certain types of dogs. As he did not measure heart rate at that time, Pavlov was able to see this effect only in certain types of dogs. Had he been measuring respiration and heart rate, he would have been able to see this effect in practically all of his dogs.

In the 1920's Pavlov performed a few experiments to duplicate the role of the person in special dogs by placing the clothing of the person to whom the dog reacted in the room with the animal; this he found elicited similar neurotic behavior as the person himself.

Since we have been routinely measuring the cardiovascular function in our dogs for the last 30 years, we have been impressed with the role of the person in the experiments in nearly all of the dogs. The person can obviously have the effect of a conditional signal based upon his past experience with that particular dog. But, in addition to this, there is abundant evidence that one individual has a powerful influence on another individual. This seems to me to reflect some type of innate responsiveness. This effect of an individual on another individual is distributed throughout the animal kingdom, from insect to human. There are many examples of how even so low on the zoological scale the presence of an insect, in some not yet understood way, influences another insect. Many individuals, deprived of the company of their mates or of their companions, decline and die (Gantt, 1960).

Numerous attempts, in one form or another, have been made to elucidate some influence of the presence of the individual. Most of these, as far as concerns the mechanism, have led to no positive results. Some Russian investigators have recently reported that mitosis in living tissue emits rays that affect the growth of yeast cells (Sneerson et al. 1961). Ranging upward from such cellular reactions are those of the alleged extrasensory perception of Rhine and Pratt (1957). There are also many observations on the effects of deprivation of person on the behavior of higher animals. Among these are those of Harlow and Zimmerman (1959), showing the marked effect on infant monkeys of deprivation of maternal care. Another example of the effect of the individual, especially at certain periods of life, is the imprinting phenomenon reported by Lorenz (1952).

In medicine, the role of the physician as the person has been recognized, although with the advance of scientific and mechanical medicine, it is likely to be swept aside. The great physician William Osler mentions that a patient with incurable cancer gained ten pounds after the visit of an optimistic physician.

This effect of person, which is more than that of a signal depending upon the past experience of the individual, i.e., some obscure, innate effect, is as real as it is obscure (Gantt, 1966).

We have found that the mere presence of the person has a certain effect upon the dog, easily demonstrable in the cardiovascular functions, either a positive, improving effect, or a negative, deleterious effect (Gantt, 1960). Neurotic dogs show the effect in a much more pronounced way than do normals (Newton and Gantt, 1968). This effect, again, may take two forms. Some neurotic dogs become wildly agitated, with greatly increased heart rate and blood pressure; while others not only fail to show the normal reactivity to a person, but show what seems to be an inhibitory shell around them, completely impervious to the person. Thus, some of the dogs studied by Murphree et al. (1967) showed no cardiovascular reaction to the presence of the person, nor even to the person petting the dog. Like a schizophrenic, they had inhibited the effect of person, or at least as expressed in the cardiovascular component.

Our standard procedure is to measure the reaction of the dog to the person standing in the room with him, and also with the person petting the dog, viz., rubbing him behind the ears. These two procedures usually produce opposite results—the first produces tachycardia; the second, bradycardia. The degree of heart rate change varies from dog to dog, and person to person (Gantt, Newton, Royer, and Stephens, 1966).

The work of Anderson (1966) has shown a marked effect of the presence of the person upon the cardiovascular reactions to a painful stimulus; the heart rate rise to a faradic shock may be reduced as much as 50% when a person is in with the dog. Studies with the coronary blood flow in an unanesthetized dog show that the increase of blood flow in response to a person petting the dog (rubbing him behind his ears) may be greater than the coronary blood flow in the same dog when he is hungry and eating (Newton and Ehrlich, 1969).

## B. Schizokinesis

Schizokinesis has two aspects: a specific one, and a more generalized form. The specific one has to do with the difference in the rate of formation and perseveration of the components of the conditional reflex. Some two decades ago, we noticed that the excitatory cardiac component of the reflex formed more quickly than the general components—secretory and motor. The respiratory component behaved more like the cardiac component. It seemed that those functions that were of a supportive nature fell into one group and the specific components into another. It is comprehensible why the supportive functions should appear before the specific. Paradoxically, however, the cardiovascular functions usually persist much longer than the general ones. In some dogs, it has been almost impossible to eradicate the cardiac conditional reflexes, once they have been formed. They are much slower to be extinguished than the secretory or motor conditional reflexes.

On the other hand, the dog takes longer to form differential cardiac reflexes than it does to form differential secretory or motor, i.e., the inhibitory cardiac conditional reflex is slower to form than the inhibitory secretory or motor reflex (Gantt, 1960). From this it appears that the cardiovascular component is more susceptible to conditioning but that once these conditional reflexes are formed they are difficult to inhibit or otherwise eradicate.

This susceptibility of the cardiovascular function to the experiences of life, as well as the stresses and emotional situations, and the comparative rigidity of these reactions, once formed, may be the basis from which originate certain cardiovascular disorders, e.g., tachycardia and hypertension. Since the cardiovascular functions are ordinarily autonomic and unconscious, this means that cardiovascular pathology may have its origin far back in the patient's life, and the original incidents may have been completely forgotten. There is, thus, a physiological subconscious, as well as a possible Freudian one.

There is another aspect of schizokinesis which derives from this split between what goes on in what may be considered the physiological concomitants of emotion and what goes on at the motor and sensory level of a specific, definable conditional reflex. It appears that the emotional system, represented in some of the autonomic functions, may persevere in a maladaptive activity, while at the conscious level there is apparent adaptation. Such a split function, insofar as we can understand the efficiency of the organism, would be an inefficient system.

This would contradict the ideas of equilibrium and harmony that have come down from the Greeks and are incorporated in Claude Bernard's constancy of the *milieu interieur*, later elaborated by Cannon into "homeostasis." Schizokinesis, on this level, is opposed to the welfare, or at least the physical efficiency of the organism, judged by the expenditure of energy. This idea first impressed me in 1937, when I referred to it as "dysharmony," later as schizokinesis (Gantt, 1937). It represents a kind of built-in liability of the organism. It is often not possible to perform efficiently at every level, and what may be effective at one time or in one system may not be effective in another. We know of many instances in pathology, e.g., where secretions of gastric juice useful in digestion of food is injurious as in a peptic ulcer. The body, fortunately, has marvelous powers for coordination and integration, which usually far outweigh its dyscoordination through schizokinesis (Gantt, 1962).

It has been argued that this overactivity of the preparatory and supporting function was necessary under more primitive conditions of attaining food and avoiding enemies, a function which has persisted though no longer useful. I am more inclined to look upon this schizokinesis as an inherent and unavoidable activity in the living organism. If, in the course of its life, or over generations when old functions no longer useful should have disappeared, the individual sometimes cannot make the proper adjustments and we have a malfunctioning organism. Everything is not always "for the best in the best of all possible worlds."

## C. Autokinesis

One of the earliest phenomena that we saw after the neurotic state was initiated by difficult differentiation was a progressive *development* of the pathology, which development occurred without repetition of the former external stress that seemed to produce it. This development was seen in the inclusion of several other physiological systems which had not been involved at the time of the original stress. But these pathological states were evoked by bringing the dog into the environment of the original stress or of several of the items present in the original stress. These items included the kind of food the dog was given at that time, the presence of the person who had worked with him, as well as the room in which he worked.

In one dog, Nick, who was studied during his life span from the age of 2 to 16 years, we saw that the development included several new systems: the genito-urinary, the cardiovascular, the respiratory. In another dog of the opposite type, V3, we also noted the progressive inclusion of new behavioral traits evoked by people who had worked with him previously and *pari passu* with the passage of time any person would evoke these reactions (Gantt, 1944).

From such studies we postulated that without the repetition of the external stress which produced a disturbance, there may be a progressive development taking place internally. This suggests that there can be interaction among the centers of activity present in the brain which have been created previously by some external stress. This brings us to view the world of the individual as not only involving reactions to an external environment but a reactivity among its own centers, among the traces in the central nervous system which have been implanted by previous experiences. There is a continuous internal interaction and development occurring within the internal universe of the individual.

In our neurotic animals we have seen especially the development which takes the animal downhill, i.e., a *negative autokinesis*. But there is reason to believe that both in the human and in the dog there can be improvement through interaction of excitatory foci in the brain, an improvement which can be designated *positive autokinesis.*

Although there are many more examples known of autokinesis than of schizokinesis, the former is not so well understood, because the subject is more complex and less well defined. Autokinesis is a function that is of great importance in the development of pathological conditions on the one hand and their remission or therapy on the other; yet very little experimental work has been done on this subject. It is first necessary to collect as many examples as possible to represent this progressive interaction of forces of excitation within the nervous system, in order that we may see where the need is for further exploration. The many phenomena representing autokinesis have to be rigidly examined to see whether they represent some interaction among the forces of excitation and inhibition, and to see if they depend upon a basic common mechanism.

I summarized my current thinking in regard to reflexology and autokinesis in an article (Gantt, 1966) from which I take the ensuing quotation:

> Man's primary battles have been practical and pragmatic—for existence, for food and for progeny. Only in the last few centuries of his long biological history has he turned his attention to the scientific study of his relationship to his surroundings. Compared with the physical conquest of Nature the understanding of his place in the universe has been indeed short.
>
> This scientific study goes back to Aristotle, but in its modern form to the ideas of Francis Bacon, Lomonosov, Locke, Descartes, and Galileo. Bacon and Lomonosov stressed the ability of science to subdue Nature. Locke emphasized the possibility of the human organism to adapt in his individual life, and also the value of observation; Descartes formulated the schematic concept of the reflex. These theoretical ideas became concrete through the experimental methodology which Galileo had done so much to establish in the physical sciences. Locke gave a tremendous impetus to the belief in the external

environment as the chief factor in behavior. The concept of reflex was strengthened by Bell and Magendia when they showed the specific function of the anterior and of the posterior nerve roots.

The tremendous advance made in the understanding of the relation of the organism to the external world resulted from the experiments of Pavlov at the turn of the century. It is important to remember that Pavlov illumined the concept of the conditional reflex not theoretically from Sechenov but as a result of careful observation made on the chronic animal in the course of his studies of digestion. It was his genius which created the methods by preserving the nerve connections and studying the animal over its life-span, enabling him to see reactions which *developed* as a result of the experience of the individual, based on the inborn, built-in activity of the animal. Thus arose the idea of the unconditional reflex and the conditional reflex, the positive and the negative, the excitatory and the inhibitory (Pavlov, 1910).

Somewhat similar experiments were performed about the same period by Thorndike in the United States and Bekhterev in Russia. However, in their relation to the inborn physiological reflex, these studies lacked the simplicity of Pavlov's. Pavlov's had a further advantage in that they were physiological. They arose from the physiological measurements of secretion involving the autonomic nervous system, while those of Bekhterev and the psychologists concerned movements in space of the "voluntary" muscular system; in the former, consciousness of the response was unessential; in the latter it was or could be involved. Thus, Pavlov's had the virtue of mostly eliminating anthromorphic explanations and of being capable of quantitative measurement.

Later work of the American School, in the footsteps of Skinner, developed *operant* or *instrumental* conditioning in which habits were impressed on the individual by food or pain avoidance reinforcement, the individual being offered an opportunity to select its response in a restricted environment. This was a readily available method of training the subject to make a required response in a short time; Skinner could demonstrate before a class of 500 the formation in a few minutes of an operant conditional reflex in a pigeon.

Several definite, new trends have come into both the American and the Russian work recently. Cybernetics has been responsible for introducing the principle of "feedback," electronic machines, the comparison of the brain to digital or analog computers, electrophysiology has made possible the use of the conditional reflex method for the study of nerve tracts and cellular physiology. The sophistication of psychologists in physiological methods has been responsible for the introduction of many new techniques—electrodes in the brain, recording from single nerve cells, injection of drugs into specific cerebral areas, etc.

There has thus been over the past few centuries an increasing emphasis on the external environment, and in spite of explicit opposition to the reflexology of Descartes, there has actually been an increasing acceptance of his mechanistic concept adorned in the clothes of the modern mechanist with his computers, electric circuitry, and feedback. Whether this be right or wrong, it is imperative, if we would see where we stand, that we recognize it for what it is worth.

Two of our studies show the importance of the internal environment and how there can be a great deal of internal conditioning: the preservation of the conditional reflex after the elimination of both afferent and efferent limbs of the reflex arc and the independence of the cardiac conditional reflex of the external movement (Gantt, 1937; 1953b). The conditional reflex can be formed and can exist internally without involvement of the external environment! If the nervous system can form conditional reflexes from a stimulus applied within, albeit an artificial one, it is reasonable to assume that it can elaborate conditional reflexes from stimuli arising from origins peculiar to itself.

Cardiovascular changes—heart rate, blood pressure, and vasomotor manifestations—have been shown to be components of the food and of the pain conditional reflexes. If the movements of the dog are prevented by curare or by crushing of the motor roots, mentioned above, the heart rate is nearly as high whether the dog makes a movement or not (Newton and Gantt, 1960; Royer and Gantt, 1966). Here again we see that the peripheral event is not necessary for the autonomic activity, it is a central affair (Brogden and Gantt, 1942).

By autokinesis I mean the development of the individual from forces within rather than from without. Several categories of autokinesis exist. On the phylogenetic level there is evolution; on the ontogenetic, embryological development and maturation. These are clearly recognized. They occur from inborn forces, inherent in the structure of the living substance, biological and organizational. But the autokinesis which I should like to discuss is an acquired autokinesis, one that is individual and that develops like the conditional reflex as the result of the experience of the individual to the accidents of life.

My realization of autokinesis came about as a result of observing dogs with experimental neurosis in the laboratory. In the dog Nick, I saw that years after the production of the symptom, after the dog was taken out of the environment and without any intervening experimentation, when he was brought back entirely new elaborations of the pathology were observed.

I have noted that sometimes *one* injection of a drug will permanently, or at least for a long time, change the level of reactivity of the dog, the size of his conditional reflexes, though the drug is not repeated. Wiener, recognizing the development of pathologic reactions to formerly innocuous stimuli, explained it by saying that the *level* of feedback had been altered (Wiener, 1956).

When the development is in the direction of making better adaptations this I call positive autokinesis, when the direction is downward, negative autokinesis.

There is likely an interaction among the foci of nervous storage depots that may discharge and stimulate other centers. If there can be interaction between the organism and the stimuli of the external environment it seems reasonable that there may be interaction within the organism on the basis of internal forces. There are evidently many means of communication among various organs, which, as we know, is at the basis of homeostasis. If the results of an infection can be stored indefinitely somewhere, if stimuli from external sense organs can be stored in the nervous system, it is reasonable to believe that stimulations from organs within may be stored probably in the nervous system and remain active or become active subsequently.

We already know something of how organs interact. A well recognized example is the interaction between the kidney and the cardiovascular system. If the blood pressure in the kidney is reduced the kidney produces renin which interacts with globulins in the blood to form angiotonin which then raises the blood pressure (Page and Helmer, 1940a; 1940b).

The individual may at any time contribute to the effects of external stimulation and modify the results. A recognition of the function of autokinesis and the recognition of the internal universe as one even more important than the external one—with which we are more familiar because of our relation of consciousness to the impulses brought over the sensory nerves and from the external sense organs—would change our reflexological view of behavior from a static to a dynamic one and open up a limitless field for investigation.

The study of the relation of the organism to the external world was given a powerful impetus by Descartes' model of the reflex. The concept developed under the genius of Pavlov's brilliant experiments. It is time now to look within the organism, to replace and supplement a static reflexology by a dynamic physiology of behavior. This is not to say that there have not been many valuable researches of what goes on inside the organism, and of internal relationships; on the other hand, a vast literature has accumulated in this field. To mention a few: the researches of Claude Bernard (1878), Irvine Page (Page and Helmer, 1940a; 1940b) on the production of angiotonin by reduced renal blood pressure of the relations between liver and kidney (Russek, 1962). Pavlov's brilliant observations have already shown us the importance of the internal environment. It now remains for us to amplify the study of the universe within us, an infinitely more complex one than all the external universes, so that we see the organism not only reacting to the forces without but to the multitude of forces and complexities within.

Everyone is acquainted with the principle of induction in his own life; after a rest of certain functions these functions are intensified and the repetition of certain activities lead to their inhibition. Many neurotic and psychotic states may be explained by the clash of excitation and inhibition and especially difficult differentiation.


## IV. CONCLUSION

It is appropriate to conclude with an editorial for the Conditional Reflex Journal (1968), in which I described how a difficult differentiation can result in disturbed or pathological behavior.

If we examine critically the causes of conflict in the human we usually can find a difficult, partial inhibition as the cause. Why does "the watched pot never boil?" Here we have simultaneous excitation and inhibition, the sight of the pot is excitatory, its not boiling inhibitory; the difficult differentiation, like other unpleasant emotions, causes the passage of time to appear slow. But let one employ external inhibition, i.e., turn his attention to another activity, not look at the pot, the difficult differentiation is removed, and time seems to go faster.

When people get angry with each other, nearly always the inhibition of an ongoing activity can be found as the basis. This is most easily seen in children, because they have not developed the ability for inhibition. If you stop a child from doing something he is doing he will cry, whether you stop him from eating or from going somewhere, or call him from play to put him to bed, etc. Nearly all daily conflicts with other persons are based on whether you encourage an ongoing activity (i.e., support the excitation) or whether you block, viz., inhibit, an ongoing activity. The frustration of politicians is related to this blocking, the anger of scientists also is related to blocking of their experimental work, refusal of grants, limitation of space, opposition to concepts. Adults are fraught with inhibition, but they show their conflicts in other, often oblique, ways, e.g., resentment, various emotional reactions.

In the human what is being inhibited in a conflict is often the role of the effect of person and all the forms of activity based on person and approval, e.g., pride, vanity, or prestige. "The main thing inhibited is what he considers as his person. When in traffic, and being held up, one may say, 'What are those idiots doing, holding *me* up?' They are hurting my image of myself as the man in a hurry to an important event." In affluent societies money usually is related to the effect of person, viz., satisfying the desire for approval, conformation to whatever is the mode, be it miniskirt or top hat, for what wins the approbation of the crowd.

Such feelings as jealousy and covetousness are based on the conflict between excitation and inhibition. If one dog sees another dog eating a bone this causes excitation of the food center in the dog that does not have the bone and inhibition is required to prevent a fight. Among scientists the excitation connected with a concept expressed by someone else is linked with a desire to appropriate the concept: inhibition of the excitation for prestige becomes difficult. Here also appears the ambition for esteem and vanity, viz., some of the manifold forms of the effect of person.

In discipline imposed from the outside without the voluntary participation of the individual, the mechanism may be entirely different. If the person is unwilling or unable to transfer the situation to another focus of activity, he may be in the situation of the dog confronted with a difficult differentiation, with a conflict between excitation and inhibition. He is still concerned with the original excitation.

In voluntary self-discipline there is no longer the preoccupation with the activity being inhibited, but there is a transfer to another activity; this places it more nearly in the mechanism of what Pavlov called external inhibition. But when inhibition is imposed from the outside and the individual is "unwilling," there may be preoccupation with the inhibited activity rather than with a rival substituted activity. Thus arises disturbed behavior in both dog and man.

# REFERENCES

Alpern, E. B., Finkelstein, N., & Gantt, W. H. Effect of amphetamine (benzedrine) sulfate upon higher nervous activity. *Bulletin Johns Hopkins Hospital,* October 1943, 73(4), 287-299.

Anderson, S., & Gantt, W. H. The effect of person on cardiac and motor responsivity to shock in dogs. *Conditional Reflex,* 1966, 1(3), 181-190.

Bernard, C. *Les phenomenes de la vie.* Paris: Hachette, 1878.

Brogden, W. J., & Gantt, W. H. Intraneural conditioning: Cerebellar conditioned reflexes. *Archives of Neurology and Psychiatry,* 1942, 48, 437-455.

Gantt, W. H. Contributions to the physiology of the conditioned reflex. *Archives of Neurology and Psychiatry,* 1937, 37, 848-858.

Gantt, W. H. (Tr. and Ed.) *Lectures on conditional reflexes,* (I. V. Pavlov). [2nd Ed. (Book) Vol. 1, 1941.] New York: International Publishers, 1928. Pp. 414.

Gantt, W. H. Origin and development of nervous disturbances experimentally produced. *American Journal of Psychiatry,* 1942, 98(4), 475-481.

Gantt, W. H. Measures of susceptibility to nervous breakdown. *American Journal of Psychiatry,* May 1943, 99(6), 839-849.

Gantt, W. H. *Experimental basis for neurotic behavior.* New York: Harper (Hoeber), 1944. Pp. 212.

Gantt, W. H. Psychosexuality in animals. In: *Psychosexual development in health and disease.* New York: Grune and Stratton, 1949.

Gantt, W. H. Effect of alcohol on the sexual reflexes of normal and neurotic male dogs. *Psychosomatic Medicine,* 1952a, 14(3).

Gantt, W. H. Postscript to experimental induction of psychoneuroses by conditioned reflex with stress. Chapter In: *The biology of mental health and disease.* New York: Harper (Hoeber), 1952b. Pp. 508-514.

Gantt, W. H. Principles of nervous breakdown: Schizokinesis and autokinesis. *Annuals of the New York Academy of Science,* 1953a, 56(2), 143-163.

Gantt, W. H. The physiological basis of psychiatry: The conditional reflex. In: *Basic problems in psychiatry.* J. Wortis (Ed.). New York: Grune and Stratton, 1953b. Pp. 778-798.

Gantt, W. H. Normal and abnormal adaptations—homeostasis, schizokinesis and autokinesis. *Diseases of the Nervous System,* (Monogr. Supl. XVIII, No. 7), 1957.

Gantt, W. H. Cardiovascular component of the conditional reflexes to pain and other stimuli. *Physiol. Rev. Suppl.* 4, 1960, 40(2), 266-291.

Gantt, W. H. Factors involved in the development of pathological behavior: Schizokinesis and autokinesis. *Perspectives in Biology & Medicine,* 1962, 5, 473-482.

Gantt, W. H. Reflexology, schizokinesis and autokinesis. *Conditional Reflex,* 1966, 1(1), 57-68.

Gantt, W. H. The role of inhibition in neurotic behavior. *Conditional Reflex,* 1968, 3(2), 65-68.

Gantt, W. H., Katzenelbogen, S., & Loucks, R. B. An attempt to condition adrenalin hyperglycemia. *Bulletin Johns Hopkins Hospital,* Vol. LX, No. 6, June 1937, 400-411.

Gantt, W. H., Pavlov and Darwin. In: *Evolution after Darwin,* Vol. 2. Chicago, Illinois: University of Chicago Press, 1960. Pp. 219-238.

Gantt, W. H., Newton, J. E. O., Royer, F., & Stephens, J. Effect of person. *Conditional Reflex,* 1966, 1(1), 18-35.

Harlow, H. F., & Zimmerman, R. R. Affectional responses in the infant monkey. *Science,* 1959, 130, 421-432.

Heath, R. G. Psychology. *Symposium, American Association Adv. Science and American Psychiatry Association,* December 30, 1954.

Krassutski, 1928.

Lorenz, K. Z. *King Solomon's ring.* New York: Crowell, 1952.

Murphree, O. D., Peters, J. E., 1969.

Murphree, O. D., Peters, J. E., & Dykman, R. A. Effect of person on nervous, stable, and crossbred pointer dogs. *Conditional Reflex,* 1967, 2(4), 273-276.

Newton, J. E. O., & Ehrlich, W. Coronary blood flow in dogs: Effect of person. *Conditional reflex,* 1969, 4(2), 81-88.

Newton, J. E. O., & Gantt, W. H. Curare reveals central rather than peripheral factor determining cardiac orienting reflex. *American Journal of Physiology,* 1960, 199, 978-980.

Newton, J. E. O., & Gantt, W. H. History of a catatonic dog. *Conditional Reflex,* 1968, 3(1), 45-61.

Page, I. H., & Helmer, O. M. Crystalline pressor substance (angiotonin) resulting from reaction between renin and renin-activator. *Journal of Experimental Medicine,* 1940a, 71, 29-42(a).

Page, I. H., & Helmer, O. M. Angiotonin-activator, renin and angiotonin-inhibitor, and mechanism of angiotonin tachyphylaxis in normal, hypertensive, and nephrectomized animals. *Journal of Experimental Medicine,* 1940b, 71, 495-519(b).

Pavlov, I. P. *Work of the digestive glands.* W. H. Thompson (Tr.). London: Griffin, 1910.

Rhine, J. B., & Pratt, J. G. *Parapsychology: Frontier science of the mind.* Springfield, Illinois: Charles C. Thomas, 1957.

Royer, F. L., & Gantt, W. H. Effect of movement on cardiac conditional reflex. *Conditional Reflex,* 1966, 1(3), 190-194.

Russek, M. Personal communication, 1962.

Sneerson, V., Gantt, W. H., & Hodes, R. (Tr. Ed. by W. H. Gantt). *The achievement of Soviet medicine* (L. Fridland). New York: Twayne Publishers, Inc., 1961.

Thomas, Caroline. Personal communication.

Wiener, N. *I am a mathematician: The later life of a prodigy.* New York: Doubleday, 1956. Pp. 291.

Wolf, Stewart. Personal communication.

# PART 2

Frustration and punishment have long been associated with the development of pathological behavior in the thinking of both educated laymen and research scientists. And for good reason. Were the approach to all goals unimpeded and the consequences of all behavior regularly predictable, and never aversive, happiness and calm (and health) would surely reign supreme. Furthermore, even cursory observation of the immediate behavioral consequences of frustration and/or punishment reveals a close similarity to the patterns of behavior shown in various types of psychopathology.

Each of the three chapters in Part 2 exemplifies the use of the two-stage research strategy mentioned in Chapter 1. Each also clearly assumes the basic principle that maladaptive patterns of behavior are built upon basically adaptive foundations. Two of the chapters, those by Abram Amsel (Chapter 4) and Kenneth B. Melvin (Chapter 6), involve considerable emphasis upon S–R behavioristic theoretical analysis. The chapter by Sandler and Davidson (Chapter 5), on the other hand, is in the radical empirical, nontheoretical tradition of Skinnerian operant conditioning.

The Hull–Spence theoretical system has contributed to experimental psychopathology importantly in two somewhat different areas. The first of these, which is an outgrowth of Spence's[1] emphasis on the associative-motivational aspects of the appetitive unconditioned reaction to the presentation of food to a hungry animal following the performance of an instrumental response, has been most fully developed theoretically and analyzed empirically by Abram Amsel. Over a period of some 15 years of systematic research and theorizing, Amsel has established the "frustration effect" as a byword in behavior theory. His most recent work demonstrating the manner in which a history of frustrative nonreward provides a mediational mechanism for regression to previously acquired response patterns in the presence of current frustration may well be a future landmark in the conceptual development of this field. In addition, his analysis of idiosyncratic frustration-mediated response sequences elegantly illustrates the manner in which nomothetic behavior theory dovetails with idiographic behavior analysis.

Kenneth B. Melvin began his work on self-punitive, vicious-circle behavior under the tutelage of Judson S. Brown and continued this early work with the editor of the present volume. The research on vicious circle behavior done by

[1] K. W. Spence. *Behavior theory and conditioning.* New Haven: Yale University Press, 1956.

Brown, Melvin, and others identifies the second major area of current experimental psychopathology with important historical roots in the Hull–Spence system. The phenomenon, in fact, was given its name and, simultaneously, its conceptual send-off by O. H. Mowrer when he and Brown were both at Yale University. Melvin's chapter in this volume summarizes the most important recent work on the topic and extends Mowrer's original conditioned-fear analysis into the more complicated domain of secondary punishment.

The contribution of Skinnerian operant conditioners to the field of experimental psychopathology, particularly on the topic of response-contingent punishment, has been of immeasurable significance. In their chapter, Sandler and Davidson organize and review some of this work, as well as describing their own recent studies on persistent self-punitive behavior. One of the more interesting sociological–historical concomitants of research in the area of experimental psychopathology has been its tendency to overcome the otherwise impenetrable barriers between researchers in the various "schools" of scientific psychology. The interface between the researches described in Melvin's and Sandler and Davidson's chapters exemplifies this point quite clearly.

# 4

## Frustration,
## Persistence,
## and Regression[1]

ABRAM AMSEL

University of Texas
at Austin

## I. INTRODUCTION

This is my first attempt—in cold blood—to try to say what some of our recent work may have to do with psychopathology, or even more generally with personality. Forgive me, then, if I approach the task timidly by first trying to place the kinds of work we do in the broader context of my interests in animal learning and motivation.

Simply to say that an investigator is interested in the psychology of learning does not begin to specify the processes with which he is concerned, or what he does in the laboratory, or even what he reads. It is usually the case, when the study of learning involves man as the laboratory subject, that psychologists are concerned with processes that are primarily human—remembering and forgetting of verbal material, processing of information, simulation of human cognitive ability by computers, formation and identification of concepts, psycho-linguistics, and so on. On the other hand, we know that a number of eminent psychologists have for many years taken the experimental particulars from which they have derived their theories from observation of, and experimentation with nonhuman animals. Many if not most of these people, who would generally be identified as learning theorists, have been less interested in the cognitive and intellectual abilities of the animals they have chosen to study than in simpler learning processes, such as Pavlovian conditioning and simple instrumental

[1] The preparation of this chapter was supported by grant GB-3772 from the National Science Foundation.

(Thorndikian) learning. They have also worked with lower animals to study basic motivational or need systems. In short, they have been involved in the scientific investigation of the more primitive processes, ontogenetically as well as phylogenetically, the more "stupid" kinds of learning that operate in man as well as in other animals.

Both C. L. Hull and E. C. Tolman, the great learning theorists of the 1930's and 1940's, introduced into psychology ingenious theoretical systems which had as their main concern the identification of the factors which contributed to the formation of habits and goal expectancies at a relatively primitive level. Hull, for example, was tremendously preoccupied with the mechanisms of adaptation and survival, although his formal theorizing did not treat these concepts specifically. The next generation of learning theorists—people like H. F. Harlow, N. E. Miller, O. H. Mowrer, B. F. Skinner, and K. W. Spence—has carried on a tradition of experimental research and theory in which the aim usually has been to understand the relatively nonintellectual, basic-motivational processes of humans by studying and understanding these same processes in lower animals. Or so, at least, it has seemed to me. True, Skinner's work with pigeons has given us a tremendous increase in our understanding of the ways of the pigeon; but I would guess that Skinner has been interested in pigeons more abstractly, as an organism for pursuing the experimental analysis of behavior, and not in the manner in which an ethologist, such as Lorenz, might be interested in pigeons. Harlow's work has been primarily with monkeys and other nonhuman primates, and this work has contributed greatly to the knowledge we have about the activities and emotional–affectional systems of primates. It has always seemed clear to me, however, that this has not been Harlow's only, or even primary, intention; that the purpose of Harlow's work is at the same time more general and more specific than this: to understand affectional (and other) systems in mammals, and to understand these systems in man. As I suggested some time ago (Amsel, 1961), in a review of Mowrer's *Learning theory and behavior,* one of the characteristics of most of the American learning theorists who have worked with animals in the last 20–30 years is that they have not been interested in the animals they are studying in the way a naturalist is, but rather have been interested in these animals as "preparations" from which it may be possible to develop hypotheses about the simpler emotional–motivational processes of higher animals in general and humans in particular. I suppose this has been nowhere more evident than in the work of N. E. Miller, from his earlier and still influential work on conflict (e.g., Miller, 1944) to his recent experiments on instrumental conditioning of autonomic responses.

Learning theorists to whom the epithet "rat psychologists" has often been applied are frequently interested in the connative and affective aspects of behavior rather than in the cognitive aspects *and they are seldom interested in the rat.* They tend to be functionalist in outlooks and to be influenced by

Darwin, by Pavlov, and by Freud in their emphasis on adaptiveness, on motivation and reinforcement, and on the nonintentional nature of a significant part of learning. On the other hand, psychologists who are students of learning and who take data from human subjects tend to be more fascinated by the cognitive–intellectual aspects of behavior. There seems to be within their ranks more of an even split between functionalist and structuralist outlook, and among the great number and variety of intellectual ancestors they would certainly include Ebbinghaus and the British Associationist philosophers.

In the sense of the distinction made in the forgoing discussion, we have for several years used the laboratory rat as a "preparation" to study certain emotional–temperamental characteristics which seem to be common to man and many other animals. One of our particular concerns, for 15 or 16 years, has been to study the effects on invigoration, inhibition, and persistence of frustrative nonreward. In this paper, I want to talk generally about some of the findings in this area of research, particularly as they relate frustrative factors to persistence and to regression. These findings will bear upon experimental psychopathology to the extent they provide hypotheses or raise questions of interest to people who work in this area.

## II. THREE FUNCTIONAL PROPERTIES OF FRUSTRATION

For some time we have taken the position that there is a kind of emotional persistence which reflects learning to continue approaching a goal in the face of anticipated frustration (Amsel, 1958, 1962, 1967; Amsel & Ward, 1965). This frustration theory of persistence emerged out of a series of experiments, beginning in the early 1950's which seemed to demonstrate that frustrative nonreward (nonreward in the presence of anticipation of reward) can be regarded as influencing behavior in at least three ways. First of all, frustrative nonreward appears to have an invigorating or potentiating effect on any behavior which immediately follows it, the so-called *frustration effect* (FE). This frustration effect can be thought of as an attribute of primary, unlearned frustration, a natural reaction of probably all higher animals to nonattainment of expected goals, to thwarting, to encountering physical or psychological barriers or deterrents in the path of goal-attainment. The original study of the FE (Amsel & Roussel, 1952) employed an experimental arrangement which has since come into fairly general use. The apparatus, shown schematically in Figure 1, has been called a double runway or tandem runway and it conceptualizes the manner in which failure to attain reward for one response has an effect on subsequent behavior. In an apparatus such as this a rat or other animal is trained to run down two alleys with two goal boxes in serial arrangement. In the simplest version of this experiment, the rat traverses runway 1 from the start box and finds food or some other rewarding agent in goal box 1, and is then released into runway 2 and finds food again in goal box 2. After a number of such preliminary trials in which the animal is rewarded successively in both goal box 1 and goal box 2, there follows a series of test trials in which the food is sometimes omitted from goal box 1 but is always still found in goal box 2. In such an experiment, the drive or arousing properties of frustrative nonreward are reflected by an increase in the speed of running in runway 2 following nonreward in the first goal box beyond what it ever was in the preliminary period (Figure 2).

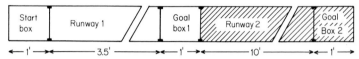

Figure 1. The double-runway apparatus for the study of primary frustration effects (Amsel & Roussel, 1952).

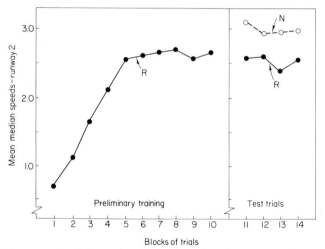

Figure 2. An example of frustration effect data taken from an experiment by Wagner (1959). R = reward, N = nonreward.

The basic conceptual features of the double runway have been incorporated into a variety of experimental situations that involve responding in two segments in series, so that rewarding or not rewarding the first may have some direct potentiating effect on the second response. Similar effects have been found with monkeys and rats in bar-pressing (Davenport, Flaherty, & Dryud, 1966); with pigeons in key-pecking (Staddon & Innis, 1966); and in a number of experiments using children as subjects (see Ryan & Watson, 1968, for a review). The FE has been demonstrated under a variety of motivational–reinforcement conditions. Recently, for example, there have been demonstrations of frustrative effects from the omission of electrical stimulation in a "rewarding" area of the brain (Johnson, Lobdell, & Levy, 1969; Panksepp & Trowill, 1968).

Nonreward in the presence of anticipated reward (frustrative nonreward) appears to increase the vigor of responses which occur at that time. The affected response presumably will be whichever is dominant when the animal is frustrated. In the experimental examples just given, running in the second alley is dominant, or key-pecking is dominant, or bar-pressing is dominant. In other recent experiments (e.g., Azrin, Hutchinson, & Hake, 1966; Davis & Donenfeld, 1967; Gallup, 1965), a response that occurs just after animals are nonrewarded seems to be striking or otherwise attacking another animal which is present, and under these conditions it is tempting to term the intensified response an aggressive response. A frustration–invigoration hypothesis seems strongly supported by a variety of studies. In some cases support for the older frustration–aggression hypothesis (Dollard et al., 1939) can be found. There are also a number of early studies which deal experimentally with regression and even relate the concept to extinction and frustration (Hull, 1934; Miller & Miles, 1935, 1936; Miller & Stevenson, 1936). Hull observed, in the context of a gradient of locomotion study, the reoccurrence in extinction of behavior that had occurred earlier; Miller specifically recognized the analogy to regression. Lewin and his associates were also interested in this same class of problems (Barker, Dembo, & Lewin, 1937).

We have been doing a variety of experiments which can be interpreted as showing that frustration not only leads to invigoration and aggression but also to persistence and to regression. To anticipate my conclusion, I will argue that primary frustration invigorates or intensifies behavior, and may lead to aggression; and that secondary or anticipated (conditioned) frustration is involved in persistence and regression.

I said that frustrative nonreward could be regarded as influencing behavior in at least three ways and I have mentioned only one—as a nonspecific arouser or potentiator of an immediately following response. It seems clear that frustration also has specific directive effects on behavior; that frustration exercises stimulus control over behavior by providing characteristic internal cues. These internal stimuli have been conceptualized as of two major sorts: those arising directly out of the primary frustration reaction itself, as a sort of feedback (Amsel & Ward, 1954; Amsel & Prouty, 1959); and those arising out of conditioned (anticipated) frustration (Amsel, 1958; Spence, 1960). It is important to draw a distinction between these two sources of internal stimulus control over behavior. Stimuli arising out of primary (unconditioned) frustration provide an animal with cues for making responses that will take him out of an existing frustrated state; those arising out of conditioned frustration are signals that alert the animal to an upcoming aversive event and provide some basis for avoiding this event. Stimulation of this second type is very important in our present account because, as the signaler of negative upcoming goal events, it provides the mechanisms for relating frustration to persistence and to regression. We will deal first with the concept of persistence and later I will attempt to show that, in terms of our analysis, regression is merely another form of persistence.

## III. FRUSTRATION AND PERSISTENCE

The term persistence, for present purposes, refers to a tendency for organisms to pursue goal-directed activities despite nonreinforcement, punishment, obstacles or deterrents or, more generally, in the face of any negative indications. For some years "resistance to extinction" has been the classical, learning-theory term that specifically identifies the kind of persistence which is related to nonreinforcement. Another kind of persistence, which is involved in the approach to punishment, has been studied less extensively (Banks, 1966; Brown & Wagner, 1964; Fallon, 1968; Miller, 1960), but to the extent it has been studied there is evidence of mechanisms operating which are similar to those operating in resistance to extinction. Persistence, then, is the more general term encompassing resistance to extinction and resistance to avoidance of punishment and seems to involve a single basic factor common to both—learning to approach to cues signaling some degree of probability of negative consequences. For persistence to develop there must be some uncertainty of outcome; there must be significant probabilities both that reward will be present and that reward will be absent following a response; or there must be significant probabilities both that a response will be terminated by a reward and that a response will be followed by punishment.

In the building of persistence, the barriers or deterrents to behavior may be objects external to the organism, including other organisms present as barriers; however, the primary factors in persistence in relation to goals are internal reactions—anticipated frustration and anticipated pain signaling the likelihood that negative consequences will result from continued approach behavior. The view has often been taken that these internal reactions are learned as simple, Pavlovian conditioned responses (e.g., Amsel, 1958; Miller, 1948; Mowrer, 1940). Such hypothetical internal conditioned responses were termed anticipatory or antedating goal responses many years ago by Hull (1931) and were used extensively by Spence (e.g., 1958) for explanatory purposes. They were designated $r_G - s_G$ to indicate that they were noncompetitive portions of the final goal response whose main function was to produce internal stimulation through direct stimulus feedback. The $r_G$ factor of early Hullian theory remains an important part of the conceptual language of the theory of learning. The anticipatory goal response is the expectancy construct in stimulus-response learning theory and we shall use this language in the next section.

## IV. WHAT IS THE BASIS FOR THE LEARNING OF PERSISTENCE?

As I indicated earlier, behavioral persistence seems to be mediated by some kind of conditioned representation of nonreward or punishment at the goal. The organism learns to approach the goal despite stimuli which signal frustration or pain. In this sense, what I would call *"active" persistence* involves conditioned emotional responses and the counterconditioning of stimuli from these emotional responses from avoidance to continued approach. The frustration theory of the partial reinforcement effect (PRE) (Amsel, 1958), in its simplest form, represents the process of acquiring persistence as a hypothetical four-stage sequence of events, and an outline of these events is described in schematic form in Figure 3. In Stage 1 of partial-reward training (see Figure 3) reward trials operate to effect the conditioning of $r_R$ ; nonreward trials cannot effect any significant amount of frustration until $r_R$ develops in strength. In Stage 2 when $r_R$ is already strong and is a factor in the evocation of the instrumental response, the occurrence of nonreward results in primary frustration ($R_F$). During this

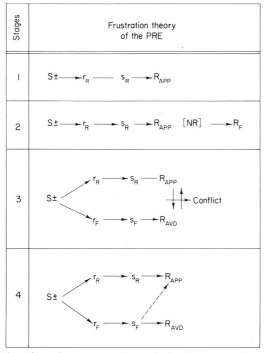

**Figure 3.** Simple schematic representation of the four-stage theory of the partial reinforcement effect. (See text for details.)

second stage there is also the beginning of a buildup of $r_F$, conditioned on the basis of primary frustration ($R_F$) as the unconditioned response. In Stage 3 $r_F$ counteracts $r_R$ —anticipatory frustration producing avoidance and anticipatory reward producing approach—and the result is conflict. Finally, in Stage 4 of partial-reward acquisition, which is reached if partial-reward acquisition is carried on long enough, the anticipatory frustration-produced cues ($s_F$) come to evoke avoidance as well as approach. This conditioning of cues ($s_F$) signaling nonreward to continued approach is the mechanism of persistence, the kind of persistence that shows up as greater resistance to extinction following partial- than following continuous-reward acquisition.

It should be obvious that a similar account could be given of the manner in which an organism can learn to approach in the face of stimuli signaling pain, the difference between pain and frustration at a goal being only that for frustration to occur there must first have been an expectancy of reward ($r_R$), while pain can be directly introduced into a previously rewarding situation at any time.

Experimental situations in which animals such as rats can be trained to persist in the face of frustrative goal indications or of signaled painful consequences of approaching a goal are exceedingly simple. The most simple experiment would involve two groups of subjects. The first group (continuous reward) is rewarded on every occasion on which a response is performed; the second group (partial reward) is rewarded on only some percentage of such occasions, often, arbitrarily, 50%. Both groups are then subjected to extinction, never again finding reward at the termination of their goal-approach response. The so-called PRE describes the fact that under these conditions the "partial" group is more resistant to extinction (persistent) than is the "continuous" group. Hundreds of variations of this simple experimental arrangement have been employed in a study of persistence effects by psychologists. There are a smaller, but still significant, number of experiments (e.g., Miller, 1960) which have investigated the manner in which animals learn to approach in the face of cues signaling pain. Miller's experiments of this sort run the animal to food at the end of the alley in the face of gradually increasing strengths of electric shock. The finding is then that the subjects are abnormally persistent in running into a strong shock. They have in this sense learned to approach to the cues of fear. They have learned "courage." Banks (1966) has shown that rats show this same kind of courageous persistence to continuous punishment after training with intermittent (partial) punishment and continuous rewards.

In experiments of this kind, we are studying the way in which an animal learns to approach a goal in the face of cues which signal that instead of being rewarded it may be frustrated or punished. The more experience of this kind an experimental animal is given, at least up to a point, the more likely it is that the animal will be persistent in these kinds of situations. The circumstances under which frustration (or fear) leads to persistence would seem to be that there must be inconsistent reward (or consistent reward and consistent or inconsistent punishment) for the same behavior from one occasion to another in approximately the same situation.

We can apply this simple principle to a nonexperimental setting. If when an infant cries he is lifted out of his crib he will learn to continue crying until picked up. If the infant is picked up sometimes, but not always, this inconsistent treatment will probably produce a persistent crier. That is to say, when the parents decide in desperation to let him "cry it out," crying will continue for a long time. If the crying is always rewarded, this will of course establish it very strongly as a response; but under these circumstances of continuous reinforcement it will also tend to extinguish very quickly. On the same principle, if what appears to the child to be the same behavior is both rewarded and punished the child will tend to persist in the face of punishment. Persistence depends on inconsistent treatment of consistent behavior.

## V. THE TRANSFER OF PERSISTENCE EFFECTS

Is the persistence pattern which is acquired under partial reinforcement highly specific to the situation in which it was learned? Or is persistence that has been learned in relation to one particular situation likely to show up in any other? Recent experiments in which the basic partial reinforcement comparison is conducted within the individual subject show that there is at least some generalization of persistence effects. The procedure of the within-subject experiment is to reinforce an approach response every time it is made in the presence of one stimulus, say in a black alley, and to reinforce that same response some lesser percentage of the time (say 50%) when it is made in a white alley. The finding is that under these circumstances, when the response is extinguished in both alleys, extinction is according to the PRE pattern in both when compared to between-subject conditions (e.g., Amsel, Rashotte, & MacKinnon, 1966; Brown & Logan, 1965). In learning theory terms, we would say that mediated generalization of the $s_F$-approach counterconditioning is operating to transfer the persistence effect from the PRF alley to the CRF alley.

As our purpose is to relate persistence to regression, perhaps a more instructive kind of experiment is one in which the PRF and CRF training occur separately in successive phases, rather than being mixed together in a single phase as was the case in the kind of experiment just described. The sequence here is as shown in the schema of Table I, the interesting feature of this paradigm being that we are looking in extinction at effects of earlier PRF training conducted in relation to a different stimulus carried through a block of CRF training trials. If we take this separate-phase within-$S$ schema as being analogous, even minimally, to learning sequences of interest in the study of

TABLE I  Outline of a Separate-Phase within-S Partial Reinforcement Experiment

|  | Phase 1 | Phase 2 | Phase 3 |
|---|---|---|---|
| Subject A | $Stim_1$-PRF | $Stim_2$-CRF | $Stim_2$-EXT |
| Subject B | $Stim_1$-CRF | $Stim_2$-CRF | $Stim_2$-EXT |

personality and psychopathology, the experiment asks whether persistence learned at some early stage will be manifested later in a slightly different situation in which the persistence training had not specifically been given.

We have known for some time that persistence effects developed in rats and pigeons through PRF training in experimental apparatuses like runways or lever boxes will survive long periods of time and/or interpolated blocks of CRF training in the same runway or lever box (Jenkins, 1962; Theios, 1962). Rather extreme versions of this finding are available from recent experiments in our laboratory (Donin, Surridge, & Amsel, 1967; Rashotte & Surridge, 1969) which show that not only PRF but also PDR training (partial *delay* of reward training in which animals are rewarded on *every* occasion but reward is delayed on some occasions) build persistence which survives extended interpolated blocks of time and/or CRF training in the same situation, and does this even though the individual trial experiences are separated by 24 or even 72 hr.

But all of these comparatively recent results on the generalized PRE and the transfer of persistence effects from one color of alley to another were really nothing more than corroborative of earlier work by Ross (1964) which provided a much more convincing demonstration than we had had before that in the partial reinforcement experiment the building of persistence has to do with counterconditioning of the $s_F$ to instrumental approach in acquisition.

## VI. THE ROSS EXPERIMENT AND "REGRESSION"

A counterconditioning view of persistence, as we employ the term, implies that a connection of some kind is formed in acquisition between an initially disruptive emotional mediating event and some ongoing behavior. If this mediational control by anticipated frustration is powerful, the argument goes, $s_F$ might elicit approach not only in the situation in which the counterconditioned connection was originally formed, but also in any other situation in which anticipated frustration comes into play. The experiment performed by Ross (1964) was to this point, and Table II is an outline of the design. The preliminary learning phase involves not one but three responses, each different from the response subsequently to be continuously reinforced in Phase 2 and extinguished in Phase 3. Running a short distance and jumping horizontally

**TABLE II**  Outline of the Design of an Experiment by Ross (1964) Showing Transfer of Persistence Effects across Responses, Situations, and Motivational-Reward Conditions[a]

| Phases of experiment | (1) Preliminary learning | (2) Acquisition running response | (3) Extinction running response |
|---|---|---|---|
| Apparatus[b, c] | A[b] | B[c] | B[c] |
| Motivation | Hunger | Thirst | Thirst |
| Experimental conditions | *Running* Continuous (RC) Partial (RP) *Jumping* Continuous (JC) Partial (JP) *Climbing* Continuous (CC) Partial (CP) | *Running* Continuous reward | *Running* Continuous nonreward |

[a] After Amsel, 1967.
[b] Short black wide box.
[c] Long white narrow runway.

across a short gap in a short black box were responses introduced in Phase 1 and designed to be compatible with the Phase 2-Phase 3 running response, in the high, long, white runway, while the climbing response of Phase 1 was meant to be incompatible with the Phase 2-Phase 3 response. Now, if under the PRF schedule in Phase 1, counterconditioning occurs, which means that the subjects learn to make the required approach response to cues from anticipated frustration, will these responses learned earlier emerge in the Phase 3 extinction of a different response, in a different situation, and under different motivational-reward conditions—in fact, under circumstances in which no persistence training at all had been given and the major similarity is that the animals are being handled by the same experimenter?

Ross's results, like the earlier work of Jenkins and Theios, and the later ones from our laboratory, demonstrated that persistence acquired in partial reward acquisition survives a later block of continuous reward to affect extinction. In addition, however, Ross demonstrated that persistence acquired in one situation can have effects in a different situation, involving different responses and different motivational-reward conditions. Reactions to anticipated frustration learned when hungry in a black box emerge when S is thirsty and anticipating frustration in a long, high, white runway, even though there had been no persistence training in that runway. Several (11 out of 13) of the animals that had learned to climb for food under PRF conditions in the black box actually climbed in the long, high, white runway when under extinction for running to water, and because climbing quickly disrupted running behavior there was the appearance, in a comparison of the two climbing groups, of a reversed PRE. These findings point up again the importance of mediational control, relative to external stimulus control, in the emergence of the partial reinforcement persistence effect in extinction. Even more, however, they make it difficult to account for the emergence of the Phase 1 response in extinction without a counterconditioning interpretation. Ross's data show that in Phase 3, under extinction conditions, the animal persists in doing what he had done in Phase 1 under PRF conditions; in a sense, he *regresses* to a mode of behavior learned in the earlier PRF acquisition.

## VII. IDIOSYNCRATIC RITUALS

The final experimental example I want to give of how persistence effects depend on counterconditioning is a derivative of the Ross experiment. We thought it would be interesting to find a within-subject experimental situation in which animals would learn *idiosyncratic response rituals* under partial-rewardlike conditions to one stimulus ($S_1$), while learning to respond under CRF conditions to another discriminative stimulus ($S_2$). This would allow each animal to form a "fixation" on a pattern of behavior under conditions of uncertainty of reward. If our view of how persistence and regression are mediated is tenable, response rituals learned to $S_1$ under PRF-like conditions should emerge in the extinction of responding to the other stimulus ($S_2$) when continuous reward training has been interpolated between training to $S_1$ and extinction of responding to $S_2$. A few years ago, Michael Rashotte and I struck upon a within-subject experiment of this sort, (Amsel & Rashotte, 1969; Rashotte & Amsel, 1968). It is based on Logan's conception of correlated reinforcement (Logan, 1960) and particularly the procedure he terms discontinuously negatively correlated reinforcement (DNC). A DNC condition in an alley is one in which the animal must run slowly to be rewarded (somewhat like Skinnerian *drl*). In our case the cutoff point is usually 5 sec., which means that, if $S$ gets to the end of the alley in less than 5 sec., it does not find food reward, but if $S$ takes 5 sec. or longer to traverse the alley it finds food in the goal box. In these experiments each $S$ runs in two 5-ft. alleys, one black and the other white. In the black alley, the DNC condition obtains; in the white alley $S$ run under conditions of uncorrelated continuous reward. Speeds are taken over five 1-ft. segments. Under these conditions, the typical rat learns some kind of ritual of slow approach to the goal in the DNC alley to consume the 5 sec. which is a very long time for this response.

We have performed a series of experiments showing quite clearly that, when

Ss are run under DNC conditions to one stimulus and under CRF conditions to another stimulus, most animals do, in fact, learn idiosyncratic response rituals to the DNC stimulus at the same time as they perform in a quite normal fashion in the stimulus alley signaling uncorrelated continuous reinforcement. This can be seen in Figure 4 which shows what we call "response profiles" over five 1-ft. segments of the alley. A response profile plots, for each subject, over individual trials (or a small block of trials), its speed over each of the five successive 1-ft. segments of the runway. Each horizontal panel plots the acquisition speed data for a single rat in the DNC and CRF alleys. Note that, in general, CRF profiles are describable as inverted Vs, while the DNC profiles by the end of training are quite idiosyncratic and ritualized. Different animals learn to respond slowly in different ways; that is to say, different animals take time in different ways in different segments of the runway.

In a series of experiments of this sort we have been successful in demonstrating that the idiosyncratic response pattern learned to one discriminative stimulus under DNC conditions does, in fact, emerge when responding is extinguished not in the DNC- but in the CRF-stimulus alley. The DNC pattern emerges most clearly in the separate-phase type of experiment (see Table I), where responding to the CRF stimulus undergoes extinction while responding to the DNC stimulus does not, which is also in broad outline the design of the Ross experiment. In this sort of experiment a yoked PRF–CRF control is included. The yoked condition is one in which, a subject in the PRF–CRF condition is paired with a subject in the DNC–CRF condition and gets, uncorrelated with his performance, the same percentage of reward under PRF conditions, and in the same positions in the sequence of trials, as its DNC mate has earned by running slowly.

An indication that the pattern of responding learned to the DNC stimulus in acquisition emerges in the extinction of responding to the continuously reinforced stimulus can be seen in Figure 5. Shown here are the data for five DNC–CRF Ss and their five PRF–CRF yoked controls over the three phases of the experiment (Rashotte & Amsel, 1968).

The remarkable thing about these data is that they show in extinction the emergence of a response ritual to a stimulus which never evoked that ritual before. It seems very likely to us that this pattern of behavior emerges because something happens in extinction which calls forth an association that was formed in acquisition in relation to a different stimulus. This series of experiments is a powerful demonstration of how mediated generalization and counterconditioning control persistence effects. Obviously I am also saying that persisting in the face of nonreward may take a form other than continuing to make a response learned in just prior acquisition. An organism may show persistence to cues signaling frustration by responding in a manner learned much earlier in a situation much different from the current one. Thus, regression is one

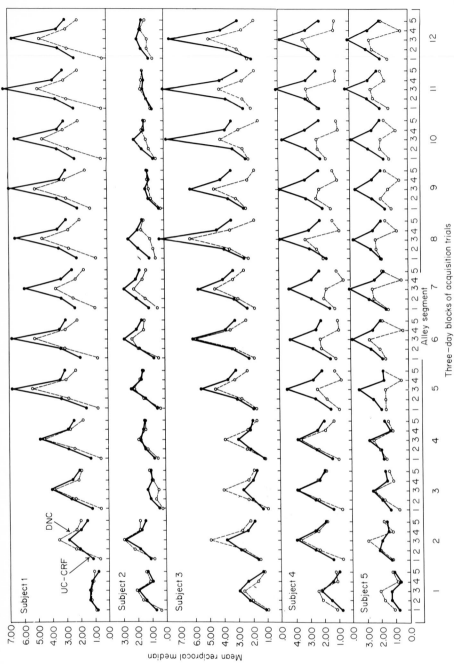

**Figure 4.** Acquisition profiles for five subjects run under both DNC and CRF conditions in a runway with five 1-ft. segments.

64

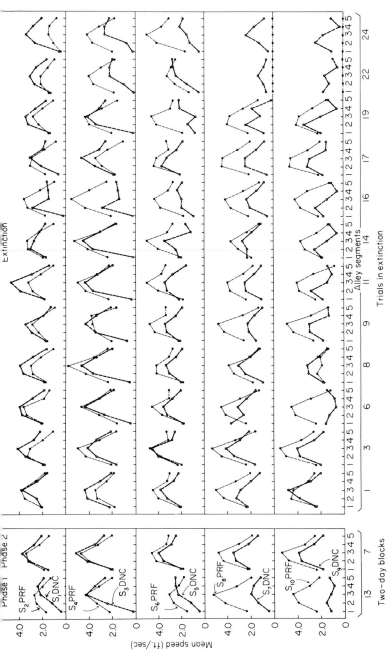

**Figure 5.** Response profiles for five subjects run under DNC–CRF conditions and five yoked controls run under PRF–CRF conditions. Phase 1 consists of DNC training for one group and uncorrelated PRF training for the yoked controls. Phase 2 was CRF training in a different alley for both groups, and Phase 3 was extinction for both groups in the alley where Phase 2 (CRF) training had been given.

65

form that persistence can take. In frustration-theory terms, a frustration-regression hypothesis is supported if frustration means anticipatory (conditioned) frustration ($r_F$). Perhaps frustration-aggression applies, when and if it does, only to primary (unconditioned) frustration ($R_F$).

When the distinction between primary and conditioned frustration has been made, a similarity between the present conclusion and a position taken by Freud (1920) with respect to regression, fixation and frustration becomes apparent. Freud held that "libidinal regression" was a result of two factors: fixation and frustration. In psychosexual development "single portions of every separate sexual impulse may remain in early stages of development" (p. 349). This process, he felt, gives rise to fixations which are predisposing toward regression when the libido, in one of the later developmental stages, is frustrated by external forces from normal gratification. Regression, then, is a return to one of the earlier fixations. If the term frustration as Freud used it is read "anticipated frustration," and if the case is made to apply more generally than to sexual motivation, and if the fixations formed at earlier stages of development are taken to depend on uncertainty of gratification (partial reinforcement), then there is some degree of similarity between this Freudian generalization and the present derivation from animal experimentation. In another sense, the present derivation may be thought to provide some of the more specific conditions under which Freud's view of regression might apply.

## VIII. BEHAVIORAL HABITUATION AND PERSISTENCE

I started this presentation by reviewing early work on the FE and the four-stage theory of frustrative persistence which has guided our work for several years. The experimental data to which I have referred make it seem plausible that a counterconditioning mechanism does operate with some degree of generality; that it is involved in delayed as well as partial reward; that it operates in the transfer of persistence effects across stimuli and across motivational and reinforcement conditions; and that it operates in the learning of response rituals which then emerge in the extinction of responses to stimuli which have never before elicited them. We have shown, then, that the classical-conditioning model in our frustration theory can be taken to apply somewhat more generally than we had initially supposed.

The four-stage frustration theory of the PRE says that stimuli from anticipatory frustration get counterconditioned in the fourth stage to goal-approach. Another language to describe these hypothetical events—and some people prefer to talk about frustration theory in this way—is that the $Ss$ competing responses to stimuli from anticipated frustration *habituate* during partial reinforcement acquisition; that habituation of responses to $s_F$ accounts for the "frustration tolerance" of partially reinforced $S$s in extinction. In extinction, the argument goes, the disruption of responding is less after PRF because the competing responses to stimuli from nonreinforcement have habituated in PRF acquisition. While it is not unreasonable to hold such a view about the habituation of responses in acquisition affecting frustration tolerance in extinction, a simple habituation concept or a simple frustration tolerance concept cannot account for the transferred persistence effects in the Ross experiment; nor can they account for the generalized partial reinforcement effect; nor for the transferred ritualized response profiles of the DNC experiment. A more active counterconditioning mechanism is required, and I have recently (Amsel, 1971) ventured to reverse the argument and to guess that this kind of active process is generally involved in behavioral habituation; that any instance of behavioral habituation to an initially disruptive event involves some degree of counterconditioning; and that this counterconditioning leads to some increment in persistence in the face of later disruptive events. If this transferred persistence effect seems to emerge abruptly and to resemble earlier modes of behavior it will have the characteristics of regressive behavior.

# REFERENCES

Amsel, A. The role of frustrative nonreward in noncontinuous reward situations. *Psychological Bulletin*, 1958, **55**, 102-119.

Amsel, A. Hope comes to learning theory. *Contemporary Psychology*, 1961, 6, 33-36.

Amsel, A. Frustrative nonreward in partial reinforcement and discrimination learning: Some recent history and a theoretical extension. *Psychological Review*, 1962, **69**, 306-328.

Amsel, A. Partial reinforcement effects on vigor and persistence: Advances in frustration theory derived from a variety of within-subjects experiments. In K. W. Spence and J. T. Spence (Eds.) *The psychology of learning and motivation, Vol. I. (Advances in research and theory)*. New York: Academic Press, 1967.

Amsel, A. Behavioral habituation, counterconditioning, and a general theory of persistence. In A. H. Black and W. F. Prokasy (Eds.) *Classical conditioning:* II. New York: Appleton-Century-Crofts, 1971.

Amsel, A., & Prouty, D. L. Frustrative factors in selective learning with reward and nonreward as discriminanda. *Journal of Experimental Psychology*, 1959, 57, 224-230.

Amsel, A., & Rashotte, M. E. Transfer of experimenter-imposed slow-response patterns to the extinction of a continuously rewarded response. *Journal of Comparative and Physiological Psychology*, 1969, 69, 185-189.

Amsel, A., Rashotte, M. E., & MacKinnon, J. R. Partial reinforcement effects within subject and between subjects. *Psychological Monographs*, 1966, **80** (20, Whole No. 628).

Amsel, A., & Roussel, Jacqueline. Motivational properties of frustration: I. Effect on a running response of the addition of frustration to the motivational complex. *Journal of Experimental Psychology*, 1952, 43, 363-368.

Amsel, A., & Ward, J. S. Motivational properties of frustration: II. Frustration drive stimulus and frustration reduction in selective learning. *Journal of Experimental Psychology*, 1954, **48**, 37-47.

Amsel, A., & Ward, J. S. Frustration and persistence: Resistance to discrimination following prior experience with the discriminanda. *Psychological Monographs*, 1965, **79**, (4, Whole No. 597).

Azrin, N. H., Hutchinson, R. R., & Hake, D. F. Extinction-induced aggression. *Journal of the Experimental Analysis of Behavior*, 1966, **9**, 191-204.

Banks, R. K. Persistence to continuous punishment following intermittent punishment training. *Journal of Experimental Psychology*, 1966, **71**, 373-377.

Barker, R. T., Dembo, T., & Lewin, K. Experiments on frustration and regression in children. *Psychological Bulletin*, 1937, **34**, 754-755.

Brown, R. T., & Logan, F. A. Generalized partial reinforcement effect. *Journal of Comparative and Physiological Psychology*, 1965, **60**, 64-69.

Brown, R. T., & Wagner, A. R. Resistance to punishment and extinction following training with shock or nonreinforcement. *Journal of Experimental Psychology*, 1964, **68**, 503-507.

Davenport, J. W., Flaherty, C. F., & Dryud, J. P. Temporal persistence of frustration effects in monkeys and rats. *Psychonomic Science*, 1966, **6**, 411-412.

Davis, H., & Donenfeld, D. Extinction induced social interaction in rats. *Psychonomic Science*, 1967, **7**, 85-86.

Dollard, J., Doob, L. N., Miller, N. E., & Sears, R. R. *Frustration and aggression.* New Haven: Yale Univ. Press, 1939.

Donin, Janet A., Surridge, C. T., & Amsel, A. Extinction following partial delay of reward with immediate continuous reward interpolated, at 24-hour intertrial intervals. *Journal of Experimental Psychology*, 1967, **74**, 50-53.

Fallon, D. Resistance to extinction following learning with punishment of reinforced and nonreinforced licking. *Journal of Experimental Psychology*, 1968, **76**, 550-557.

Freud, S. *A general introduction to psychoanalysis.* (Trans. by G. S. Hall) New York: Liveright, 1920.

Gallup, G. G., Jr. Aggression in rats as a function of frustrative nonreward in a straight alley. *Psychonomic Science*, 1965, **3**, 99-100.

Hull, C. L. Goal attraction and directing ideas conceived as habit phenomena. *Psychological Review*, 1931, **38**, 487-506.

Hull, C. L. The rat's speed of locomotion gradient in the approach to food. *Journal of Comparative Psychology*, 1934, **17**, 393-422.

Jenkins, H. M. Resistance to extinction when partial reinforcement is followed by regular reinforcement. *Journal of Experimental Psychology*, 1962, **64**, 441-450.

Johnson, R. N., Lobdell, P., & Levy, R. S. Intracranial self-stimulation and the rapid decline of frustrative nonreward. *Science*, 1969, **164**, 971-972.

Logan, F. A. *Incentive.* New Haven: Yale Univ. Press, 1960.

Miller, N. E. Experimental studies of conflict. In J. McV. Hunt (Ed.), *Personality and the behavior disorders.* Vol. I. New York: Ronald Press, 1944.

Miller, N. E. Studies of fear as an acquirable drive: I. Fear as motivation and fear-reduction as reinforcement in the learning of new responses. *Journal of Experimental Psychology*, 1948, **38**, 89-101.

Miller, N. E. Learning resistance to pain and fear: Effects of overlearning, exposure, and rewarded exposure in context. *Journal of Experimental Psychopathology*, 1960, **60**, 137-145.

Miller, N. E., & Miles, W. R. Effect of caffeine on the running speed of hungry, satiated, and frustrated rats. *Journal of Comparative Psychology*, 1935, **20**, 397-412.

Miller, N. E., & Miles, W. R. Alcohol and removal of reward: An analytical study of rodent maze behavior. *Journal of Comparative Psychology*, 1936, **21**, 179-204.

Miller, N. E., & Stevenson, S. S. Agitated behavior of rats during experimental extinction and a curve of spontaneous recovery. *Journal of Comparative Psychology*, 1936, **21**, 205-231.

Mowrer, O. H. Experimental analogue to "regression" with incidental observation on "reaction formation." *Journal of Abnormal and Social Psychology*, 1940, **35**, 56-87.

Panksepp, J., & Trowill, J. Extinction following intracranial reward: Frustration or drive decay? *Psychonomic Science*, 1968, **12**, 173-174.

Rashotte, M. E., & Amsel, A. Transfer of slow-response rituals to the extinction of a continuously rewarded response. *Journal of Comparative and Physiological Psychology*, 1968, **66**, 432-443.

Rashotte, M. E., & Surridge, C. T. Partial reinforcement and partial delay of reinforcement effects with 72-hour intertrial intervals and interpolated continuous reinforcement. *Quarterly Journal of Experimental Psychology*, 1969, **21**, 156-161.

Ross, R. R. Positive and negative partial-reinforcement extinction effects carried through continuous reinforcement, changed motivation, and changed response. *Journal of Experimental Psychology*, 1964, **68**, 492-502.

Ryan, T. J., & Watson, P. Frustrative nonreward theory applied to children's behavior. *Psychological Bulletin*, 1968, **69**, 111-125.

Spence, K. W. A theory of emotionally based drive (D) and its relation to performance in simple learning situations. *American Psychologist*, 1958, **13**, 131-141.

Spence, K. W. *Behavior theory and learning*, Englewood Cliffs, New Jersey: Prentice-Hall, 1960.

Staddon, J. E. R., & Innis, N. K. An effect analagous to "frustration" on interval reinforcement schedules. *Psychonomic Science*, 1966, **4**, 287-288.

Theios, J. The partial reinforcement effect sustained through blocks of continuous reinforcement. *Journal of Experimental Psychology*, 1962, **64**, 1-6.

Wagner, A. R. The role of reinforcement and nonreinforcement in an "apparent frustration effect." *Journal of Experimental Psychology*, 1959, **57**, 130-136.

# 5

# Psychopathology:
# An Analysis of Response
# Consequences

JACK SANDLER

University of South Florida

ROBERT S. DAVIDSON

VA Hospital, Miami

## I. INTRODUCTION

Attempts to apply learning models to the study of psychopathology have had a long history. The case was first stated by Pavlov, and has been repeated numerous times by others, including Watson, Liddell, and Dollard and Miller. The basic assumption has been that pathological behavior is learned according to the same principles and classes of variables which determine normal behavior (Sidman, 1960). These variables may be combined or permutated in different ways to produce many variations in behavior, some of which may be classified as abnormal or pathological. For example, extreme social or sensory deprivation may produce hallucinatory or autisticlike behaviors (Bexton, *et al.*, 1954; Harlow, 1958), deprivation of a loved one, for example, through death may result in extreme depression demonstrated in chimps by Ferster (1966), punishment of avoidance behavior may lead to "masochism" (Brown *et al.*, 1964; Sandler, 1964, Sandler *et al.*, 1966a, 1966b, 1966c), punishment of eating behavior may result in food rejection and eventual starvation (Masserman, 1961) and "inappropriate" stimulus generalization may lead to phobic behavior (Watson & Raynor, 1920).

Despite the intrinsic appeal and scientific merit of this approach, a retrospective analysis of its impact upon clinical theory and practice would reveal it to be minimal. "This body of research, which clearly satisfies the criteria of being objective and controlled, has not been embraced by clinicians, mainly because its significance for human pathology is somewhat obscure, and the experimentalists themselves have made only nominal efforts to integrate their results with clinical data" (Wilson, 1963, pp. 130-131).

Recently, however, the extension of operant principles into many levels of complex behavioral inquiry gives reason to reconsider the manner in which learning theory may advance the study of pathological processes. The most important components of this attack are proceeding along two related lines:

1. Research at the animal level identifies principles relevant to the etiology of pathological behavior;

2. The growing application of operant principles in the clinical arena provides evidence of its value in the treatment of pathological behavior.

These recent advances support the traditional clinical belief that pathological conditions are complex and multiply determined, but they also endorse the classical scientific strategy of initiating investigations at the simple level first and proceeding to the more complex in a systematic manner.

This is not to say that all of the problems have been resolved. Despite a burgeoning body cf information, especially in the area of behavior modification, there is still little known regarding the manner in which learning principles can explain the acquisition and maintenance of pathological behavior. Such information would seem to be a necessary prerequisite before a more complete integration of principles and applications can be realized. Operant investigators analyzing basic processes in the laboratory often assume that these principles can be extended to those complex events encompassed by the term psycho-pathology, and operant therapists take it for granted that the target behavior they wish to modify has been acquired via the operant model, but these are still theoretical stances in need of empirical justification.

This paper is concerned with a proposed research model which may offer some clues in such an endeavor. Although any such undertaking must, at present, be programmatic, relevant literature suggests that such a model may be feasible. The fundamental requirement is that investigations at the basic level can be demonstrably related to more complex investigations of the multiple determinants of pathological behavior.

One must first define the term "behavior pathology"—no mean task in itself. Neither clinicians nor experimentalists have been of much assistance in this regard. Nor has any single definition encompassing the entire range of pathological events been universally accepted. Often it is even unclear why an investigator regards his results as an example of pathological behavior, other than that such "strange" or "unusual" behavior is unexpected on the basis of some theory, prior observation, common sense, and/or appears to resemble what is conventionally regarded as pathological. Clearly, more attention must be directed at resolving this basic issue.

Many forms of pathological behavior may be distinguished from normal behavior by the persistence of behavior which is nonproductive, i.e., does not lead to rewards, and may, in fact, result in punishment, despite the availability of nonpunishing or rewarding alternatives. Another distinguishing characteristic of psychopathology is the presence, at some frequency, of behavior which is not normally maintained by the reinforcing community, as well as the possible absence of behaviors which are normally reinforced by the environment. Thus, for example, the presence of depressive behavior (e.g., crying, inactivity, and blaming oneself) may be tolerated at low frequencies of occurrence since we all behave that way occasionally, but such behavior is rarely reinforced in our society when it occurs at high frequency. Or, for example, in some pathological states a limited number of different behaviors may be observed and manv of these may be low in frequency. The individual's behavioral repertoire is said to be "impoverished." Such a state of affairs is again rarely tolerated in our active society, and individuals exhibiting such deficits are most frequently committed to an institution or excluded from society in other ways.

There are other pathological behaviors which do not readily conform to this analysis, such as alcoholism and psychopathic deviance. Certain potentially pathological behaviors are promoted in our society, which, through advertising and competitive enterprises, reinforces drinking and the "manipulation" of others. Thus, with these behaviors, many of the immediate consequences are reinforcing while the long-range consequences may be severely punishing.

The emphasis upon behavioral consequences in these examples is clearly congruent with operant principles. In operant terms, what the clinician may highlight as specific instances of pathological behavior, for example, persistent behavior which results in punishing effects, may be represented as behavior under the control of multiple consequences. Each new manifestation provides further evidence of the magnitude and range of the psychopathology. However, in order to understand this "bizarre" behavior, one must analyze the interaction between the processes involved in the history of the response, i.e., the variables which determined the acquisition of the behavior, and the current determinants of the behavior (McKearney, 1968). Such an approach brings more sharply into focus the importance of the history of the response in determing pathological outcomes.

At one level of analysis, there is nothing new in this formulation. It is almost commonplace to acknowledge that behavior is a function of past experiences plus those stimuli currently impinging upon the individual. This principle is the cornerstone of the learning theory approach to personality, and had historical antecedents at least as far back as Locke's concept of the "tabula rasa." Unfortunately, little genuine progress has been made in isolating the variables which influence the interaction between the acquisition processes and current determinants. Furthermore, the overemphasis upon the abnormal behavior of the moment has tended to obscure the study of the historical components of the interaction.

The analysis of such an interaction may be based upon a model of behavior which advances from the study of relatively simple events consisting of a single response history or acquisition process, to the more complex events involved in the multiple determination of psychopathology at the human level. Figure 1 provides a schematic description of how such an analysis might proceed. As the figure illustrates, either a straightforward acquisition process, or some combination of acquisition variables and maintenance variables (which may vary from the training schedule) constitute the background of any current response.

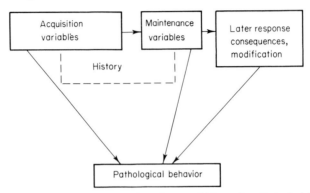

Figure 1. Schematic diagram illustrating the acquisition of pathological behavior at various stages in the history of the organism.

The division is arbitrary, of course, since it is difficult and, sometimes, impossible to distinguish between acquisition and maintenance processes, especially when considering behavior in the natural environment. The use of such a scheme is offered purely on the grounds of convenience. Since pathological behavior may conceivably arise at any one of these levels, the rest of this chapter will be devoted to an analysis of some of the conditions which may determine such outcomes. Our first consideration will focus upon those acquisition variables which might produce the kinds of behavior previously specified as pathological.

## II. ACQUISITION VARIABLES

As previously indicated, the crux of the operant approach is its emphasis upon the consequences of behavior: those responses which are reinforced should increase in frequency, while those which are not reinforced or result in aversive stimulation (punishment) should decrease in frequency. The five most basic response-consequence arrangements for predicting the course of behavior are schematically presented in Table I (adapted from Holland & Skinner, 1961). Thus, presentation of any response consequence which increases the future

TABLE I    Five Most Common Types of Consequence Which May Come to Control a Response[a]

| Class of stimulus[b] | Contingency with behavior | Name of procedure[c] | Expected outcome |
|---|---|---|---|
| 1. $S^+$ | Present | Positive reinforcement | Increase |
| 2. $S^-$ | Present | Punishment | Decrease |
| 3. $S^+$ | None (no stimulus present) | Extinction | Decrease |
| 4. $S^-$ | Withdraw or postpone on response | Negative reinforcement | Increase |
| 5. $S^-$ | None (no stimulus present) | Extinction | Decrease |

[a]Adapted from Holland and Skinner (1961).
[b]$S^+$ and $S^-$ refer to classes of stimuli which are identified according to their functional relationship to behavior.
[c]Examples of each procedure and the contribution to the formation of pathological behavior are discussed in the text.

probability of that response constitutes positive reinforcement (row 1), while the withdrawal of such an event (row 3) defines the extinction arrangement. Similarly, the presentation of any response consequence which *decreases* the future probability of a response defines the punishment procedure (row 2), while response contingent withdrawal of such a stimulus (row 4) constitutes negative reinforcement, as in escape or avoidance conditioning. Row 5, which refers to those arrangements in which the aversive stimulus is withdrawn subsequent to a history of negative reinforcement, defines the extinction of such behavior. This effect parallels that of extinction of positively reinforced behavior (row 3). While such arrangements are probably never present in their "pure" form in the natural environment, we obviously cannot understand their effects under natural conditions without first referring back to systematic observations conducted under controlled conditions.

This analysis makes no assumptions regarding the nature of the stimuli involved, therefore the same stimulus might conceivably serve any or all of the various functions specified in the table. Thus, Azrin (1958) demonstrated that noise had a punishment effect when response-contingent; functioned as a negative reinforcer when *terminated* by the same response, and also functioned as a conditioned positive reinforcer when paired with another positive reinforcer.

It is also important to recognize that arrangements 2, 3, and 5 encompass circumstances which usually obtain at some stage *subsequent* to acquisition. Thus, when they are in effect, they represent a change in response consequences from reinforcing events, to nonreinforcing events. For example, in considering the punishment arrangement, prior conditions are assumed to have prevailed which determined the initial acquisition of such behavior. Similarly, the extinction arrangement, by definition, can only be introduced after a response has been acquired by either positive or negative reinforcement.

How, then, can acquisition principles be used to explain the occurrence of pathological behaviors? If Sidman's thesis is correct, pathological behavior must have been acquired in the same manner as normal behavior. Thus, bizarre responses may occur as a function of positive or negative reinforcement. Ayllon (1965), for example, has provided an elegant instance of the development of aberrant broom-holding behavior in a psychotic patient as a consequence of positive reinforcement.

However, the mere existence of a reinforcing arrangement *per se* provides only a partial explanation of such effects. Consider the case of negative reinforcement, where the attempt is to establish an instrumental avoidance response. Dinsmoor (1954) has suggested that all negative reinforcement paradigms involve a punishmentlike effect in the sense that all responses other than the avoidance response are followed by aversive stimulation. Furthermore, in such arrangements, the frequency and distribution of noxious events vary with the performance of the organism. For example, the slow learner obviously receives a higher density of aversive stimulation than the fast learner. This, in turn, will probably have a drastic effect on his behavior, perhaps including complete response suppression, another form of pathological behavior. In operant terms, the *actual schedule* (as differentiated from *programmed schedule*) of events may constitute a critical determinant in reinforcing arrangements and this variable may function even during initial acquisition. Furthermore, other forms of psychopathology, such as persistent responding in the face of aversive consequences, or nonrewarding circumstances, actually appear to be contradictory to a simple reinforcement principle.

Clearly, then, if we are to apply our model to such forms of behavior, as well as to psychopathological events in the natural environment, other variables in addition to positive and negative reinforcement must be taken into consideration. Thus, it is probably inadequate if not misleading to analogize directly from simple principles to pathological behavior. To provide a more veridical analysis, we must consider other variables which may be present during acquisition. In this connection, let us examine the acquisition process in relation to reinforcement schedules, and possible interactions between reinforcing events and associated stimuli.

## A. Reinforcement Schedules

Response characteristics are profoundly influenced by the manner in which reinforcement is distributed or scheduled. Furthermore, as previously indicated, such schedule effects may be present in many situations where they are overlooked. For example, Wilcoxon (1952) argued that the neurotic behavior (fixation) produced by the Maier procedure (Maier, 1949) is partially attributable to the reinforcement schedules. There are probably many such examples in the experimental psychopathology literature. Most behaviors in the natural environment are also probably influenced by reinforcement schedules, although here again, this factor is often difficult to isolate since more than one schedule may be operating and the reinforcement may be obscure.

For these reasons, it might best serve our purposes to refer to systematic attempts to investigate schedule effects (Ferster & Skinner, 1957). Initial acquisition is most efficiently accomplished where every response is reinforced (CRF), but it is behavior acquired under intermittent or partial reinforcement schedules which appears to be most relevant to the current analysis.

The change from CRF to intermittent reinforcement introduces new response consequences, in the sense that the first time reinforcement is withheld an extinctionlike process is in effect. An arbitrary distinction may be made, however, between those situations in which response rates decline, and those arrangements in which responding is maintained, and sometimes actually strengthened. The former will be considered in detail in a later section. Where the latter effect is accomplished, the procedure usually involves only subtle changes which do not result in extinction, and, therefore, these arrangements will be considered in the context of variables associated with initial acquisition.

Sometimes, under positively reinforcing conditions, the change from CRF to a partial schedule may actually result in an increase in response rates, an interesting effect which may be of some relevancy in the current analysis. For the most part, however, where the change in reinforcement schedule is presented in a systematic and gradual manner, the accompanying changes in behavior are appropriate to the changes in schedule.

All reinforcement schedules fall into one of two categories: thus, reinforcement may occur after $X$ number of responses (ratio schedule), or after an $X$ period in time (interval schedule). In addition, the reinforcement may be regular or random, thus describing four major schedule possibilities, each of which results in a characteristic behavioral effect. For example, where reinforcement occurs after an irregular number of responses (Variable Ratio schedule), extremely high, stable rates may be generated in relation to relatively few reinforcements. This may explain the maintenance of behavior under many normal circumstances as well as contributing to an understanding of a variety of pathological phenomena, such as "pressure of speech," manic behavior, and the persistence of responding under "nonreinforcing" circumstances, especially if our observations are restricted to those periods during which reinforcements are not available.

Perhaps the most commonplace example of a partial reinforcement effect occurs in the case of compulsive gambling. Such behavior is characterized by frequent and persistent wagering over long periods of time, despite the relatively infrequent payoffs (reinforcements).

Another schedule which appears to be of applicability in the present analysis occurs when an organism is differentially reinforced only for a particular response dimension. For example, where only a low frequency of responding is reinforced, the characteristic pattern generated by such an arrangement is a slow, but relatively stable rate, perhaps analogous to lethargy and passivity. Extreme or exaggerated forms of normal behavior may be acquired by means of differential reinforcement, as in the case of the mother who rarely responds to her child when called in a normal tone of voice but does react when vocal intensity is raised.

There are still other reinforcement schedules which may generate pathological effects. It is possible, for example, to arrange conditions in which increasing effort results in a decrement of reinforcement magnitude. Obviously, where an animal is working for food, at some stage it might reach the critical point of no return and starve to death, or rather, work itself to death. Wiener has described a situation which would enable the analysis of similar processes in humans (1962, 1965). To carry this approach further, it would be interesting to determine whether humans could be trained to earn a progressive decrement of reward over time, yet continue to respond. The analogy between such behavior and certain instances of suicide seems evident.

It is also possible to produce an experimental analog of superstitious behavior by the use of another type of reinforcement schedule, in which strange or unusual reactions are produced as a consequence of adventitious positive reinforcement. The term "adventitious" refers to an arrangement in which reinforcement is administered independently of any specific response rather than contingent on a particular response as in the typical operant arrangement. In this type of arrangement, the response is not instrumental in producing reinforcement as in the usual reinforcement paradigm. This allows accidental correlations to develop between any behavior which might occur and reinforcement, and the organism reacts as if the behavior were functionally related to reinforcement. Skinner's (1948) examples of the stereotyped, ritualistic behavior of pigeons which turned in circles or stretched their necks repeatedly, stand out as classic experimental prototypes of such behavior.

It is difficult to draw a direct parallel to the human level, because the relationships between responses and their controlling contingencies are often obscure, but several observations will illustrate the process. Skinner (1969) recently reviewed a report that the Kaingang Indians "shout at thunderstorms to make them go away." Clearly, "continuous shouting is guaranteed by the fact that sudden squalls always go away" (p. 24). Skinner's point is that "the contingencies are not unlike those in which a hungry pigeon is given food periodically by a clock mechanism. In pigeon and Indian alike, adventitious reinforcement generates ritualistic behavior" (p. 24).

Such effects sometimes occur as incidental by-products of studies but are rarely investigated for their own sake. The most dramatic example of the relationship between superstitious behavior and reinforcing contingencies was observed by us in a verbal conditioning study. Subjects were provided with a voice key and a point recorder and simply instructed to earn a certain number of points without being informed of the contingency between verbal behavior and reinforcement. In one instance, the experimenter inadvertently presented a point in response to the sound made when the subject's hand fell on the desk. The subject immediately repeated the response, and the experimenter continued to reinforce this behavior. Within a relatively short time, by means of successive approximations, the subject was making full sweeping motions with both arms. An uninformed person walking in on this scene would have observed the subject standing in the middle of the room engaged in what looked like practice for the swimming team. Perhaps this is analogous to the peculiar kinds of rituals displayed by patients in mental institutions.

## B. Interaction between Acquisition Schedules and Associated Stimuli

As in the case of reinforcement schedules, there is convincing evidence that stimuli which are present and systematically associated with reinforcing events during acquisition may also exert considerable influence over behavior. Zimmerman (1957) demonstrated that a stimulus regularly paired with reinforcement during acquisition could maintain behavior indefinitely, as long as it intermittently accompanied reinforcement. The conditioned reinforcing function of the stimulus was demonstrated by the "new response" technique, in which the subject learned to make a new response under the control of the conditioned reinforcer alone.

Stimuli also may be associated systematically with responses which lead to reinforcement, extinction, punishment, etc. This procedure produces discriminative stimuli ($S^D$) in the presence of which an appropriate response is manifested. This effect has most frequently been revealed in animals using multiple and chained schedules of reinforcement where, for example, responding is maintained in the presence of a stimulus associated with reinforcing conditions, and extinguished in the presence of a stimulus associated with the withdrawal of reinforcement.

It is also now clear, as indicated earlier, that the same stimulus may reveal several functions, depending upon its association with reinforcing events. Azrin (1958) obtained both conditioned reinforcing and discriminative effects with a single stimulus which also suppressed behavior when response-contingent, thus demonstrating its initial punishment effect. Following a period in which noise was presented only when responding was reinforced, and withdrawn when responding was not reinforced, the behavior was maintained in the presence of the noise, and extinguished in the absence of the noise. Following another period in which noise was systematically associated with reinforcement, subjects worked for the noise alone, thus demonstrating a conditioned reinforcement effect.

Davidson (1969) found that alcoholic patients would respond at higher rates when shock of low or intermediate intensities was paired with alcohol reinforcement than they would for the alcohol alone, revealing the conditioned reinforcement effects of the shock. Subsequently, the subjects learned to stop responding when each response illuminated (produced) a red light which signaled that strong shock would be presented after every 30th response. Here, the red light functioned as a discriminative stimulus for a punishing event.

The implications of such findings for analyzing pathological processes seems clear. Many events defined as pathological on the basis of their deviancy from the reinforcing practices of the community may occur as a function of conditioned reinforcement. Perhaps the clearest example is in fetishism. However, even ordinarily aversive events may also acquire conditioned reinforcement properties under appropriate circumstances, thus resulting in the paradoxical state of affairs characterized by masochism (Sandler, 1964), regarded by Mowrer as the core characteristic of all neuroses (Mowrer, 1948).

Similarly, behavior which increases in the presence of "inappropriate" stimuli (warning gestures, threats of punishment, etc.) may also be accounted for on the basis of stimulus discrimination.

While it is true that these processes have been investigated only under laboratory conditions, the principles are easily generalizable to behavior in the natural environment. Perhaps the most commonplace example is the red traffic light which may represent a discriminative stimulus for avoidance behavior (applying the car brakes to prevent a collision). However, we also learn to talk in the presence of people who are "interested" in what we have to say (i.e., who provide discriminative stimuli for our verbalizations) and we are pleased (reinforced) when they agree with us through head nodding, smiles, and verbal approval (conditioned reinforcers). Similarly, the frequency of smoking and drinking increases at parties, coffee breaks, etc. because of the discriminative stimuli which are present, and because of the reinforcements, both primary and conditioned, which follow such behavior under these circumstances.

While more research is critically needed to demonstrate these processes in the natural environment, a number of observations have already revealed the extent to which a variety of pathological behaviors, from delusions (Rickard, *et al.,* 1960) to temper tantrums (Williams, 1959) and antisocial behavior (Allen, *et al.,* 1964; Hart, *et al.,* 1964) occur as a function of discriminative and/or conditioned reinforcing stimuli in a social context.

## III. LATER MODIFICATION

Pathological behaviors of long standing cannot properly be analyzed without considering what happens to the behavior after initial acquisition. It has already been noted that variables associated with acquisition may also influence behavior, but, in addition to these variables, any of the five basic response consequences may also be present at any time subsequent to acquisition, thus further influencing response characteristics. For example, a response acquired via positive reinforcement may subsequently also produce additional and different positive reinforcement, or negative reinforcement, or punishment, etc. Obviously, the number of possible permutations and combinations can be multiplied very rapidly. To simplify matters, we will consider only those arrangements which have been adequately investigated and which appear to have the greatest relevance for an understanding of pathological behavior.

### A. Acquisition Followed by Extinction

The introduction of an extinction procedure (i.e., withdrawal of the reinforcing contingency) represents, of course, a classical arrangement in learning research. However, analysis of such events, and the concomitant changes in behavior, also provides information relevant to an understanding of certain forms of pathology.

In a very real sense, extinction may be considered the ultimate change in reinforcement schedules from some magnitude of reinforcement to 0 reinforcement. In the previous section, we described some of the effects of gradual and systematic changes in reinforcement schedules, where behavior is maintained. Here we consider the conventional extinction arrangement in which all reinforcement is withdrawn.

Of course, extinction like effects can occur under certain changes in reinforcement schedules (Table II, row 1). For example, where a new schedule is suddenly introduced which requires a large increment in responding to obtain

TABLE II  Four[a] Common Combinations of an Acquisition or Training Schedule and Modification due to a Change in Schedule or Procedure

|   | Acquisition schedule | Modification |
|---|---|---|
| 1. | Positive reinforcement (1) | Positive reinforcement (2) |
| 2. | Positive reinforcement | Extinction |
| 3. | Positive reinforcement | Punishment |
| 4. | Negative reinforcement | Punishment |

[a]Examples of each are discussed in the text.

reinforcement relative to the previous schedule, an organism may simply stop responding and, in some cases, risk starvation. Since it appears as if the organism has suddenly lost the "will to work" Skinner (1953) termed this outcome "abulia." Perhaps these observations are related to the reduction in behavior which sometimes follows a shift from vocational or occupational training (with a relatively high density of reinforcement, or relatively simple requirements) to on-the-job training. In such cases, the behavioral deficits which occur (and are sometimes attributed to laziness, incompetence, etc.) may be attributed to the sudden change in schedule requirements.

Even closer parallels between extinction effects and pathological behavior can be drawn from conventional extinction arrangements (Table II, row 2). For example, the death of a loved one (withdrawal of positive reinforcement) may result in extensive behavioral deficits, or a generalized reduction in behavior, classified as depression. Ferster (1966) reported an observation of such behavioral deficits in a chimpanzee following the removal of its mate.

Related to the extinction process, research on deprivation may also provide information relative to the current analysis. Harlow (1958) has provided us with the clearest example of the manner in which an extended history of deprivation may result in a variety of pathological behaviors, especially characterized by deficits in the behavioral repertoire. Such procedures may be regarded as massive extinctionlike programs, in the sense that extrinsic, response-produced reinforcers were not available at any time during the deprivation period.

Other investigators have demonstrated similar extinction effects as well as a variety of inappropriate behaviors as a function of sensory deprivation (Heron, Bexton, & Hebb, 1953).

Ferster (1961) and Lovaas (1967) have both commented on the possible role played by insufficient reinforcement, or extinctionlike arrangements in the etiology of behavioral deficits. Ferster (1961) has further suggested that any hiatus in the parent–child relationship during critical periods of development may result in later behavioral deficits, such as those revealed in autism, since reinforcement for appropriate behavior is unavailable at such times, thus resulting in a restricted behavioral repertoire, and the extinction of important social functions.

Perhaps the most pertinent findings in this area, however, are related to those arrangements which reveal considerable resistance to extinction. Some of these examples have been specified in the previous section, but these effects are not necessarily restricted to behavior acquired via positive reinforcement. Thus, Solomon et al. (1953) report extensive durability of avoidance behavior with no evidence of extinction over hundreds of trials. This "inappropriate" behavior (persistent, stereotyped responding of a nonfunctional nature) is the consequence of the highly traumatic conditions and the presence of exteroceptive pre-aversive stimuli, which prevail during the acquisition of the avoidance response. Under these circumstances, merely presenting the preaversive stimulus during extinction is sufficient to insure continued avoidance behavior over an indefinite period of time. Such findings may have considerable relevance for understanding the development and maintenance of phobic behavior.

## B. Punishment

Even casual observation reveals the extensive use of aversive controls in human interactions, from social prohibitions, to aversive systems of discipline in the family and school, to punitive legal codes. Also, punishment processes have long been regarded as playing a pivotal role in the production of pathological behavior. A number of writers have commented on the immediate effects which such experiences have on pathological behavior. "Trauma"-inducing circumstances leading to suppression and repression are central to psychoanalytic theory. Similarly, social learning theory also stresses the relationship between early punitive experiences and subsequent psychopathology.

Less directly, some of the side effects of aversive control may also contribute to pathological behavior. Thus, many aggressive, assaultive and law-breaking responses may be regarded as attempts at counter control induced by aversive experiences. Escape behavior, such as school and work dropouts also increase under continuing aversive schedules. Alcoholism and drug addiction are popularly placed in the context of escape behavior.

Such arguments have a powerful common sense appeal, and there is much evidence to support these views. However, once again, a more thorough analysis of the relationship between punishment and psychopathology must consider such variables as the history of the response being punished, the interaction between punishment and reinforcement, the nature, magnitude, and schedule of the punishment, etc.

In line with our previous analysis of responses acquired via positive or negative reinforcement, let us consider some of the effects produced by changes from schedules of positive or negative reinforcement to punishment schedules.

*Positive reinforcement followed by punishment*: Under many circumstances, the introduction of a punishing consequence (Table II, row 3), results in a decrement in response frequency (Church, 1964). Folk wisdom as well as a good deal of experimental evidence supports this generalization. Such arrangements are regarded in many quarters as being largely responsible for much of what is termed behavior pathology. Perhaps the strongest argument can be drawn in terms of behavioral deficits, i.e., a restricted behavioral repertoire which is the result of early and extensive repressive and suppressive experiences. Thus, Masserman (1961) demonstrated that punishment in the form of air puffs and electric shock, contingent on a food-reinforced response, suppressed the response to the point where the animals risked starvation. Conger *et al.* (1958) and Sawrey *et al.* (1966) showed that strong shock, superimposed over food reinforced behavior, resulted in bleeding ulcers.

It has been further demonstrated that a stimulus associated with unavoidable shock may also suppress behavior maintained by positive reinforcement (Estes & Skinner, 1941). Sidman (1960), noting the emotional behavior of the organisms during the preaversive stimulus, has argued that such effects resemble the characteristics of anxiety neurosis.

As indicated above, punishment may also elicit various forms of aggressive responses, which appear to have pathological effects. It is a commonplace observation that many animals, when subjected to various punishment schedules, engage in self-mutilation, following shock delivery. Ulrich *et al.* (1962) have observed shock-elicited aggression between animals when exposed to punishing experiences. There is certainly ample reason to believe that punitive experiences are intimately involved in many forms of psychopathology. What remains to be isolated, however, is a more precise analysis of this relationship, especially with regard to more clearly circumscribed forms of clinical phenomena. In this fashion, for example, we might explicate the putative influence of punishment on such sexual problems as frigidity and impotence.

Any such analysis, however, must also consider the "paradoxical" effects which often occur during punishment arrangements. Many studies have demonstrated that punishment, superimposed over a positively reinforced response, may result in *increased* responding (Sandler, 1964). Thus, Masserman (1961), by simply introducing punishment in a reduced form, and only gradually increasing its aversive properties, produced a situation in which animals ultimately worked for the noxious stimulus alone. A similar effect was observed by Sandler (1964) where the schedule of punishment was only gradually increased, and the schedule of positive reinforcement was held constant.

An example of how such an effect may occur is shown in Figure 2. The upper record reveals the high stable response rate generated by a marmoset monkey maintained for about 20 sessions on VR 50 liquid reinforcement. In the second hour of this session (bottom record) strong shock was delivered on every 500th response. Under other circumstances, such as lower response rate, shorter positive reinforcement history, more frequent shock, etc., such a procedure usually results in rapid and complete suppression. Note that in this instance, however, the suppressive effects of the shock diminished. Responding stopped for about 20 min. after the first shock, but for only about 2 min. after the last shock.

When the shock no longer produced long delays, the shock frequency was gradually increased. Ultimately, each response produced shock (FR 1) while the VR 50 liquid schedule was maintained. Observation of the monkey under these conditions would have revealed an animal receiving, on an average, one

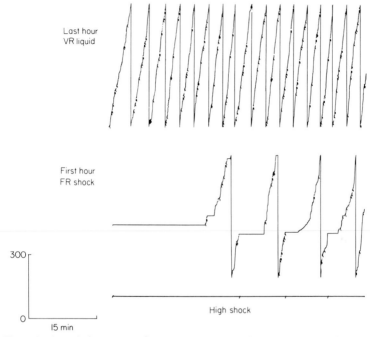

**Figure 2.** Cumulative record for a marmoset monkey maintained of VR 50 liquid reinforcement (upper Panel) and VR 50 liquid reinforcement, FR 500 shock (lower panel). Each pip on the cumulative record represents liquid presentation; each pip on the event pen represents shock presentation.

reinforcement and 50 shocks per 50 responses, plus, a higher overall rate than that obtained prior to the introduction of the shock (Sandler, 1964). Davidson (1968) also demonstrated that organisms would respond at higher rates during mild or moderate punishment than they would under conditions of positive reinforcement alone.

Such findings suggest that the use of term "punishment" may be questionable. It certainly seems inappropriate to refer to an event which increases response rate as punishment, despite any *a priori* judgments to the contrary. Such events may also be analyzed in terms of their discriminative or conditioned reinforcement properties, which may resolve the "paradox." And, most important, these findings suggest the means for investigating many forms of pathological behavior characterized by persistent responding in the face of normally aversive consequences. What is missing is a closer inspection of the manner in which self-punishing behavior is established and maintained by social variables.

We may thus find that pathological behavior is actually promoted and maintained by individuals, agencies, and institutions whose ostensible purpose it is to reduce the frequency of such maladaptive behavior. Although this concern has frequently been expressed, it might be more instructive if we were to explicate the cause and effect relationships which up to now have only been suspected.

*Negative reinforcement followed by punishment*: A number of studies (Brown *et al.*, 1964; Morse & Kelleher, 1966; Sandler, 1964; Sandler, *et al.*, 1966a, 1966b, 1966c; Sidman, *et al.*, 1957) have investigated the effects of punishment following negatively reinforced behavior. Church (1963) observed that, in the majority of instances, these arrangements resulted in the maintenance of behavior involving aversive consequences.

Consider the results shown in Figure 3. Representative records for animals maintained in a signal avoidance paradigm (5-sec. tone followed by shock) are on

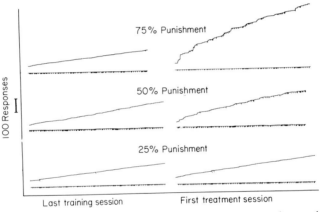

Figure 3. Representative cumulative records for three marmoset monkeys maintained in a signal avoidance paradigm before response shock (left) and after response shock (right). Trial onset and duration are indicated by the bottom event pen, and trial run-outs (avoidance shocks) by deflections of the cumulative response pen.

the left-hand side. Trial onset and duration are indicated by the bottom event pen. Avoidable shocks are revealed by deflections of the cumulative response pen. Note the stable, efficient pattern of performance. When response shock of varying intensities was introduced (right-hand side records) two changes occurred, both of which were related to punishment intensity; avoidance efficiency declined, but overall response rate increased.

Sandler *et al.* (1966b) have previously described the manner in which such effects can be even more clearly ascertained. Where there is a relatively long history of negative reinforcement, and where the suppressive effects of punishment are circumvented, procedures can be employed which insure the maintenance of response-produced aversive stimulation, even after the negative reinforcement has been withdrawn (Sandler, *et al.*, 1966c). The end result reveals organisms continuing to respond over extremely long durations, despite the fact that the only consequence for their behavior is a normally noxious event (Morse & Kelleher, 1966; McKearney, 1968). In these instances, the appropriate manipulation of relevant variables resulted in durable behavior patterns representative of organisms maintained on fixed-interval positive reinforcement, except that the only consequence of their behavior was an extremely strong noxious shock.

Although such findings have been largely neglected by reinforcement theorists, once again, it would seem that they represent special extensions of the principles rather than contradictions. However, to reveal this underlying consistency, one must focus upon the interaction between the history of the response and the current consequences.

Representative histories of negatively reinforced behavior have already been described. In these cases, the animal's history involves punishment prior to the establishment of the escape and/or avoidance response. While the punishment is not response-produced in the usual sense, all responses except those specifically related to the removal of the aversive event *are* followed, to one degree or another, by noxious stimulation (Dinsmoor, 1954). The aversive event may come to serve as a discriminative stimulus for the escape-avoidance response. When this same stimulus is now made contingent upon the response, earlier training conditions are reinstated, and the organism responds to the aversive event as a discriminative stimulus. Evidence to support such an argument stems from a variety of sources. Thus, when such an arrangement is first superimposed over an avoidance baseline, response rates often increase dramatically (Sandler, 1964).

In general, the greater the similarity between the current aversive events and the aversive events initially employed to generate escape and avoidance behavior, the greater the probability that response rates will be maintained. Conversely, if the new aversive event is dissimilar, suppression, the typical punishment effect, will result.

It may be possible to identify those circumstances which may result in the maintenance of negatively reinforced behavior despite the presence of new aversive consequences. For example, if the various aversive consequences of behavior are specifically programmed such that responding is discriminatively less noxious than not responding, we would predict the maintenance of behavior providing the organism has an opportunity to evaluate two alternatives. This is nothing more than specifying a "lesser of two evils" situation where the lesser evil occurs as a consequence of continued responding. Once this effect has been achieved, conditions may be altered such that the effect can be maintained. An example of this would be to randomly alternate unpunished avoidance conditions with punished-extinction conditions, followed by a gradual increase in number of punished-extinction trials. The result may be an organism responding to produce noxious stimulation with no evidence of extinction (Sandler, *et al.*, 1966b).

This is, of necessity, only an abbreviated summary of a few possible arrangements and their concomitant effects which may be considered in analyzing various response histories. There are, of course, an infinite number of variations on the theme and probably none of them completely describes the history of any given form of pathological behavior in the natural environment. Nevertheless, it seems reasonable to assume that as the many permutations and combinations of variables are analyzed, closer and closer approximations to clinical phenomena will be observed. For example, little has been done with procedures which involve a transition from an acquisition history of positive reinforcement to a maintenance schedule involving negative reinforcement, and vice versa. Yet, it seems reasonable to assume that many responses which occur in the natural environment involve just such features.

## IV. MAINTENANCE

With a proper analysis of the history of a response (including the acquisition conditions and associated stimuli as well as the secondary determinants which influence the maintenance or absence of the behavior), we are in a position to assess the effects of any current conditions which may be imposed. Such an analysis may be considered within the context of a three-part schedule.

Any such division is, of course, arbitrary, and it is probably the case that most contemporary responses can be understood as extensions of two-part schedules, since most of the current determinants are extensions of variables present during acquisition and maintenance. In other words, behavior is relatively stable because the environment is relatively stable. The conditions which prevail today are highly similar to those present yesterday and the day before, and the number of dramatic changes in relation to the "stable" determinants are relatively few. Thus, the phobic individual whose behavior is determined by reinforcing events such as those outlined above will manifest the same behavior in the presence of strangers to the degree that these individuals also provide similar reinforcement.

Nevertheless, and quite obviously, occasions arise in which an individual is faced with a "new" situation, i. e., a response learned and maintained under prior conditions comes under the control of new determinants. This can be as commonplace as encountering a traffic obstacle on a familiar route to work, or as significant as seeking treatment for a behavior disorder. In each case, the effect of the new condition will be determined, in large measure, by the prior determinants, and the prediction of the individual's reaction to these new circumstances must consider these antecedent events.

In analyzing three-part schedules, we have made an arbitrary distinction in terms of those situations where an established response encounters a "new" consequence, or a "significant" change from prior conditions. Examples of several possible arrangements appear in Table III. Thus, one elementary case might (row 1) include acquisition under positively reinforcing circumstances, followed by an extinction procedure and then, subsequent to complete extinction, the reintroduction of positive reinforcement.

TABLE III An Extension of Table II Including a Three-Component History or Combination of Acquisition, Maintenance, and Modification Stages, Variables, or Procedures[a]

|    | Acquisition schedule | Maintenance schedule | Modification |
|----|----------------------|----------------------|--------------|
| 1. | Positive reinforcement | Extinction | Positive reinforcement |
| 2. | Negative reinforcement | Extinction | Negative reinforcement |
| 3. | Negative reinforcement | Punishment + negative reinforcement | Punishment + extinction |

[a]Examples of each are discussed in the text.

Investigations using such procedures reveal the development of a rapid discrimination between the reinforcing and the extinguishing conditions. The same results (i.e., rapid discrimination) might not obtain with negative reinforcement where, at high levels of avoidance efficiency, there may be little stimulus change accompanying the changes in determinants (row 2). Any attempt to employ an extinction arrangement to reduce the frequency of pathological behavior, therefore, must consider at least the degree to which reinforcing events are present in the environment as well as the history of the response. An example of such a procedure is Brady's work (Brady, 1958) involving shifts from a schedule of negative reinforcement to extinction and back to negative reinforcement which produced ulcers in monkeys.

We have conducted a series of studies based upon this three-part schedule model using changes in schedules in acquisition, maintenance, and extinction (Table III, row 3). In these studies, animals are initially trained in a discriminated shock avoidance procedure. At varying stages during acquisition and maintenance, punishment is superimposed over the avoidance response in various ways. Subsequently, the avoidance contingency is withdrawn (extinction), but the punishment is maintained.

Three major schedule variations and their typical effects are shown in Figure 4. The left-hand side records show the behavior of the last avoidance training session for three marmosets. All three animals were maintained on a typical Sidman avoidance schedule, except that each response by animal C10 also produced a response shock (indicated by pen deflections).

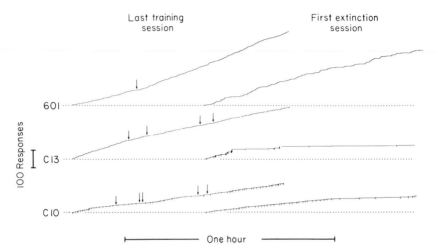

Figure 4. Three major schedule variations and their typical effects. Each arrow represents an avoidable shock and each pen deflection a response shock.

During extinction (right-hand side records) the avoidance contingency was withdrawn but the punishment condition was maintained for C10, and first introduced to C13. In addition, all aversive consequences were withdrawn for 60I. Note the rapid suppression which obtained in the last case as contrasted with the more durable response pattern for C10. One might argue that this S's three-part schedule history enhanced the probability of maladaptive behavior, in the sense that each response produced unnecessary self-aversive stimulation.

In our first study designed to explore such three-part schedules (Sandler *et al.*, 1966a), punishment intensity was varied during a 10-day maintenance period, after which avoidance shock was deleted. Under these conditions, bursting during the maintenance condition was positively correlated and resistance to extinction negatively correlated with shock intensity. In a second study (Sandler, *et al.*, 1966b), it was found that animals could be maintained indefinitely on punished-extinction schedules as long as they were interchanged on some regular basis with avoidance sessions. During a final extinction phase of this experiment, one S continued responding, producing punishment shock with each response, through more than 40 sessions. In a third study, Sandler and Davidson (1967) demonstrated that the maintenance of punished avoidance behavior in the presence of a nonpunished alternative is a function of the length of initial avoidance training. That is, animals with a long avoidance-training history were more likely to continue the response they learned initially, despite the occurrence of strong shock contingent on each response, and even though a more adaptive alternative (a second response lever) was available.

We are currently exploring the further possibilities of such arrangements for their relevancy to human psychopathology. Table IV schematically outlines one

TABLE IV Schematic Outline of Punished-Avoidance–Punished-Extinction Paradigm

| | Punished avoidance | | Punished extinction |
| --- | --- | --- | --- |
| | Response options | Aversive consequences | Aversive consequences |
| 1. | Bar A | No avoidable shock (punishment) | Punishment |
| 2. | Cessation | Avoidable shock (no punishment) | None |
| 3. | Bar B | No avoidable shock (no punishment) | None |

such arrangement. During an avoidance condition in which responding on one lever is punished and responding on a functionally equivalent lever is not, three options are available. The animal may continue to respond on the punished bar (1) in which case he does not receive the avoidable shock, but does receive response shock; he may stop responding (2) with its attendant consequences; or he may make the avoidance response on the alternative lever (3), the most adaptive alternative since this removes all aversive consequences. Relevant variables can be easily introduced for the purpose of determining their effect on each of these alternatives. Maladaptive behavior in extinction (thus completing the three-part schedule) can be analyzed in a similar fashion.

Several variations on the three-part schedule model have been reported but these have been restricted to the analysis of "normal" processes rather than analyzing pathological behavior. Most of the possible variations on this complex paradigm relevant to the current analysis remain to be investigated.

# REFERENCES

Allen, K. Eileen, Hart, Betty, Buell, Joan S., Harris, Florence R., & Wolf, M. M. Effects of social reinforcement on isolate behavior of a nursery school child. *Child Development*, 1964, **35**, 511-519.

Ayllon, T., Haughton, E., & Hughes, H. B. Interpretation of symptoms; factor fiction. *Behaviour Research and Therapy*, 1965, **3**, 1-7.

Azrin, N. H. Some effects of noise on human behavior. *Journal of the experimental Analysis of Behaviour*, 1958, **1**, 183-200.

Bexton, W. H., Heron, W., & Scott, T. H. Effects of decreased variation in the sensory environment. *Canadian Journal of Psychology*, 1954, **8**, 70-77.

Brady, J. V. Ulcers in "executive" monkeys. *Scientific American*, 1958, **199**, 95-100.

Brady, J. V. & Polish, E. Performance changes during prolonged avoidance. *Psychological Reports*, 1960, **7**, 554.

Brown, J. S., Martin, R. C., & Morrow, M. W. Self-punitive behavior in the rat: Facilitative effects of punishment on resistance to extinction. *Journal of Comparative and Physiological Psychology*, 1964, **57**, 127-133.

Church, R. M. The varied effects of punishment on behavior. *Psychological Review,* 1963, 70, 369-402.

Conger, J. J., Sawrey, W. L., & Turrell, E. S. The role of social experience in the production of gastric ulcers in hooded rats placed in a conflict situation. *Journal of Abnormal and Social Psychology,* 1958, 57, 214-220.

Davidson, R. S. Effects of increasing intensity shock contingent on reinforced responses on a variable interval schedule. Paper presented at APA, 1968.

Davidson, R. S. Research design and the aversive conditioning of alcoholic behavior. Paper presented to SEPA, 1969.

Dinsmoor, J. A. Punishment. I. The avoidance hypothesis. *Psychological Review,* 1954, 61, 34-46.

Dollard, J., & Miller, N. E. *Personality and psychotherapy.* New York: McGraw-Hill, 1950.

Estes, W. K., & Skinner, B. F. Some quantitative properties of anxiety. *Journal of Experimental Psychology,* 1941, 29, 390-400.

Ferster, C. B. Reinforcement and punishment in the control of human behavior by social agencies. *Psychiatric Research Reports,* 1958, 10, 101-118.

Ferster, C. B. Positive reinforcement and behavioral deficits of autistic children. *Child Development,* 1961, 32, 437-456.

Ferster, C. B. Animal behavior and mental illness. *Psychological Record,* 1966, 16, 345-356.

Ferster, C. B., & Skinner, B. F. *Schedules of reinforcement.* New York: Appleton-Century-Crofts, 1957.

Harlow, H. F. The nature of love. *American Psychologist,* 1958, 13, 673-685.

Hart, Betty M., Allen, K. Eileen, Buell, Joan S., Harris, Florence R., & Wolf, M. M. Effects of social reinforcement on operant crying. *Journal of Experimental Child Psychology,* 1964, 1, 145-153.

Heron, W., Bexton, W. H., & Hebb, D. O. Cognitive effects of a decreased variation in the sensory environment. *American Psychologist,* 1953, 8, 366.

Holland, J. G., & Skinner, B. F. *The analysis of behavior.* New York: McGraw-Hill, 1961.

Lovaas, O. I. A behavior therapy approach to the treatment of childhood schizophrenia. In J. Hill (Ed.) *Minnesota Symposium on Child Psychology.* Minneapolis: University of Minnesota Press, 1967.

Maier, N. R. F. *Frustration: the study of behavior without a goal.* New York: McGraw-Hill, 1949.

Masserman, J. H. A biodynamic psychoanalytic approach to the problems of feeling and emotions. In M. E. Reymert (Ed.) *Feelings and emotions.* New York: McGraw-Hill, 1950.

Masserman, J. H. *Principles of dynamic psychiatry.* Philadelphia: W. B. Saunders, 1961.

McKearney, J. W. Maintenance of responding under a fixed-interval schedule of electric shock-presentation. *Science,* 1968, 160, 1249-1251.

Miller, N. E. Learnable drives and rewards. In S. S. Stevens (Ed.) *Handbook of experimental psychology.* New York: Wiley, 1951.

Morse, W. H., & Kelleher, R. T. Schedules as fundamental determinants of behavior. Paper presented at APA, 1966.

Mowrer, O. H. Learning theory and the neurotic paradox. *American Journal of Orthopsychiatry,* 1948, 18, 571-610.

Mowrer, O. H. *Learning theory and personality dynamics.* New York: Ronald Press, 1950.

Rickard, H. C., Dignam, P. J., & Horner, R. F. Verbal manipulation in a psychotherapeutic relationship. *Journal of Clinical Psychology,* 1960, 16, 364-367.

Sandler, J. Masochism: An empirical analysis. *Psychological Bulletin,* 1964, 62, 197-204.

Sandler, J., & Davidson, R. S. Punished avoidance behavior in the presence of a non-punished alternative. *Psychonomic Science*, 1967, 8, 297-298.

Sandler, J., Davidson, R. S., Greene, W. A., & Holzschuh, R. D. Effects of punishment intensity on instrumental avoidance behavior. *Journal of Comparative and Physiological Psychology*, 1966a, 61, 212-216.

Sandler, J., Davidson, R. S., & Holzschuh, R. D. The effects of increasing punishment frequency on Sidman avoidance behavior. *Psychonomic Science*, 1966b, 5, 103-104.

Sandler, J., Davidson, R. S., & Malagodi, E. F. Durable maintenance of behavior during concurrent avoidance and punished-extinction conditions. *Psychonomic Science*, 1966c, 6, 105-106.

Sawrey, W. L., Conger, J. J., & Turrell, E. S. An experimental investigation of the role of psychological factors in the production of gastric ulcers in rats. *Journal of Comparative Physiological Psychology*. 1966. 49. 457-461.

Sidman, M. Normal sources of pathological behavior. *Science*, 1960, 132, 61-68.

Sidman, M., Hernstein, R. J., & Conrad, D. G. Maintenance of avoidance behavior by unavoidable shocks. *Journal of Comparative and Physiological Psychology*, 1957, 50, 553-557.

Skinner, B. F. "Superstition" in the pigeon. *Journal of Experimental Psychology*, 1948, 38, 168-172.

Skinner, B. F. *Science and human behavior*. New York: Macmillan, 1953.

Skinner, B. F. The machine that is man. *Psychology Today*. 1969, 2, 20-25.

Solomon, R. L., Kamin, L. J., & Wynne, L. C. Traumatic avoidance learning: the outcomes of several extinction procedures with dogs. *Journal of Abnormal Psychology*, 1953, 48, 291-302.

Staats, A. W., & Staats, Carolyn K. *Complex human behavior*. New York: Holt, Rinehart and Winston, 1963.

Ulrich, R. E., & Azrin, N. H. Reflexive fighting in response to aversive stimulation. *Journal of Experimental Analysis of Behaviour*, 1962, 5, 511-520.

Watson, J. B., & Raynor, R. Conditioned emotional reactions. *Journal of Experimental Psychology*, 1920, 3, 1-14.

Weiner, H. Some effects of response cost upon human operant behavior. *Journal of Experimental Analysis of Behaviour*, 1962, 5, 201-208.

Weiner, H. Conditioning history and maladaptive human operant behavior. *Psychological Reports*, 1965, 17, 934-942.

Weiner, H. Controlling human fixed-interval performance. *Journal of Experimental Analysis of Behaviour*, 1969, 12, 349-373.

Wilcoxon, H. C. "Abnormal fixation" and learning. *Journal of Experimental Psychology*, 1952, 44, 324-333.

Williams, C. D. The elimination of tantrum behavior by extinction procedures. *Journal of Abnormal Social Pyschology*, 1959, 59, 269.

Wilson, R. S. On behavior pathology. *Psychological Bulletin*, 1963, 60, 130-146.

Zimmerman, D. W. Durable secondary reinforcement: method and theory. *Psychological Review*, 1957, 64, 373-383.

# 6

# Vicious Circle Behavior

KENNETH B. MELVIN

University of Alabama

## I. INTRODUCTION

In 1937, K. Horney used the term, "vicious circle behavior," to describe the self-perpetuating, self-punitive, compulsive behaviors of the neurotic. Several years later, a possible subhuman analog of this process was discovered by J. S. Brown (as reported by Mowrer, 1947). Brown observed that rats trained to escape shock by traversing a straight alley and entering a "safe" area would later persevere in running from an unshocked starting area if the shock remained in some subsequent section. Mowrer (1947, 1950) noted the similarity of this phenomenon to the "neurotic paradox," wherein punishment of anxiety-motivated behavioral symptoms leads to their reoccurrence. He theorized that the rat leaves the presently safe start box due to conditional fear; fear is then maintained by the onset of punishment. The instrumental running response is reinforced by fear reduction. Furthermore, punishment-induced fear generalizes through the generally homogeneous alley and start box.

The first definitive study on vicious circle behavior was that of Brown, Martin, and Morrow (1964). They showed that punishment of an ongoing escape response during extinction increased response speed and tended to increase the number of trials run until the rat met the extinction criterion (one trial of at least 60 sec.). Their "long" shock punishment (6 ft.) was more facilitative than a delayed "short" shock of 2 ft. The primary results of the Brown, Martin, and Morrow experiment were soon supported by other research findings (Brown, Anderson, & Weiss, 1965; Martin & Melvin, 1964; Martin, 1964; Melvin, 1964). In fact, since Brown et al. (1964), there have been approximately 30 studies confirming the basic vicious-circle effect. Certain of these experiments are especially valuable in clarifying theoretical considerations, especially in relation to secondary sources of motivation.

The present paper will evaluate recent data in terms of variables determining vicious-circle behavior, relating these findings to those examined by Brown (1969). Furthermore, it will illustrate possible commonalities between self-punitive locomotor behavior and other types of punishment-induced facilitation involving aversive motivation.

## II. INTENSITY OF PUNISHMENT

As the intensity of punishment is increased, positively rewarded responses are increasingly suppressed (Church, 1963). In the vicious-circle paradigm, however, the intensity variable tends to work in an opposite fashion, i.e., the vigor of the response and resistance to extinction are an increasing function of punishment intensity, up to a certain limit. This conclusion was initially supported by Gwinn (1949). He found that, during extinction, an escape response was faster and continued longer with a "strong" shock punishment than a "weak" shock punishment. These results were generally supported by data reported by Hurwitz, Bolas, and Haritos (1961) for escape-trained rats.

A more elaborate experiment by Martin (1964) involved various combinations of shock intensity during escape training and punishment–extinction. He trained rats to escape shock by leaving a 1-ft. start box and traversing a 6-ft. alley. Voltage levels during training were 40, 60, 80, or 100 V. for four groups of subjects. These groups were further subdivided so that there were (a) four nonpunished groups designated 100-0, 80-0, 60-0, and 40-0, (b) four groups which continued on the same voltage from training to punishment–extinction (100-100, 80-80, 60-60, and 40-40), and (c) two "shifted" groups (80-60 and 60-80). Shock-punishment was administered on the first 14 in. of the alley.

Alley speed during extinction was a significant function of shock intensity during both training and punishment. Comparison of each punished group with its respective nonpunished control group revealed significant facilitative effects of punishment, except for Group 40-40.

Martin's (1964) findings have been generally confirmed and extended in an avoidance paradigm. Beecroft, Bouska, & Fisher (1967) trained rats to avoid 55 V. (through 10 k$\Omega$). During the first 10 trials of extinction, speed in the first 4 ft. of the alley appears to be an increasing function of the intensity of a near-goal 1-ft. shock (0, 40, 55, and 70 V.). Number of trials to extinction increased as a function of intensity up to 55 V., but the shift from 55 V. in training to 70 V. during punishment–extinction reduced resistance to extinction relative to a constant 55 V.

Melvin and Bender (1968) trained rats to avoid shock (55 V., 10 k$\Omega$) by traversing a start box and 4-ft. runway within 5 sec. In Experiment I, Ss were given 15 extinction trials, (0 V.) followed by 60 punishment–extinction trials. During the latter series, three groups of rats were punished with shock of decreasing, increasing, or constant intensities in the first 2-ft. section. Figure 1 shows the mean alley speed across voltage levels. As Figure 1 indicates, running speed was a significantly increasing function of punishment intensity under several conditions, thus confirming and extending prior results (e.g., Martin, 1964; Beecroft *et al.*, 1967). Experience with gradually ascending intensities of punishment reduced the facilitative effect of a more intensive shock.

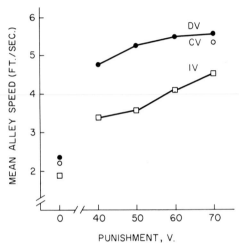

PUNISHMENT, V.

**Figure 1.** Mean alley speeds for three groups as a function of punishment voltage. Group IV received 0, 40, 50, 60, and 70 V. in that order. After the initial 0-V. trials, Group DV was given 70, 60, 50, and then 40 V. Group CV initially received 0 V., followed by 70 V. for the next 60 trials (from Melvin & Bender, 1968).

It thus appears that if strong and stable vicious-circle behavior is once established, the vigor of the response is enhanced as a function of punishment intensity. While a marked increase in intensity of the noxious stimulus from training to extinction may reduce the persistence of responding, gradual shifts in intensity during punishment–extinction do not have this effect.

## III. LOCATION OF PUNISHMENT

In the straight alley, shock punishment has been administered at various locations, and thus, at various points in the response sequence. Punishment administered in the goal box suppresses rather than facilitates avoidance responding (Seligman & Campbell, 1965)—a fact consistent with major theoretical explanations of vicious circle behavior.

An optimal punishment location is the middle of the alley, e.g., the center 2 ft. of a 4-ft. alley. In one study, Brown, Horsfall, and Van Bruggen (1969) trained rats to run a 6-ft. alley to escape shock. During extinction, a group punished in a middle 1-ft. section ran faster than rats given immediate punishment or delayed punishment. Melvin and Stenmark (1968) established a new response (running) which was motivated by conditioned fear. Again, a shock given in the second foot of a 4-ft. alley was more facilitative than a delayed punishment in the last foot. Finally, Melvin and Bender (1968) reported two experiments involving avoidance training in a 4-ft. alley. Cross-experiment speed comparisons suggest that a middle 2-ft. shock was more facilitative than an immediate (initial 2 ft.) shock-punishment.

Whereas immediate or "near" shock seems slightly less facilitative than a middle shock, it has usually proven superior to even more delayed shock. Martin and Melvin (1964), using escape training and 8-in. punishment segments in either end of a 4-ft. alley, first reported this relation. Melvin, Athey, and Heasley (1965) confirmed these initial results with 1-ft. shocks given in the first or last segment of a 4-ft. alley.

Campbell, Smith, and Misanin (1966) also compared immediate and delayed shocks. After rats were trained to traverse a start box and 6-ft. alley to avoid shock, they received one of the following three treatments: (a) regular (nonpunished) extinction (b) immediate punishment—a .15-sec. shock given at a point 4 in. beyond the start box and (c) delayed punishment—a .15-sec. shock was delivered at a point 8 in. before the goal box. The start and goal boxes were interchangeable.

During extinction, the immediate-punishment group ran faster and showed slightly more resistance to extinction than a nonpunished group. Unlike former results, delayed punishment led to faster extinction than no punishment. This outcome was attributed, in part, to the use of a temporally rather than spatially controlled shock (Campbell et al., 1966). However, more recent research has indicated that this variable is not a crucial one (Anson, Bender, & Melvin, 1969; Beecroft & Fisher, 1969; Melvin & Martin, 1966).

A possible explanation for the suppressive effect of delayed shock may involve the length of the punishment zone and its interaction with goal box cues. It may be that the use of a short shock zone succeeds in pairing punishment onset with (a) the act of entering the goal box and (b) the goal box itself. A conditioned fear hypothesis (Brown, 1969; Mowrer, 1960) holds that the shock punishment elicits fear which generalizes throughout the homogeneous alley and start box (but not into the markedly different goal box). In the Campbell et al. (1966) study, however, fear would generalize into the nondistinctive goal box rather than the distant (64 in. away) start box. This analysis is supported by the findings of Delprato and Denny (1968). They varied the duration of confinement in the goal box, (2 versus 30 sec.), finding that punishment prolonged extinction only with the 30-sec. confinement. Delprato and Denny invoke the concept of "relief" to explain these results. In any case, the role of the goal box appears crucial: Thus, interchangeable start-goal boxes such as those used by Campbell *et al.* (1966), confound two important sets of cues and should not be used.

Mowrer (1960), Brown *et al.* (1964), and others have invoked the generalization of punishment-induced fear as a theoretical mechanism. I shall attempt to specify the operation of this mechanism, and thus to account for the punishment-location results. Assume that (a) fear generalizes throughout the alley from the specific shock-punishment area and (b) the more remote the rat is in space and time from the point of shock, the less will be its fear from this source. Figure 2 illustrates hypothetical generalization gradients of conditioned

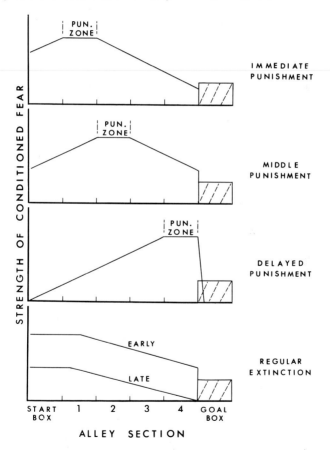

Figure 2. Hypothetical gradients of conditioned fear. The lower curves represent fear conditioned during training as it exists during "early" ( e.g., trials 1–5) and "late" phases of regular (nonpunished) extinction. The other curves represent the generalization of *punishment-induced* fear over the runway as function of punishment location. Theoretically, the summation of fear from these two sources provides a basis for predicting speed at a specific location in the runway (after allowance for the effects of the shock itself, if it is used on these test trials).

fear with shock-punishment (1 ft.) at different locations or absent. These gradients are not unlike the speed gradients over alley sections reported in several investigations. Both Brown *et al.* (1964, Fig. 5), and Melvin (1964, Fig. 2) reported that rats given regular extinction (RE) gradually slow as they approach the goal box. The slope of this gradient could be attributed to greater fear induced by shock onset during training plus some inhibition of fear as the *S* nears the safe goal box. Assuming that the extinction of escape responses is due to a progressive loss of conditioned fear, the generalization of fear from the point of punishment would be crucial in maintaining the running response. This explanation is compatible with the progressive speed increase over sections found by Brown *et al.* (1964), with a delayed shock (see their Fig. 5). Furthermore, with a constant-length shock, a middle location would yield more facilitation than other locations in longer runways. This deduction is in line with the results of Brown *et al.* (1969) showing superiority for an intermediate punishment in a 6-ft. alley.

A further prediction can be made from this fear-gradient hypothesis: If shock-punishment is presented in a variable location, punishment-induced fear would be equivalent in all alley sections. Thus, if a rat locked into vicious-circle behavior was given a nonshocked test trial, it should show only a slight decline in speed as it approaches the goal. After continued self-punitive running, the gradient should be even flatter, as the contribution of fear due to shock during training is reduced.

## IV. TYPE OF TRAINING

### A. Escape, Avoidance, and Avoidance–Escape

Most investigators have used either escape or avoidance training prior to punishment–extinction. Also, there have been several experiments directly comparing the two procedures. In the first of these, Hurwitz, Bolas, and Haritos (1961) presented data which suggested that avoidance-trained rats resisted punished extinction more strongly than escape-trained subjects.

In a more complex experiment, Beecroft and Brown (1967) examined the effects of three types of training. During this training, the CS–UCS interval ranged from 0 sec. (escape) through 1 or 2 sec. (avoidance–escape) to 4 sec. (avoidance). In the avoidance–escape paradigm, the rat always received some shock; however, his speed determined the length of electrified grid and the duration of shock. Following training, a 55-V. shock was present in the last 2-ft. segment of the 6-ft. alley. Even though escape-trained rats were intermediate in speed during acquisition, they were the least resistant as well as the slowest subjects by the end of the punished extinction. Beecroft and Brown thus established that punishment–extinction following avoidance training is generally more facilitative than it is after escape training, a finding later confirmed by Bender and Melvin (1967).

## B. Training with Positive Reward

Brown (1969) reported the results of attempts to convert food-reinforced approach behavior into fear-motivated self-punitive behavior. After training rats to run a 6-ft. alley for food, shock was introduced gradually in the center of the alley. However, the shock was never paired with food. Also, hunger was progressively reduced. Nonpunished Ss extinguished quite rapidly, as did most punished Ss. In four studies of this type, Brown reported that only 20% of the punished animals showed vicious-circle behavior.

A study by Cloar (1970) yielded somewhat similar results. Two groups of rats were trained in daily sessions to run a 4-ft. alley for food or to escape shock. The two groups were equivalent in asymptotic speed during training as well as resistance to extinction (in the nonpunished control condition). Cloar did not use a gradual increase in shock for the two punished subgroups, but rather the standard vicious-circle procedure. While shock-trained rats showed punishment-induced facilitation, punished rats trained with positive reward typically extinguished quite rapidly. However, two food-trained rats (about 10%) became locked in the vicious circle.

A recent study by Martin (1969b) provides further evidence that appetitively motivated subjects generally fail to show vicious-circle behavior. A food-rewarded group receiving moderately intense punishment was *suppressed* relative to its control group, whereas an escape-trained shock-punished group ran faster and longer than its nonpunished control group. In training, Martin's escape rats were running at about 4.6 ft./sec. while the food-rewarded rats were considerably slower (3.0 ft./sec.). However, this slow speed in the latter group can not account for the different outcomes, since avoidance-trained rats are equally as slow but are facilitated under similar conditions (e.g., Melvin & Smith, 1967; Beecroft, 1967).

While prior training with positive reward is generally ineffective in producing vicious-circle behavior, what about those few food-trained subjects that do show this effect? Brown (1969) attributes their behavior to punishment-induced generalized conditioned fear. Recent data indicating that *some* rats can learn to run an alley on the basis of only 1 or 3 fear-conditioning trials provide some support for this notion (Galvani, 1969).

## V. LEARNING SELF-PUNITIVE BEHAVIOR

While the punishment–extinction procedure typically results in continued responding, under certain conditions it may actually lead to a progressive increase in performance. This "learning" effect was first noticed by Melvin and Martin (1966) when rats trained to escape noxious noise received shock-punishment during extinction (see Figure 4).

Incomplete escape training was used by Beecroft and Bouska (1967), who also found this learning effect in self-punitive running. Independently, Melvin and Smith (1967) obtained strong evidence for this phenomenon after (a) avoidance training and (b) after 30 avoidance–extinction trials. Data from both of these experiments revealed curves typical of learning during the initial phase of punishment–extinction. Further evidence was provided by other investigators, e.g., Beecroft and Brown (1967) and Melvin and Stenmark (1968).

Anson et al. (1969) examined the role of shock in this type of learning. Their escape-trained rats were punished by equivalent fixed-distance or fixed-duration shocks during extinction. The two types of punishment did not significantly differ in their effects; both facilitated performance relative to a nonpunished control condition. A second experiment showed the basic self-punitive effect with avoidance-trained rats on a 50% (fixed-duration) punishment schedule. Speed increased progressively over trials, this increase in speed occurring in the punishment section of the alley, but appeared on nonpunished as well as punished trials. These results relegate the reduction of punishment duration to a minor explanatory role and are supportive of a modified conditioned fear interpretation.

## VI. PERCENTAGE OF PUNISHMENT

For purposes of comparison, Figure 3 shows approximate relationships found between resistance to extinction (typically represented by trials to extinction or running speed) and percentage of punishment. The data shown for Bender and Melvin (1967) diverges slightly from that of Martin and Moon (1968) and Beecroft et al. (1967); however, the 50%-punishment condition was not significantly different from 100%. Still, a 10%-punishment schedule was not as effective as the higher percentages, although it led to faster running than no (0%) punishment. The most recent experiment (Bender, 1969) represents an intermediate relationship. As Figure 5 indicates, Bender found that 33% punishment led to more resistance to extinction than no punishment, but less resistance than 100% punishment. She used secondary punishment, however, a procedure which may provide a clue to a variable interacting with punishment percentage. This variable is probably either (a) the *intensity* of punishment and/or (b) the intertrial interval. Martin and Moon (1968) and Beecroft et al. (1967) used moderately strong shock; Bender and Melvin (1967) used a moderate shock (50 V.). However, Melvin (1964), who found the weakest effects of partial punishment, used a relatively "weak" shock of 45 V. as well as

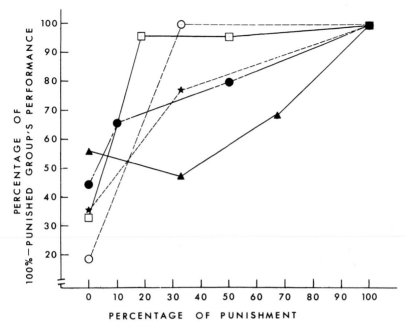

Figure 3. The results of five experiments involving intermittent punishment. The major interest was in comparisons between 100%-punished groups and partially punished groups; therefore, the latter groups' data are plotted as percentages of the 100%-punished groups performance for each experiment. The basic measure of response was number of trials to extinction, except for alley speed in one case (Bender & Melvin, 1967). Groups split on the basis of other variables were combined where warranted. Key: (○) Martin & Moon, 1968; (□) Beecroft et al., 1967; (●) Bender & Melvin, 1967; (▲) Melvin, 1964; (★) Bender, 1969.

daily 12-trial sessions with spaced trials. The other four experiments were conducted with massed trials. A study employing varied levels of percentage (e.g., 0, 10, 30, 60, and 100%), different punishment intensities ("weak," e.g., 40 V. versus "strong," e.g., 60 V.) and perhaps different intertrial intervals should further elucidate these relationships.

## VII. GENERALITY OF THE VICIOUS-CIRCLE PHENOMENON

As has been indicated, the self-punitive phenomenon has been obtained under various conditions. Experimenters have used different strains of hooded as well as albino rats, different shock sources, alleys of various widths, lengths, and types of door construction, etc. But until quite recently, vicious-circle behavior was shown primarily with rats motivated and punished by electric shock in a straight alley. The following studies indicate that the effect is not this limited.

Melvin and Martin (1966) examined the effects of two quantitatively different noxious stimuli used as motivation and/or punishment, i.e., a loud buzzer (101 dB., .0002 dyn./cm.$^2$) or shock (50 V., 10 k$\Omega$). Whereas the buzzer was quite aversive to the experimenters, it appeared to be only mildly so to the rats: They learned to escape it, but ran slowly as compared to animals trained with shock. During extinction, shock-trained rats were punished with a .30-sec. shock or a .30-sec. buzzer or given regular extinction. Buzzer-trained animals received similar extinction conditions.

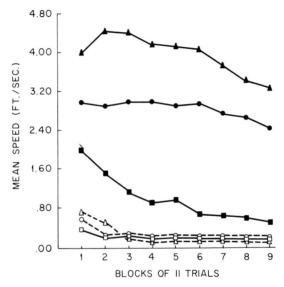

Figure 4. Mean alley speeds for six groups of rats trained to escape either a noxious buzzer or a 50-V. shock. Two groups were punished with shock (Sk–Sk(●), Bz–Sk(▲)), two with buzzer (Sk–Bz(■)), Bz–Bz(□)) and two received nonpunished regular extinction (Sk–RE(○), Bz–RE(△)) (from Melvin & Martin, 1966).

The two shock-punished groups showed little tendency to extinguish; 17 of these 18 subjects ran to the 100-trial limit. Intermediate in speed and resistance to extinction was the shock–buzzer group, which was significantly superior to the remaining three groups. These relationships are reflected in the speed data shown in Figure 4. The one punished group that was not facilitated was the buzzer–buzzer group. This lack of "vicious circle" behavior may be ascribed to the "mild" aversiveness of the buzzer. Martin (1964) also found no facilitative effect with a group trained and punished with a mild aversive stimulus (a 40-V. shock).

These results extend the boundary conditions under which this self-punitive behavior appears, i.e., the *nature* of the facilitative punishment can be different from that of the escape–training stimulus. In fact, given identical punishment conditions, shifted groups ran faster than their respective nonshifted groups. The different manner in which the punishment was controlled (temporally rather than spatially) and the observation of a within-subjects facilitative effect also broaden the generality of this phenomenon.

One theoretical explanation of vicious-circle behavior holds that the greater the similarity between acquisition and extinction conditions, the greater will be resistance to extinction (cf., Church, 1963). However, Melvin and Martin's data reveal that these relations were reversed.

An alternative explanation (Mowrer, 1960; Brown et al., 1964), invokes the mechanism of conditioned fear. In general, performance during punished extinction is consistent with this hypothesis. The shock-punished rats should run longest, which they did, since the more noxious shock should elicit stronger fear. The buzzer is too weak an aversive stimulus to elicit much fear, except possibly in case of rats originally trained to escape shock. This interesting interaction may be due to some type of "sensitization."

There is further evidence that a punishment qualitatively different from that aversive stimulus used in training can be facilitative. Rollings and Melvin (1970) trained rats to escape shock by traversing a 4-ft. alley. One group of subjects were then given 60 regular extinction trials. A second group received a shock-punishment in the first 2-ft. section for 60 trials. The third group received a similar shock, but the overall level of punishment was increased through the *addition* of a noxious buzzer (101 dB.) on Trials 16–60. This summation of two aversive stimuli significantly increased running speed, whereas rats continued on shock punishment alone ran at constant or decreasing speeds. Both punished groups were more resistant to extinction than the nonpunished control group.

A relatively neglected but promising area for establishing the generality of the vicious-circle effect is that of comparative research. A recent study by Martin, Ragland, and Melvin (1970) involved standard techniques and a simple two-group design. Clear facilitative effects of shock punishment on running speed were shown with the gerbil (*Meriones unguiculatus*). While fellow members of the order *Rodentia*, the gerbil and the laboratory rat are classified in different families. Another promising species requires study; in fact, this species *(Homo sapiens)* exhibits considerable self-punitive behavior in its natural habitat.

The most direct attempt to obtain bar-pressing behavior analogous to vicious-circle running is that of Wells and Merrill (1969). They developed a fixed-ratio (FR) bar-press escape response in 12 rats. A retractable lever was inserted with shock onset; its retraction initiated a 30-sec. intertrial interval. During extinction, six rats were assigned to a nonshocked control group. A second group was punished after the first four presses of the FR 12. This punishment procedure is similar to that used in the runway, i.e., punishment is administered during an *ongoing* chain of responses. Wells and Merrill reported that the punished group made significantly more individual responses and had shorter latencies than the control group. However, just two of the punished subjects exhibited sustained self-punitive behavior, a result which may be due to the weak response tendency during extinction. While the results of this study are not as compelling as those typically obtained in the runway, nevertheless, they point the way for further investigations.

Lever pressing was used by Sandler, Davidson, Greene, and Holzschuh (1966), involving discriminated avoidance, and Sandler, Davidson, and Holzschuh (1966), who employed a Sidman avoidance procedure with FR punishment. In the latter study, punishment frequency was increased as the ratio decreased from FR 12 to FR 2 across sessions. Their marmosets showed an initial increase and then a decrease in response rate. Powell and Morris (1969) also punished free-operant avoidance but used a CRF punishment schedule. Aside from a temporary facilitation of rate in the first session, the Ss (rats) showed response suppression as an increasing function of shock-punishment intensity.

Recent experiments using free-operant avoidance provide further information on punished key- or lever-pressing behavior (McKearney, 1968; Stretch, Orloff, & Dalrymple, 1968). Unlike the experiments just cited, punishment was administered at long intervals (300–600 sec.) during extinction. McKearney (1968) trained three squirrel monkeys *(Saimiri sciureus)* to press a response key to postpone the delivery of shock for 30 sec. Following 11–17 such sessions, an FI 10-min. shock-presentation schedule was programmed concurrently with the shock-postponement schedule. After these sessions, the shock-postponement schedule was eliminated, introducing a "punishment–extinctiion" contingency, i.e., the Ss' responses did not result in avoidance but eventually in a shock after each of the 10-min. periods. In certain sessions, a 30-sec. time-out period followed each shock.

McKearney found little effect of the concurrent schedules, but introduction of the FI 10 punishment–extinction schedule increased and maintained response rates. In fact, these three Ss produced over 3000 intense electric shocks. The FI punishment resulted in the "scallops" typical of positively reinforced FI schedules, especially with the time out. Thus, punishment appears to have signalled a "safety" period. As the next shock and the "safety" period became closer in time, responding increased, perhaps due to increased conditioned fear. Stretch *et al.* (1968), found similar results, as did Byrd (1969) who used cats as Ss. McKearney (1969) later found that response rate increased as a function of shorter FI punishment schedules (5, 3, and 1 min.) and higher shock-punishment intensities—results quite similar to those reported in the runway literature.

Certain other instances of punishment-induced facilitation should also be noted. In these situations, the motivational state may be classified as aversive, but this classification is open to dispute. Imprinting represents one such paradigm. Hess (1959) provided evidence in support of his theory that the motivation for imprinting is fear. Furthermore, investigators found that punishment of an ongoing following response may strengthen imprinting (e.g., Kovach & Hess, 1963). At least in one case, the imprinting object administered the punishment and no suppression was observed (Melvin, Cloar, & Massingill, 1967). Melvin *et al.* (1967), imprinted quail chicks to a small hawk. The hawk, having missed its daily feeding one day, sought to remedy this oversight and seized a subject. The experimenter quickly intervened, causing the hawk to release the "shaken" but undamaged quail. After a 2-min. rest, this quail was reinserted into the apparatus where it resumed following. Furthermore, it exhibited strong imprinting in later sessions. This observation may reflect a process similar to that shown by the infant monkey which clings more tightly to its pain-inflicting "evil" mother (Harlow, 1962; Rosenblum & Harlow, 1963).

## VIII. SECONDARY MOTIVATIONAL SYSTEMS

If the vicious-circle phenomenon is limited to the partial reinstatement of a primary aversive stimulus (typically electric shock), it does not seem very relevant to the fear and/or anxiety motivated behaviors of the neurotic (cf., Mowrer, 1947, 1950). In fact, the neurotic rarely encounters electric shock unless he interacts with either a behavior therapist or some defective wiring. Therefore, some of the most significant evidence regarding the generality of the vicious-circle phenomenon has been obtained from experiments involving secondary motivational systems. The term, "secondary motivational system," is taken from Brown and Farber's (1968) review; it describes a stimulus-response associative relation which increases level of motivation. Conditioned fear is defined as such a system and is established through pairings of a neutral stimulus (CS) and a known aversive event. Through such pairings, some of the aversive properties of the primary motivator are transferred to the CS. The CS then should be able to energize responses and its offset should be reinforcing. The CS can also serve as a punishment; however, in the vicious-circle paradigm its action should be similar to that of primary punishment, i.e., facilitation.

### A. Fear as Motivator

Until 1968, published research reporting vicious-circle behavior involved the extinction of an escape or avoidance response established through the use of electric shock, or, in one instance, noxious noise. While one may hold that the *S* responds during extinction due to fear, a direct test of the conditioned fear assumption can be made through the use of the classic procedure developed by Miller (1948).

Melvin and Stenmark (1968) employed this technique to assess the role of conditioned fear in the establishment of self-punitive running. They gave rats 18 paired presentations of a buzzer and a shock (65 V., 10 kΩ) in the start box of an alley; however, the animals were prevented from escaping this area and the shock. After three prepunishment trials, on which the rats began to learn to escape the CS by traversing the 4-ft. alley, Ss were assigned to a nonshocked control group (NS) or one of four punished groups. The latter groups received shock in a middle location or a delayed location: Location was combined factorially with punishment intensity (55 or 75 V.).

While Group NS learned to run the alley to escape from the CS complex (the buzzer plus the static cues of the start box), further trials led to a progressive decrement in performance. All punished rats showed dramatic increases in speed, providing further evidence for the "learning of self-punitive running." The middle shock location resulted in faster running than delayed shock. Although 75 V. generally led to faster running than 55 V., this comparison was not statistically significant (perhaps due to use of the short 1-ft. shock zone). Since all four punished groups showed faster speed and more stable performance than the control group, the vicious-circle effect was actually replicated four times with this fear-motivated running response.

These results are compatible with the conditioned fear explanation of vicious-circle behavior. Furthermore, they extend the boundary conditions under which this self-punitive behavior appears, i.e., it is not limited to a previously learned escape or avoidance response punished during *extinction*. In fact, these animals had never learned to run on an electrified grid prior to the application of punishment.

Further evidence indicating that fear is a prominent factor in self-punitive running was furnished by Galvani (1969). He reasoned that the probability that the subject will exhibit self-punitive running should be an increasing function of the strength of fear aroused in the start box. Furthermore, fear (and thus self-punitive behavior) should increase as a function of number of conditioning trials (cf., McAllister & McAllister, in press).

In general, Galvani's results suggest that the greater the amount of fear conditioned to the CS and start box cues, the stronger the tendency for Ss to run in the presence of these cues. If the S ran and thus encountered shock-punishment, it tended to become locked into the vicious-circle and continued to respond. These findings are clearly in accord with the Mowrer–Brown conditioned fear interpretation as well as the results obtained by Melvin and Stenmark.

DeLude (1969) has argued that experimental support of the Mowrer–Brown hypothesis is "artifactual." He holds that the punitive shock compels the rat to run in the alley: Therefore alley speed is not a proper measure. This argument is blunted by the findings of Anson et al. (1969), that intermittently punished rats run faster than controls even on nonshocked trials. DeLude insists also that the focus of the hypothesis is on the prepunishment area; his results for starting speed, although consistently favoring the punished group, were nonsignificant. However, an experiment just completed in our laboratory showed conclusively that punishment sustained speed and resistance to extinction in the prepunishment area (Siegel, Melvin, & Wagner, in press). We used a longer prepunishment area and more optimal conditions for vicious-circle behavior than did DeLude.

## B. Conditioned Fear as Punishment

One of the most significant experiments on the conditioned fear hypothesis is that of Bender (1969). She used a secondary punishment, i.e., a stimulus eliciting conditioned fear, instead of primary punishment. Initially, rats were given a series of 15 "conditioning" trials. Four of the six groups (CS-100, CS-33, CS-0, CS-SK) were given identical treatment during this phase: a 3-sec. buzzer CS terminated simultaneously with onset of a 1-sec. 80 V. shock. Shock-UCS trials were given in a "conditioning" box rather than in the runway. The $S$s were then given training in the runway until they made five consecutive avoidances. No CS other than alley/start box cues was utilized; an $S$ could avoid shock by traversing the 4-ft. runway within 3 sec.

Immediately following avoidance training, the $S$s received extinction trials. For Group CS-100, interruption of a photobeam placed 1 ft. from the start box/alley junction initiated the buzzer formerly used in the conditiong phase. For Group CS-SK, this response delivered a 60-V. shock; for Group CS-33, the buzzer was delivered on 33% of the trials. A control group (CS-0) did not receive punishment. When the shock or buzzer was initiated, it lasted for 3 sec. or until the $S$ entered the goal box.

Bender's results were highly supportive of a conditioned-fear explanation of the vicious-circle effect. This effect was obtained not only with secondary punishment, but also with *intermittent* secondary punishment. Furthermore, these findings indicate that self-punitive running is maintained through the generalization of fear established through Pavlovian classical conditioning. Her results are also compatible with Rescorla and Solomon's (1967) theoretical treatment of the effects of Pavlovian conditioning in instrumental behavior, i.e., Rescorla and Solomon imply that an ongoing fear-motivated avoidance response should be strengthened by presentation of the classically-conditioned "excitatory" buzzer-CS (cf., Rescorla, 1968).

## C. Evidence for Fear Induced by Primary Punishment

Punishment-induced fear is held to be another crucial source of motivation for self-punitive running. Some evidence for fear derived from punishment has already been cited (Anson *et al.*, 1969; Brown *et al.*, 1964). Recently, Klare (1969) has provided further data on this phenomenon.

Klare used a 24-hr. intertrial interval, thus excluding postshock emotionality from shock on previous trials as a motivational factor. However, for some animals, postshock emotionality was induced by a shock in a different apparatus shortly before each runway trial. Klare gave 64 rats shock-escape training trials in a runway, while 56 additional rats received identical treatment, but no shock in the runway. Half of both groups were then given 30 regular extinction trials, while the remaining Ss were given 30 punishment–extinction trials. An objective measure of the degree of activity of the S in the start box immediately before the trial was used as an index of the level of conditioned fear. Those Ss receiving shock during acquisition were significantly less active than the controls not receiving shock. During extinction, shock-escape Ss that were punished for responding both ran longer and were less active in the start box than those not punished. This supported the conditioned fear hypothesis, that punishment of running retards extinction of the fear that motivates running. When postshock emotionality was introduced (through a shock shortly before the trial), it tended to suppress vicious-circle behavior.


## IX. BREAKING THE VICIOUS CIRCLE

So far, most investigators have been primarily interested in the production of the vicious-circle phenomenon. Now that this type of behavior can be reliably induced, a logical next step would be to determine how to stop it. R. C. Martin and his associates have initiated research on this problem.

In the first such study, Martin (1969a) investigated the role of the after-effects of the noxious stimulus. After massed-trials shock-escape training in a 6-ft. alley, rats were assigned to three groups: (a) a nonpunished control group (b) a group punished with 1.0-mA. nonscrambled shock (c) a group given an extra-situational 18-min. rest interval after the first 20 trials of punished extinction, but otherwise treated the same as the standard punished group. Since the intertrial interval was held at approximately 30 sec. throughout the experiment, the 18-min. delay was assumed to allow the dissipation of residual emotionality, thus reducing motivational level. However, it also eliminated internal response-produced cues derived from the aftereffects of shock. Up to the twentieth trial, both punished groups were similar in alley speed, and both were faster than the control group. The delay interval significantly reduced the speed of the delay/punished group relative to the nondelay punished group. In terms of number of trials to extinction, the standard punishment group was superior to the delay/punishment group, which in turn completed more trials than the control group.

A second study in this series was done by Ervey (1969). He varied the point at which an 18-min. delay was inserted during regular or punished extinction (after 0, 5, 20, or 80 trials). Two additional groups (one punished and one control group) were given the full 100 trials without the delay interval.

Ervey's results indicated that all punished (1.0-mA. shock) groups ran faster and longer than the control groups. The delay interval significantly reduced vicious-circle behavior only after 80 punishment–extinction trials. However, it did reduce speed on the first trial after the delay as a function of number of prior punished trials. Unlike Martin (1969a) little reduction of self-punitive running was seen with the delay after 20 trials. This divergence may be due to the stronger vicious-circle behavior obtained by Ervey, who used a different strain of rats and scrambled shock.

Given the assumption that fear plays a key role in self-punitive running, one way to reduce such fear (and thus the response tendency) might be through the administration of tranquillizing drugs. Martin, McArdle, Deemer, and Steiner (1968) reported a study in which rats were given three dosages (5.82, 1.20 or .30 mg/kg.) of the tranquillizer, Chlorpromazine, between escape training and extinction. Control subjects received injections of saline. During extinction, one-half of the subjects in the above groups were punished in the alley. Martin *et al.*, found the typical facilitative effects in the punished groups given saline injections. However, Chlorpromazine prevented the occurrence of vicious-circle behavior. Also, it generally hastened the extinction of the nonpunished control groups.

With the lowest dosage, the two nonpunished groups were not significantly different, whereas the punished Chlorpromazine group was significantly inferior in performance to the punished saline group. Thus, the effects of Chlorpromazine were not apparent unless punishment was applied. Even after the lowest dosage, a retest without the drug revealed no recovery of the self-punitive response. Thus, these effects do not appear to be "state-dependent."

## X. CONCLUDING REMARKS

This review points out the crucial nature of where and when a punishment is applied. In the case of aversive motivation, punishment administered during an ongoing response may lead to vicious-circle behavior. Here, the response-punishment-response chain is followed by reinforcement (fear and typically, pain reduction). If punishment is delivered at the completion of a response sequence, and the contingency is delineated by spatial or other cues, the reinforcement is reduced, eliminated or delayed, and little or no facilitation (or even suppression) would be expected.

As Brown (1969) stated, the type of response which is punished, in conjunction with the response elicited by punishment, is quite important. In this respect, it should be noted that the punishment procedure *always* facilitates some type of behavior. That is, if a stimulus is intense enough to elicit escape, when used as a punisher it will intensify or elicit: (a) autonomic, "emotional," responses and/or (b) ongoing aversively-motivated responses *if* they are not incompatible with (c) learned, reflexive, or species-specific responses to the punitive aversive stimulus. These latter responses are not only salient factors in determining the effects of punishment, but also the ease of aversive learning. For example, the rat usually responds to primary or conditioned aversive stimuli by running, jumping, or freezing—responses which compete with and thus hinder barpressing (especially in the avoidance paradigm).

So far, little research has been done on another type of response-punishment contingency—that where reinforcement is immediate but punishment is delayed. It is likely that punishment-induced facilitation of an aversively motivated response might be obtained in such a paradigm. An exception to this would be when the punishment was paired with spatial reinforcement cues, i.e., a goal box. Another factor would be whether or not escape from the punitive stimulus was allowed. This delay paradigm seems more analogous to *certain* clinical examples of vicious-circle behavior than the typical runway situation. For example, Mowrer states that "Many children have been so harshly dealt with in connection with toilet training that they live in real terror of nocturnal lapses; and once the disgracefulness of bedwetting, as reflected by the attitudes of adults, is accepted by the child and 'internalized,' a kind of vicious circle is often set up, the enuresis creating further shame and apprehensiveness, which in turn may further aggravate the enuresis" (1950, p. 398).

Another variable of further interest is the variability of training and/or punishment conditions. Such variability should make efforts to disrupt self-punitive behavior through stimulus changes more difficult. For example, shifting to high levels of shock-punishment from lower intensities of training shock may reduce the vicious-circle effect. However, subjects trained with *variable* shock intensities might continue to run with high intensity punishment, and even increase their speed.

The above paragraph indicates the present bias that, while a "generalization decrement" may play a minor explanatory role, Mowrer's fear hypothesis, as modified by Brown (1969), provides a better account of vicious-circle behavior.

Certainly, the punishment procedure is one marked "handle with care": It can be a potent behavioral suppressor, but in certain instances it is also a powerful facilitator. This paper should serve to delineate some conditions increasing the probability of these "paradoxical" facilitative effects of punishment.

# REFERENCES

Anson, J. E., Bender, L., & Melvin, K. B. Sources of reinforcement in the establishment of self-punitive behavior. *Journal of Comparative and Physiological Psychology,* 1969, 67, 376-380.

Beecroft, R. S., & Bouska, S. A. Learning self-punitive running. *Psychonomic Science,* 1967, 8, 109-110.

Beecroft, R. S., Bouska, S. A., & Fisher, B. G. Punishment intensity and self-punitive behavior. *Psychonomic Science,* 1967, 8, 351-352.

Beecroft, R. S., & Brown, J. S. Punishment following escape and avoidance training. *Psychonomic Science,* 1967, 8, 349-350.

Beecroft, R. S., & Fisher, B. G. Avoidance punishment and self-punitive behavior. *Psychonomic Science,* 1969, 15, 243-244.

Beecroft, R. S., Fisher, B. G., & Bouska, S. A. Punishment continuity and self-punitive behavior. *Psychonomic Science,* 1967, 9, 127-128.

Bender, L. Secondary punishment and self-punitive avoidance behavior in the rat. *Journal of Comparative and Physiological Psychology,* 1969, 69, 261-266.

Bender, L., & Melvin, K. B. Self-punitive behavior: Effects of percentage of punishment on extinction of escape and avoidance responses. *Psychonomic Science,* 1967, 9, 573-574.

Brown, J. S. Factors influencing self-punitive locomotor behavior. In B. A. Campbell & R. M. Church (Eds.), *Punishment and aversive behavior.* New York:: Appleton-Century-Crofts, 1969. Pp. 467-514.

Brown, J. S., Anderson, R. C., & Weiss, C. G. Self-punitive behavior under conditions of massed practice. *Journal of Comparative and Physiological Psychology,* 1965, 60, 451-453.

Brown, J. S., & Farber, I. E. Secondary motivational systems. *Annual Review of Psychology,* 1968, 19, 99-133.

Brown, J. S., Horsfall, R. S., & Van Bruggen, P. J. Self-punitive behavior as a function of the position of the shock in the behavior sequence. Unpublished study cited in Brown, 1969.

Brown, J. S., Martin, R. C., & Morrow, M. W. Self-punitive behavior in the rat: Facilitative effects of punishment on resistance to extinction. *Journal of Comparative and Physiological Psychology,* 1964, 57, 127-133.

Byrd, L. D. Responding in the cat maintained under response-independent electric shock and response-produced electric shock. *Journal of the Experimental Analysis of Behavior,* 1969, 12, 1-10.

Campbell, B. A., Smith, N. F., & Misanin, J. R. Effects of punishment on extinction of avoidance behavior: Avoidance-avoidance conflict or vicious circle behavior? *Journal of Comparative and Physiological Psychology,* 1966, 62, 495-498.

Church, R. M. The varied effects of punishment on behavior. *Psychological Review,* 1963, 70, 369-402.

Cloar, F. T. The effects of type of training and fixed vs. variable shock location on vicious circle behavior. Unpublished doctoral dissertation, Univ. of Alabama, 1970.

Delprato, D. J., & Denny, M. R. Punishment and the length of non-shock confinement during the extinction of avoidance. *Canadian Journal of Psychology,* 1968, 22, 456-464.

DeLude, L. A. The vicious circle phenomenon: A result of measurement artifact. *Journal of Comparative and Physiological Psychology,* 1969, 69, 246-252.

Ervey, D. H. *The effectiveness of a delay in stopping self-punitive behavior.* Unpublished master's thesis. Hollins College, Virginia: Hollins College, 1969.

Galvani, P. F. Self-punitive behavior as a function of number of prior fear-conditioning trials. *Journal of Comparative and Physiological Psychology,* 1969, 68, 359-363.

Gwinn, G. T. The effects of punishment on acts motivated by fear. *Journal of Experimental Psychology*, 1949, **39**, 260-269.

Harlow, H. F. The heterosexual affectional system in monkeys. *American Psychologist*, 1962, **17**, 1-9.

Hess, E. H. Imprinting. *Science*, 1959, **130**, 133-141.

Horney, K. *The neurotic personality of our time.* New York: Norton, 1937.

Hurwitz, H. M. B., Bolas, D., & Haritos, M. Vicious circle behavior under two shock intensities. *British Journal of Psychology*, 1961, **52**, 377-383.

Klare, W. F. Motivational factors in vicious-circle behavior. Unpublished doctoral dissertation, Univ. of Iowa, 1969.

Kovach, J. K., & Hess, E. Imprinting: Effects of painful stimulation on the following response. *Journal of Comparative and Physiological Psychology*, 1963, **56**, 461-464.

Martin, R. C. Vicious circle behavior and escape conditioning as a function of intensity of punishment. Unpublished doctoral dissertation, Univ. of Florida, 1964.

Martin, R. C. Self-punitive behavior: One way to stop it. *Psychonomic Science*, 1969(a), **14**, 25-26.

Martin, R. C. Differential effects of punishment on appetitively and aversively established behavior. Unpublished manuscript, 1969(b).

Martin, R. C., McArdle, N., Deemer, B., & Steiner, S. Stopping self-punitive behavior with a tranquilizer. Paper presented at the meeting of the Psychonomic Society, St. Louis, November, 1968.

Martin, R. C., & Melvin, K. B. Vicious circle behavior as a function of delay of punishment. *Psychonomic Science*, 1964, **1**, 415-416.

Martin, R. C., & Moon, T. L. Self-punitive behavior and periodic punishment. *Psychonomic Science*, 1968, **10**, 245-246.

Martin, R. C., Ragland, E., & Melvin, K. B. Self-punitive locomotor behavior in the Mongolian gerbil. *Psychonomic Science*, 1970, **20**, 183-184.

McAllister, W. R., & McAllister, D. E. Behavioral measurement of conditioned fear. In F. R. Brush (Ed.), *Aversive conditioning and learning.* New York: Academic Press, in press.

McKearney, J. W. Maintenance of responding under a fixed-interval schedule of electric shock-presentation. *Science*, 1968, **160**, 1249-1251.

McKearney, J. W. Fixed-interval schedules of electric shock presentation: Extinction and recovery of performance under different shock intensities and fixed-interval durations. *Journal of the Experimental Analysis of Behavior*, 1969, **12**, 301-313.

Melvin, K. B. Escape learning and "vicious circle" behavior as a function of percentage of reinforcement. *Journal of Comparative and Physiological Psychology*, 1964, **58**, 248-251.

Melvin, K. B., & Martin, R. C. Facilitative effects of two modes of punishment on resistance to extinction. *Journal of Comparative and Physiological Psychology*, 1966, **62**, 491-494.

Melvin, K. B., & Smith, F. H. Self-punitive avoidance behavior in the rat. *Journal of Comparative and Physiological Psychology*, 1967, **63**, 533-535.

Melvin, K. B., & Stenmark, D. E. Facilitative effects of punishment on the establishment of a fear motivated response. *Journal of Comparative and Physiological Psychology*, 1968, **65**, 517-519.

Melvin, K. B., & Bender, L. Self-punitive avoidance behavior: Effects of changes in punishment intensity. *Psychological Record*, 1968, **18**, 29-34.

Melvin, K. B., Athey, G. I., Jr., & Heasley, F. H. Effects of duration and delay of shock on self-punitive behavior in the rat. *Psychological Reports*, 1965, **17**, 107-112.

Melvin, K. B., Cloar, F. T., & Massingill, L. S. Imprinting of Bobwhite Quail to a hawk. *Psychological Record*, 1967, **17**, 235-238.

Miller, N. E. Studies of fear as an acquirable drive: I. Fear as motivation and fear reduction as reinforcement in the learning of new responses. *Journal of Experimental Psychology,* 1948, **38,** 89-101.

Mowrer, O. H. On the dual nature of learning: A reinterpretation of "conditioning" and "problem solving." *Harvard Educational Review,* 1947, **17,** 102-148.

Mowrer, O. H. *Learning theory and personality dynamics.* New Yorkk: Ronald Press, 1950.

Mowrer, O. H. *Learning theory and behavior.* New York: John Wiley & Sons, Inc., 1960.

Powell, R. W., & Morris, G. Continuous punishment of free-operant avoidance in the rat. *Journal of the Experimental Analysis of Behavior,* 1969, **12,** 149-157.

Rescorla, R. A. Pavlovian conditioned fear in Sidman avoidance learning. *Journal of Comparative and Physiological Psychology,* 1968, **65,** 55-60.

Rescorla, R. A., & Solomon, R. L. Two-process learning theory: Relationships between Pavlovian conditioning and instrumental learning. *Psychological Review,* 1967, **74,** 151-182.

Rollings, J. P., & Melvin, K. B. Effects of a punitive noise on self-punitive running established with shock. *Psychonomic Science,* 1970, **21,** 313-314.

Rosenblum, L. A., & Harlow, H. F. Approach-avoidance conflict in the mother-surrogate situation. *Psychological Reports,* 1963, **12,** 83-85.

Sandler, J., Davidson, R. S., & Holzschuh, R. D. Effects of increasing punishment frequency on Sidman avoidance behavior. *Psychonomic Science,* 1966, **5,** 103-104.

Sandler, J., Davidson, R. S., Greene, W. E., & Holzschuh, R. D. Effects of punishment intensity on instrumental avoidance behavior. *Journal of Comparative and Physiological Psychology,* 1966, **61,** 212-216.

Seligman, M. E. P., & Campbell, B. A. Effect of intensity and duration of punishment on extinction of an avoidance response. *Journal of Comparative and Physiological Psychology,* 1965, **59,** 295-297.

Siegel, P. S., Melvin, K. B., & Wagner, J. D. Vicious circle behavior in the rat: Measurement problems visited again. *Journal of Comparative and Physiological Psychology,* in press.

Stretch, R., Orloff, E. R., & Dalrymple, S. D. Maintenance of responding by fixed interval schedule of electric shock presentation in squirrel monkeys. *Science,* 1968, **162,** 583-585.

Wells, M. G., & Merrill, H. K. Self-punitive behavior in the rat: A free-operant demonstration. *Psychonomic Science,* 1969, **15,** 7-8.

# PART 3

The role of the autonomic nervous system in mediating emotional manifestations of maladaptive behavior is of such significance as to render any treatment of experimental psychopathology incomplete without substantial attention being given to it. The three chapters in this section of the book deal with some of the important approaches currently being taken to the study of this topic. The senior author of Chapter 7, Joseph V. Brady, has been in the forefront of experimental research on abnormal behavior for almost twenty years. His experimental production of gastrointestinal ulcers in "executive" monkeys and his earlier work on conditioned emotional reactions were both contributions of the first magnitude to this field. In his current chapter, co-authored by Jack D. Findley, a series of studies elucidating the relationship between experimentally-produced behavioral and biochemical-hormonal manifestations of emotion and emotional pathology is presented and systematically analyzed.

The subsequent chapter (Chapter 8) by Morse *et al.*, is concerned with the development of the blood-pressure symptoms of essential hypertension in monkeys placed in protracted stressful situations. One of the more intriguing findings in this work and that described in the previous chapter is that normal recovery patterns following the removal of stressful response demands gradually give way to chronic hypertension which is present even when the animal is relieved from the requirement of stressful responding.

In Chapter 9, written by the editor, an effort is made to bring together within a single conceptual framework the results obtained in studies of "learned helplessness" in dogs and on inhibition of conditioned fear in humans. The human work described in this chapter differs from the previous two in that autonomic nervous system reactions are taken to be the equivalent of any other peripheral responses, rather than being examined as part of the physiological "substrate" of skeletal behavior. It differs also from all of the other chapters in this book in its use of human rather than subhuman experimental subjects. The work on learned helplessness, although not done by the author, is one of the most interesting recent developments in experimental psychopathology. The possibility of its relationship to fear-inhibition in humans, although far from firmly established, is of sufficient promise to justify its consideration here.

# 7

# Experimental Psychopathology and the Psychophysiology of Emotion

JOSEPH V. BRADY,
JACK D. FINDLEY,
and ALAN HARRIS

The Johns Hopkins University

## I. INTRODUCTION

The psychophysiological analysis of emotional response patterns has continued, since at least the time of James and Cannon, to provide an important point of departure for the laboratory development of models for experimental psychopathology. Early research (Pavlov, 1879; Cannon, 1915; Gantt, 1944; Mahl, 1949; Malmo, 1950; Liddel, 1956) focused upon classical or respondent conditioning models emphasizing adjustments of the internal economy, though more recent psychophysiological experiments (Mason, et al., 1957; Brady, et al., 1958; Wenzel, 1961; Perez-Cruet. et al., 1963; DeToledo & Black, 1966; Brady, et al., 1969) have directed attention to the interaction between respondent conditioning processes and the instrumental or operant performances which make more direct contact with the external environment. Relatively transient visceral changes in relationship to emotional behavior situations have been described most frequently in such psychophysiological studies (Eldridge, 1954; Shapiro & Horn, 1955; Porter, et al., 1959; John & Killam, 1959; Black, 1959; Hearst, et al., 1960; Wenzel, 1961; Malmo, 1961; Berlanger & Feldman, 1962; Ross, et al., 1962; Stern & Word, 1962; Hahn, et al., 1962; Perez-Cruet, et al., 1963; Lacey, et al., 1963; Stebbins & Smith, 1964; Smith & Stebbins, 1965; Snapper, et al., 1965; DeToledo & Black, 1966; Banks, et al., 1966; Brener, 1966; Frazier, 1966; Engle & Hansen, 1966; Webb & Obrist, 1967; Parrish, 1967; Trowill, 1967; Miller & Di Cara, 1967; Nathan & Smith, 1968; Di Cara &

Miller, 1968; Ferreira, et al., 1969). Recent reports of more enduring endocrinological and autonomic effects, however, (Brady, 1965, 1966, 1967, 1970; Mason, et al., 1966; Brady, et al., 1969) would seem to bear more directly upon the problem of which this volume is addressed.

## II. EARLY ENDOCRINE STUDIES

This latter series of studies, initiated well over a decade ago, has now documented the marked sensitivity of endocrinological and autonomic processes to relatively well-specified emotional conditioning situations and provided a basis for investigating the development of chronic somatic changes within the framework of such psychophysiological models. Chair-restrained monkeys (Mason, 1958) were found, for example, to show substantial and consistent increases in pituitary-adrenocortical activity (as reflected in markedly elevated 17-hydroxycorticosteroid levels) in relationship to both the acquisition and maintenance of a conditioned emotional response (Estes & Skinner, 1941) characterized by behavioral suppression of ongoing food-reinforced lever pressing during presentation of an auditory warning stimulus terminated by shock (Mason, Brady & Sidman, 1957; Mason, Brady & Tolson, 1966). Additionally, differential participation of adrenal medullary systems in the elaboration of such emotional behavior patterns has been suggested by the results of studies involving concurrent measurements of plasma epinephrine, norepinephrine, and 17-OH-CS levels during repeated exposure to such emotional conditioning. Under such conditions, elevations in norepinephrine consistently accompanied the marked increases in 17-OH-CS, but little or no change could be discerned in epinephrine levels (Mason, et al., 1961).

## III. AUTONOMIC CHANGES

Observations of autonomic changes related to this same conditioned emotional response model were also obtained with a series of monkeys catheterized for cardiovascular measurements (Brady, et al., 1969). Stable heart rate and both systolic and diastolic blood pressure were reliably recorded during experimental sessions involving lever pressing alone for a food reward, although dramatic alterations in the cardiovascular response pattern developed rapidly upon exposure to the conditioned emotional response procedure. During the early acquisition phase, suppression of lever pressing during warning stimulus (clicker) presentation was accompanied by a sharp drop in heart rate and consistent decreases in both systolic and diastolic blood pressure. Significantly, however, continued pairings of clicker and shock superimposed upon the lever-pressing performance produced abrupt reversals in the direction of these autonomic changes, with cardiac acceleration and blood pressure elevation appearing and persisting in response to the clicker during the later stages of emotional conditioning. With this series of animals, behavioral suppression characteristically appeared during presentation of the clicker on the third or fourth conditioning trial (accompanied by the decelerative cardiovascular change) and continued to recur in essentially the same form throughout the ensuing trials which numbered up to 100 in some cases. Usually by the eighth to tenth conditioning trial however, marked increases in heart rate (approximately 40–60 beats/min. in some cases), accompanied by substantial increases in both systolic and diastolic blood pressure (e.g., 20–40 mm Hg), appeared precipitously and were sustained throughout the remaining trials despite the maintenance of continued lever-pressing suppression during clicker presentations.

When the conditioned emotional response was extinguished by repeated presentations of clicker alone without shocks during daily lever-pressing sessions with such animals following extended exposure to recurrent emotional conditioning of this type, a further divergence between autonomic and behavioral responses was observed. There was a characteristic difference in extinction rates for the cardiovascular and skeletal components of the conditioned emotional response. Although virtually complete recovery of the lever-pressing rate in the presence of the clicker generally occurred within ten presentations of clicker alone without shock, both heart rate and blood pressure elevations in response to the clicker persisted well beyond 30 or 40 extinction trials. It is also noteworthy that reconditioning of the emotional response after all behavioral and cardiovascular reactions to the clicker had been eliminated by 50–100 extinction trials, produced immediate behavioral suppression accompanied by the tachycardiac and pressor responses following only a few clicker-shock re-pairings. During such reconditioning, moreover, none of the animals showed the initial cardiac decelerative response characteristic of the early original conditioning trials.

## IV. CONDITIONED AVOIDANCE STUDIES

The conditioned emotional response model which provided the initial focus for such psychophysiological analyses placed heavy emphasis upon behavioral suppression effects. Alternative procedures involving aversive contingencies which generate marked increases in escape and avoidance behaviors, however, have also provided a basis for analyzing the psychophysiology of emotional response patterns relevant to experimental psychopathology. The conditioned avoidance model, first described by Sidman (1953) for example, has been extensively studied in relationship to endocrine and autonomic changes characteristic of emotional behavior situations. Briefly, the basic procedure involved programming shocks to the feet of a chair-restrained monkey every 20 sec. unless the S pressed a lever within that interval to postpone shock another 20 sec. The stable and durable lever-pressing performance generated by this procedure has been shown to be consistently associated with twofold to fourfold rises in 17-OH-CS levels for virtually all Ss during 2-hr. experimental sessions even in the absence of shock (Mason, et al., 1957; Brady, 1966). And repeated exposure to extended experimental sessions requiring continuous 6-hr. avoidance performances alternating with 6-hr. "rest" periods over several weeks has been found to produce an increase in the concentration of free acid in the gastric juice (Polish, et al., 1962) and a high incidence of pathological gastrointestinal changes in Ss subjected to such "stress" conditions (Brady, et al., 1958; Porter, et al., 1958; Rice, 1963). Quantitative relations have also been demonstrated between the rate of avoidance responding and the level of pituitary-adrenal cortical activity, independently of shock frequency (Sidman, et al., 1962). When the avoidance procedure included a discriminable exteroceptive warning signal presented 5 sec. prior to shock whenever 15 sec. had elapsed since the previous response, however, consistently reduced corticosteroid response levels were associated with the performance (Mason, et al., 1966). Conversely, when "free" or unavoidable shocks were superimposed upon a well-established avoidance baseline without warning, corticosteroid levels rose to more than double those observed in response to the regular nondiscriminated avoidance requirement alone (Mason, et al., 1966).

Confirmation of the previously described emotional response pattern involving 17-OH-CS and norepinephrine elevations with no significant change in epinephrine levels has also been obtained in the course of several avoidance experiments with concurrent plasma corticosteroid and catecholamine determinations (Mason, et al., 1961). Variations in the behavioral procedures, however, have been shown to produce significant deviations from this basic "emotional stress" hormone pattern. When a well-trained monkey was presented with the avoidance signal following removal of the response lever from the restraining chair for example, making his learned "coping" response impossible under circumstances which had previously required such a performance, an elevation in epinephrine was observed with no change in norepinephrine (Mason, et al., 1966). This effect occurred within 1 min. of the signal presentation and could not be observed after 10 min. of exposure to such conditions. Other variations in the pattern of catecholamine levels were observed in a series of experiments which involved the administration of "free" or unavoidable shocks to a well-trained monkey, producing dramatic elevations in both epinephrine and norepinephrine even though the S received no more shock than during previous regular avoidance sessions characterized by high norepinephrine and 17-OH-CS levels and no change in epinephrine (Mason, et al., 1966). More complex emotional behavior situations involving ambiguity with respect to which of several components in a required performance sequence would follow presentation of a "ready" signal have also been observed to produce marked elevations in both epinephrine and norepinephrine, though epinephrine levels invariably fall precipitously once the first unambiguous performance signal is presented (Mason, et al., 1961).

A broader spectrum of hormonal and autonomic changes in relationship to emotional behavior situations has been examined more recently in a series of experiments involving continuous exposure to extended sessions (72 hr. or more in duration) of required shock avoidance performances. The pattern of corticosteroid and pepsinogen changes observed before, during, and after such a continuous 72-hr. avoidance experiment for example, has been found to be characterized by the expected elevation in 17-OH-CS throughout the 72-hr. session while pepsinogen levels were consistently depressed below baseline levels during this same period. Marked and prolonged elevations in pepsinogen levels (enduring for several days beyond the 48-hr. period required for postavoidance recovery of the preavoidance corticosteroid baseline) were observed however, during the postavoidance recovery period (Mason, et al., 1961). Repeated exposure to such continuous 72-hr. avoidance requirements over extended periods up to and, in some cases, exceeding one year has also been studied in relationship to the pattern of thyroid, gonadal, and adrenal hormone secretion. One group of animals participated in the 72-hr. avoidance experiment on six separate occasions over a six-month period with an interval of approximately four weeks intervening between each exposure. Another group performed on a schedule which repeatedly programmed 72-hr. avoidance cycles followed by 96-hr. nonavoidance "rest" cycles (3 days "on," 4 days "off") for periods up to and exceeding a year.

The first group of animals exposed to repeated 72-hr. avoidance sessions at monthly intervals for six months showed a progressively increasing lever-pressing response rate over the six successive exposures (Brady, 1965), although the hormone changes developed as a consistent and replicable pattern (Mason, 1968). Twofold to threefold elevations in 17-OH-CS levels occurred repeatedly during the 72-hr. avoidance and returned to near baseline levels within four to six days after termination of the three-day experimental session. Significant changes were also observed in catecholamine, gonadal, and thyroid hormone levels though the recovery cycles in some instances (thyroid) extended well beyond three weeks following cessation of the 72-hr. avoidance performance. The remaining group of monkeys required to perform on the three-day "on", four-day "off" avoidance schedule showed an initial increase in lever-pressing response rates for approximately the first ten avoidance sessions similar to that seen in the animals exposed to the repeated monthly sessions. Within 30 weeks however, the lever-pressing response rates for these animals during the 72-hr. avoidance periods had decreased to a level well below that observed during the initial sessions and the performance stabilized at this new low level for the ensuing weeks of the experiment (Brady, 1965). The initial 72-hr. avoidance sessions characterized by progressive increases in lever-pressing rates were invariably accompanied by elevations in 17-OH-CS levels. By the 20th weekly "avoidance-rest" cycle however, steroid levels had dropped below even the initial basal levels and no elevation occurred during the avoidance performance. By the 30th weekly session, however, 17-OH-CS levels had returned to their preexperimental basal values, though continued exposure to the three-day "on," four-day "off" schedule failed to produce any further steroid elevation in response to the 72-hr. avoidance requirement even after 65 or more weeks of continuous performance on the program. Significantly, shock frequencies remained at a stable low level following some initial adjustments during the early sessions, and normal food and water intake were maintained essentially unchanged throughout the extended course of the experiment.

## V. CHRONIC BEHAVIORAL STRESS AND CARDIOVASCULAR RESPONSE

This emphasis upon more extended time lines in the laboratory analysis of experimental psychopathological phenomena has been more recently reflected in a long-term psychophysiological study of autonomic effects (e.g., cardiovascular changes) associated with both acute and chronic emotional stress in the chair-restrained baboon. Animals have now been monitored for over one year in an experiment involving continuous recording of heart rate and both systolic and diastolic blood pressure during shock-avoidance and food-reinforced performances within the context of a 24-hr. behavior program which provided scheduled rest and sleep periods (Findley, et al., 1969). Two male dog-faced baboons, each weighing approximately 25 lb., served as subjects in the initial studies. The Ss were restrained in a specially designed chair (Findley, et al., 1970) constructed around an arm-cuff device which held the S in the sitting position, limited movement, and controlled the location of the hands, as illustrated in Figure 1. An expandable metal coil spring fitted around the S's abdomen as a waist electrode provided for delivery of brief electric shocks, with the remaining portions of the chair serving as the grounded second electrode. A sound-attenuated double box served as the experimental chamber, as illustrated in Figure 2. The chair-restrained S was positioned in the chamber facing a work panel containing multiple stimulus lights, push-button switches, a Lindsley lever manipulandum, and a food-pellet tray. Water was also available to the animal through an overhead nipple and gravity feed system mounted in front of the work panel. Additionally, a urine collector was mounted below the front portion

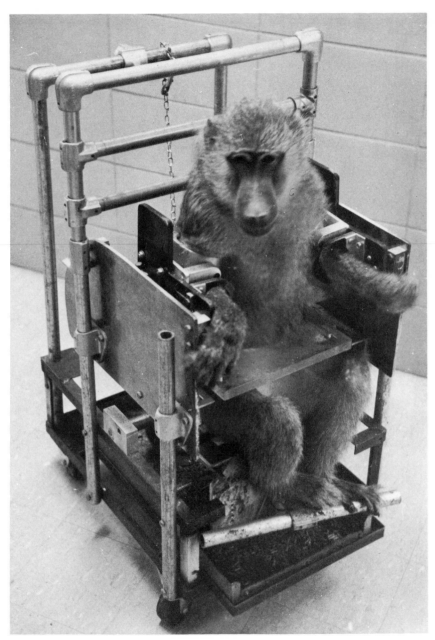

**Figure 1.** Baboon confined to restraint cart by arm cuffs and waist plate. The arm cuffs may be moved forward and backward on a track and allow considerable freedom in movement of the upper body.

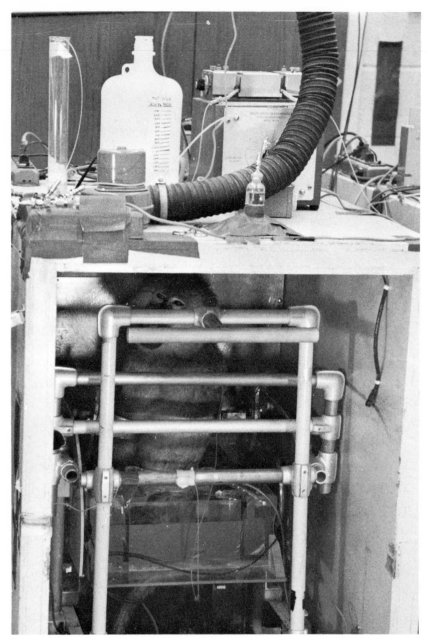

**Figure 2.** Experimental chamber with animal and cart placed inside facing intelligence panel. Blood pressure transducer, calibration equipment, and infusion pump are shown on top of chamber.

of the chair seat to permit metabolic samples to be drained through a tube and frozen in a dry ice container external to the chamber.

Each S was surgically implanted with a polyvinyl femoral artery catheter employing a modification of the technique described by Werdegar, et al. (1964), and Perez-Cruet, et al. (1966). The catheter was tunneled under the skin, up the leg, around the side just below the waist, and up the body to a point of exit just below the shoulders. The distal end of the catheter was fitted with an 18-gauge Luer stud adapter and attached through a system of valves and fittings to a Statham P23De transducer which was shock-mounted on the outside top of the experimental chamber. Patency of the catheter was maintained by continuous infusion of heparinized saline at a very slow rate and by a more rapid flush once per day. The output of the transducer was cabled to a polygraph recorder (Offner Type R) which provided a continuous display of the beat-by-beat blood pressure signal. Recordings of mean heart rate, lever pressing responses by the S, shock, and food-pellet delivery, as well as light stimulus presentations and durations were also displayed on the polygraph chart to provide for fine-grain correlations and analysis of environmental, behavioral, and physiological changes. Additionally, the blood pressure and heart rate signals were averaged electronically (Swinnen, 1968) over prespecified time intervals and printed-out in the form of mean systolic and mean diastolic pressures as well as mean heart rate at successive 10-min. intervals or at the time of programmed activity changes. Baseline pressure and rate measurements together with heart-size X-rays, urinary cathecholamines, 17-OH-CS, creatinine, albumin, cholesterol, electrolyte balance, and routine hematological determinations, completed after adaptation to the restraint chair, provided for appropriate comparisons after extended exposure to the behavioral stress program.

The sequence and duration of continuously programmed behavioral events which provided daily requirements for food, rest, escape–avoidance, and sleep are summarized in Figure 3. Three successive 8-hr. cycles were repeated once each 24 hr. with differently colored lights signaling each major activity. Beginning at 10 a.m. each day, a white light was presented for 40 min. in the presence of which each block of 150 responses (FR 150) on the Lindsley manipulandum produced six 1-gm. food pellets. Repetition of this 40-min. food cycle on three separate occasions during each 24-hr. period provided the total daily ration for the Ss. Periodic fruit and vitamin supplements were also provided during morning prefood rest cycles which served as a housekeeeping, S, and equipment checking interval. Water was freely available to the Ss throughout the experiment.

The escape–avoidance procedure remained in effect for six continuous hours on two occasions during each 24-hr. period. The onset of this activity cycle was signaled by a red light which reappeared intermittently on the average of once every 5 min. In the presence of the red light, shocks (10 mA. for .25 sec.) were

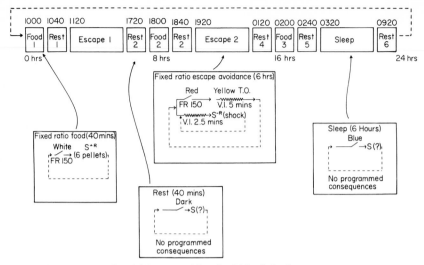

Figure 3. Sequence of activities comprising the 24-hr. behavior program.

programmed randomly on the average of once every 2½ min. independently of the S's lever responding. Completion of 150 responses (FR 150) on the Lindsley manipulandum however, terminated the red light and shock programming, and produced a "safe" period of variable duration (average 5 min.) signaled by a yellow light. The yellow light was terminated by the reappearance of the red light signaling onset of the next escape–avoidance trial. Delivery of the independently programmed shocks occasionally occurred before the S could complete the required FR 150 to terminate the red light and such shock delivery was accompanied by a brief flash of a separate white stimulus light. Under these conditions, however, the S maintained a high steady rate of lever responding which avoided all but a few shocks in the presence of the red light throughout the two 6-hr. escape–avoidance intervals each day. The third 6-hr. interval beginning at 3:20 a.m. each morning was provided for a sleep activity signaled by a blue light in the presence of which no contingencies were programmed.

As indicated in Figure 3, rest periods of a constant 40-min. duration, signaled by darkness of the work panel, were interspersed between the end of one major activity (i.e., food, escape–avoidance, sleep) and the beginning of the next. No contingencies were programmed during these recycling rest intervals.

Continuous recordings of blood pressure and heart rate, were begun following cannulations, and over a three-month period prior to establishment of the full behavioral program, baseline recordings yielded pressures on the order of 100–120 mm Hg systolic, and 65–90 mm Hg diastolic, and heart rates on the order of 65–100 beats/min. Diurnal variations were observed, with pressures and heart rate rising modestly from morning until late afternoon, then declining to a minimum around 5 a.m. During food activity periods the pressures were generally elevated on the order of 10–20 mm Hg. The pressures however, typically rose prior to the initiation of fixed ratio responding, and declined with delivery of the pellets. Heart rate during the food activity, on the other hand, showed essentially no elevation, providing a convenient control suggesting that little pressure elevation or heart rate increase was to be expected from the physical work of responding *per se.*

Introduction of the escape–avoidance activity into the behavioral program rapidly generated high response rates on the fixed ratio schedule topographically similar in all essential respects to the rates characteristic of the food-maintained performance on the same schedule, as illustrated in Figure 4. Comparisons of the acute cardiovascular changes occurring during the escape–avoidance activity with

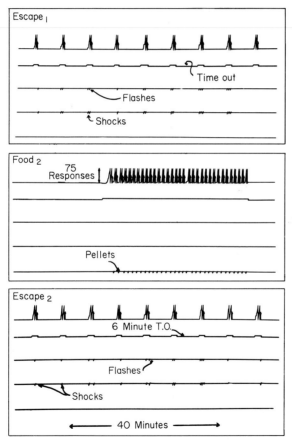

**Figure 4.** Samples of daily cumulative records from "escape" and "food" portion of the program for baboon "Sport".

those recorded during food and sleep activities however, revealed dramatic differences. Figures 5 and 6 show typical polygraph recordings of blood pressure and heart rate during intervals of escape–avoidance, food-maintained responding, and sleep. Figure 5 compares the acute changes in blood pressure and heart rate observed during an escape–avoidance performance (top panel) for one of the Ss (Sport) with those recorded during a topographically similar food-maintained

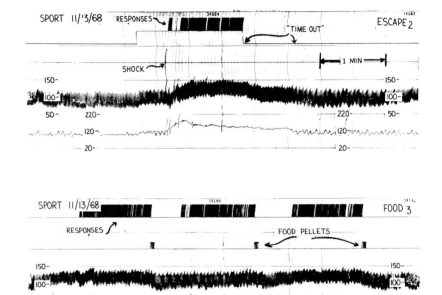

Figure 5. Sample polygraph recording for baboon "Sport" comparing typical blood pressure and heart rate changes during escape activity (top panel) with typical changes during food activity (bottom panel).

performance (bottom panel) for the same animal. Though identical performance requirements (FR 150) were programmed (top pen, each panel), the elevations in blood pressure during escape–avoidance (approximately 40 mm Hg for both systolic and diastolic, as shown on the middle pen, top panel) contrasted sharply with the more modest increases recorded during the food performance (approximately 10–20 mm Hg, as shown on the middle pen, bottom panel). Similarly, acute elevations in heart rate approximating 40 beats/min. or more accompanied onset of escape–avoidance responding (bottom pen, top panel) while virtually no heart rate change can be observed during food activity (bottom pen, bottom panel). Over the extended course of the experiment, literally thousands of such comparisons confirm the differential cardiovascular effects of the aversively and appetitively maintained components of the program.

Figure 6 compares the acute elevations in blood pressure and heart rate during an escape–avoidance performance (top panel) for the second baboon (Folley) with the cardiovascular levels observed for the same S during sleep

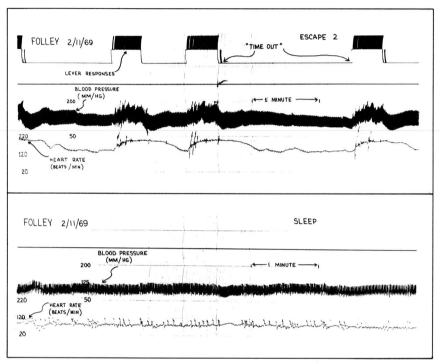

**Figure 6.** Sample polygraph recording for baboon "Folley" contrasting typical blood pressure and heart rate changes during escape activity (top panel) with typical levels during sleep (bottom panel).

(bottom panel). Again, elevations in blood pressure of the order of 40–50 mm Hg (middle pen, top panel) and increases in heart rate of approximately 50–60 beats/min. (bottom pen, top panel) during the escape–avoidance performance even in the absence of shock contrast sharply with the stably lower blood pressure (middle pen, bottom panel) and heart rate (bottom pen, bottom panel) maintained throughout sleep. In fact, the cardiovascular levels reflected in this sleep record for Folley (blood pressure: 120/80 mm Hg; heart rate: 100 beats/min.) were quite typical of the baseline values obtained for this same S over the three-month chair-restraint adaptation period prior to training on the behavioral program. Similarly, the basal values obtained for Sport (blood pressure: 100/65 mm Hg; heart rate: 80 beats/min.) during the three-month preexperimental period were generally recovered during rest and sleep intervals with only modest diurnal variations apparent for both Ss.

Acute changes in blood pressure and heart rate of considerable interest have also been consistently observed *within* the escape–avoidance activity and in comparison with other activities. In terms of mean pressures and heart rate, highest values were generally found in escape–avoidance, lower in food, and still lower in sleep. Blood pressure and heart rate were consistently elevated for both animals during escape–avoidance in comparison with other activities, however. Specifically, with the onset of the red light, and as the Ss began responding on the fixed ratio requirement, blood pressure typically rose at least 30–40 mm Hg and heart rate rose on the order of 60–80 beats/min. These acute elevations in pressure and heart rate were both reliable and clearly not directly dependent upon the delivery of electric shocks. Following the completion of a typical escape from the red light, the pressure declined abruptly, predominately showing a greater decline in diastolic, and hence an increased pulse pressure. Systolic pressure, after this initial drop, generally remained stable, while diastolic gradually increased on the order of 15–20 mm Hg as the heart rate continued to decline to the minimum resting level found during the "safe" period. This divergence from the more usually observed positively correlated changes in blood pressure and heart rate was consistently found in both Ss, and has been tentatively interpreted as reflecting peripheral changes in the cardiovascular system mediated by the central nervous system. Sample recordings illustrating these changes are shown in Figures 6 and 7. Since the basis for these changes appears to be related to the programmed environmental contingencies, the prospects for developing an experimental psychopathological model for at least the laboratory conditions which produce chronic psychophysiological changes in cardiovascular function may not be unduly remote.

Observations of more chronic cardiovascular response patterns were also made for both Ss over the extended course of the experiment. Figures 8 and 9 show successive three- to seven-day averages of mean blood pressures and heart rates during each of the major activities (i.e., escape–avoidance, food, and sleep) for Sport (Figure 8) and Folley (Figure 9) starting with the beginning of the full program and extending over a period of some ten months. As might be expected on the basis of the acute cardiovascular changes, blood pressure, and heart rate during the escape–avoidance activity were generally maintained consistently above food and sleep levels for both Ss throughout the extended course of the observation period. Heart rate increases during escape–avoidance were proportionately greater than blood pressure elevations though more variability was also apparent in the heart rate measures. Some tendency toward slightly elevated pressures and rates during the food activity could also be discerned over

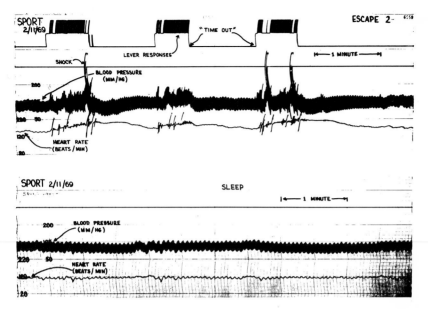

Figure 7. Sample polygraph recording for baboon "Sport" contrasting typical blood pressure and heart rate changes during escape activity (top panel) with typical levels during sleep (bottom panel).

the course of the program but considerable overlap between food and sleep values characterized the records of both Ss.

During the initial two months of exposure to the full program, one of the Ss (Sport, Figure 8) showed a progressive increase in heart rate and both systolic and diastolic blood pressure levels. Increases of the order of 40–50 beats/min. in heart rate and 20 mm Hg in both systolic and diastolic blood pressure occurred during all activities including sleep over this first 60-day period as shown in Figure 8. Upon removal of the escape–avoidance component of the activity program over the ensuing 30-day interval however, both blood pressure and heart rate levels can be seen (Figure 8) to have returned to basal levels within ten days for this animal. When the escape–avoidance activity was reintroduced following this one-month "vacation," dramatic but somewhat transient elevations in heart rate and at least systolic blood pressure, above even the prevacation levels, can be seen to have characterized Sport's cardiovascular response pattern. Over the remaining months of the full program, however, punctuated by a recurrent kidney infection as indicated, both blood pressure and heart rate gradually declined to approximately preexperimental baseline levels and remained relatively stable until the development of pyonephritis necessitated termination of the experiment.

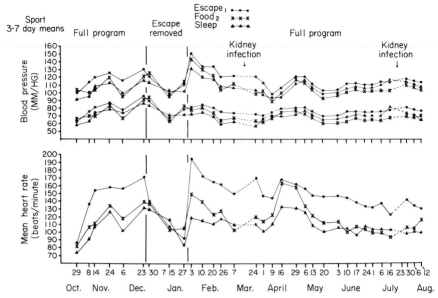

**Figure 8.** Mean systolic, mean diastolic, and mean heart rate during escape, food, and sleep for baboon "Sport" plotted at approximately weekly intervals over the course of the experiment.

With the second S (Folley, Figure 9), no dramatic or durable cardiovascular changes could be discerned in the course of the extended ten-month program. A mild elevation in systolic blood pressure accompanied by a rather sharp increase in heart rate (30–40 beats/min.) occurred during escape–avoidance upon reintroduction of this activity following the "escape removed" (Figure 9) vacation, but only the heart rate response to escape–avoidance persisted beyond the seventh or eighth month of the program. Again, some apparatus breakdowns and the development of a hernia requiring surgical repair as indicated (Figure 9) interrupted the program midway in the course of the extended observation period. The most noteworthy aspect of Folley's record, as well as that of Sport however, was the striking similarity between the blood pressure and heart rate values at the beginning and at the end of the ten-month performance program. Significantly as well, both Ss maintained a relatively stable behavioral performance baseline during all phases of the activity program throughout the extended course of the experiment.

The results of this study clearly demonstrate the adequacy of the animal restraint, cardiovascular monitoring, and behavioral programming systems for continuous long-term psychophysiological observation and experiment with the baboon. In addition, the results reliably demonstrate that substantial elevations in both blood pressure and heart rate can be selectively and differentially related

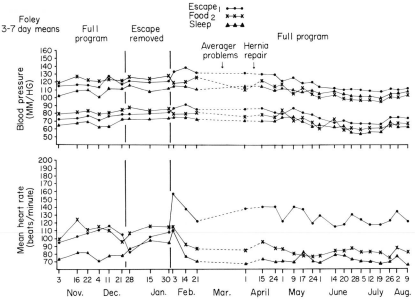

**Figure 9.** Mean systolic, mean diastolic, and mean heart rate during escape, food, and sleep for baboon "Folley" plotted at approximately weekly intervals over the course of the experiment.

to behavioral performance requirements involving aversive contingencies. These acute elevations in blood pressure and heart rate during escape–avoidance were consistently observed even in the absence of shock. This fact, plus the failure of topographically-similar food maintained performances to produce comparable elevations, confirms the importance of the contingency relations between environmental events, rather than work requirements or the occurrence of stimuli and responses *per se,* as critical determinants of psychophysiological changes.

Significantly, the results of this study with baboons fail to confirm the reports of chronically-maintained blood pressure elevations in both squirrel monkeys (Herd, *et al.,* 1969) and Rhesus macaques (Forsyth, 1969) observed under similar performance-requirement conditions. Although aversively main-tained shock–avoidance procedures provided the basis for the performance requirement in both previous studies, and observations were carried out over extended periods exceeding one year in some cases, many other procedural differences make direct comparisons with the present study hazardous. One important feature of all three studies however, was the lack of any explicit contingency relationship between the cardiovascular response levels and the occurrence of either escape–avoidance responses or shocks. With the two baboons in the present experiment for example, escape from the red light condition, which can be assumed to be positively reinforcing, occurred equally as often following either rising or falling blood pressure changes. Similarly, the delivery of electric shock in the presence of the red light was observed to occur on occasions when the pressure was falling as well as when it was rising. Although the predominance of these reinforcing events might be assumed to favor reinforcement of elevated pressure, the actual relationships provided by the present experiment were noncontingent, and chance reinforcement of lowering blood pressure could have occurred on numerous occasions. Indeed, previous reports of sustained hypertension may well have capitalized upon the consistent occurrence of critical contingent interactions not maintained with animals in the present study. Clearly, the arrangement of more explicit contingent relationships between blood pressure changes and reinforcing environmental events as suggested by the work of DiCara and Miller (1968) and Benson, *et al.* (1969) might be expected to produce more durable changes.

## VI. CARDIOVASCULAR INSTRUMENTAL CONDITIONING

Explorations of this "contingent model" for generating environmentally-related cardiovascular alterations have been most recently pursued in experiments with two baboons trained to elevate their blood pressure levels in order to avoid shock alone $(S_1)$ or to avoid shock *and* obtain a food reward $(S_2)$. Both $S$s were initially trained, using an operant "shaping" procedure, to raise and maintain diastolic pressure levels above 125 mm Hg for periods of at least 5 sec. at a time. Two feedback lights, which signaled when diastolic blood pressure was either above or below a prescribed criterion, were provided to the $S$s. In addition, the $S$s were in the presence of one of three added light conditions: "white," during which food could be obtained and no shocks ever occurred; "green," an intermediate condition which was followed by the "white" or "red" condition; and "red," a condition during which shocks could occur and no food was available. All changes from "white" to "red" or from "red" to "white" were made through the intermediate "green" condition during which two contingencies obtained: (1) if diastolic blood pressure remained *below* criterion (125 mm Hg) for 90 consecutive seconds (momentary rises above criterion reset the 90-sec. clock), the condition changed from "green" to "red"; and (2) for every 5 consecutive seconds the diastolic blood pressure remained above criterion, a "unit" was earned. Momentary drops in diastolic blood pressure (below 125 mm Hg) reset the 5-sec. unit clock. Accumulation of a prescribed number of 5-sec. units changed the condition from "green" to "white".

In the "red" condition: (1) every 30 consecutive seconds below criterion produced a 9 mA, ¼-sec. electric shock delivered via the stainless steel waistband. Momentary rises above criterion reset the 30-sec. clock; (2) twenty responses (FR 20) when the pressure was above criterion changed the condition back to "green." In the "white" condition: (1) lever responses earned food (5 pellets) on a fixed ratio (FR) 20 reinforcement schedule only when diastolic blood pressure was *above criterion* (same contingency as for escape from the shock condition in "red"). Falls in pressure below criterion not only made the lever functionally inoperative, but also reset any count already accumulated toward the FR 20 requirement; (2) when 40 min. of accumulated "down" time (time below criterion) was reached, the condition changed back to "green." If diastolic blood pressure remained above criterion, the "white" condition (including the food schedule) remained in effect indefinitely.

Stimulus changes were programmed in such a way as to establish an environment in which elevated diastolic blood pressure was rewarded by both food delivery and safety from electric shock. Low pressure (i.e., below criterion) on the other hand, resulted in frequent shocks and no food. During the course of the experiment, both the amplitude and duration requirements of the blood pressure response were systematically increased. For $S_1$ the unit number was increased to 32 through the following step sizes: 1, 2, 4, 8, 16, 20, 24, 28, 32. For $S_2$ unit number was increased to 14 through steps of 1, 2, 4, 8, 12, 14. Increments for both Ss were made at approximately ten-day intervals.

Figure 10 summarizes graphically the general procedure which remained in effect continuously (except for 1-hr. maintenance and data recording periods each day) for $S_1$ and 12 hr. each day for $S_2$. Additionally, the procedure for $S_2$ differed from that for $S_1$ in the following respects: (1) the "white" condition

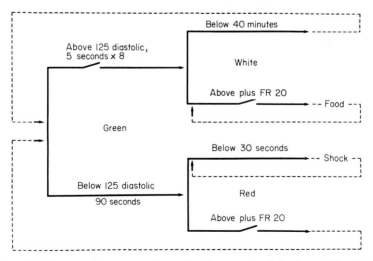

**Figure 10.** Diagram of programmed procedure for arranging behavior and blood pressure contingencies.

was a fixed (independent of blood pressure) 10-min. period with no food contingencies, which served as a time out (TO) or intertrial interval (ITI) between presentations of "green"; (2) conditioning sessions ("red"–"green"– "white") were of 6 hr. duration twice a day (at 10 a.m. and 6 p.m.) and there were separately programmed 6-hr. periods of sleep and food (FR 150 for ten pellets) which served, in part, as a control for the effects of lever pulling *per se*, and the establishment of baseline (sleep) pressures and heart rate levels.

BABOON ONE

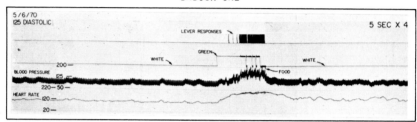

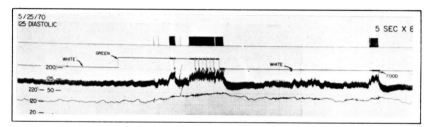

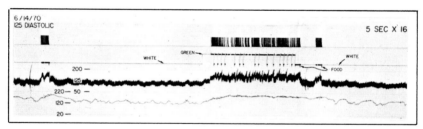

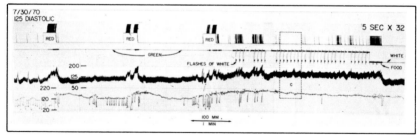

Figure 11. Sample polygraph recordings for $S_1$ showing changes in blood pressure and heart rate in response to four progressively higher contingency unit requirement conditions.

Under these experimental conditions, both Ss produced the required elevations in diastolic blood pressure above 125 mm Hg and maintained this 50–60 mm Hg rise above resting levels for specified intervals of at least 3 min., as illustrated in Figures 11 and 12. Elevations of similar magnitude (60 mm Hg) were also observed in systolic blood pressure under such conditions, and both animals maintained an essentially shock-free, food-abundant environment as indicated. Figure 11, for example, shows a sample of four separate record strips illustrating characteristic performances under each of four progressively higher unit requirement conditions. With only four 5-sec. intervals of elevated diastolic pressure (125 mm Hg) required (top panel), the rise in both heart rate (bottom line) and blood pressure (second line from bottom) can be seen to develop soon after presentation of the "green" panel light following termination of the "white" condition. Within 30–40 sec., the diastolic pressure rose above 125 mm Hg, remained at that level for the required four 5-sec. units, and reinstated the "white" condition. Following completion of the FR 20 for food with the pressure remaining above 125 mm Hg as required, a precipitous drop in pressure accompanied by a more gradual decline in heart rate can be seen to have occurred. Similar changes are shown in the second and third panels of Figure 11 for the same animal with unit requirements of eight and sixteen 5-sec. intervals, respectively. These two panels also show additional instances of food-reinforced performances with diastolic blood pressure levels above the required 125 mm Hg criterion. Significant variations in the strength of the performance did appear however, when the requirement was increased to thirty-two 5-sec. units as shown in the bottom panel of Figure 11. Alternations between the "red" (shock) condition and the intermediate "green" condition can be seen to predominate in contrast to the previously observed alternation between "green" and "white" conditions. Although the S did in fact meet the stringent unit requirement on this occasion, the performance could not be reliably maintained at this increased level. The Ss thus received frequent shocks, failed to obtain enough food to meet adequate body weight requirements, and was terminated on the program at this point.

Figure 12 shows a similar series of record strips for $S_2$. The onset of the green light can be seen to have produced a somewhat more gradual increase in pressure until the diastolic level reached 125 mm Hg. This was maintained until the unit requirement indicated for each panel (e.g., "5 sec. x 4") was satisfied and the "white" condition reinstated. Heart rate increases usually accompanied at least the onset of the blood pressure rise but there were instances (e.g., point C in the second panel from the top on Figure 12) when heart rate actually declined during periods of heightened blood pressure. Appearance of the "white" light however, invariably resulted in a precipitous fall in blood pressure accompanied by more gradual heart rate decreases. And at a requirement level of fourteen 5-sec. units (bottom panel, Figure 12), $S_2$ showed a deterioration in perfor-

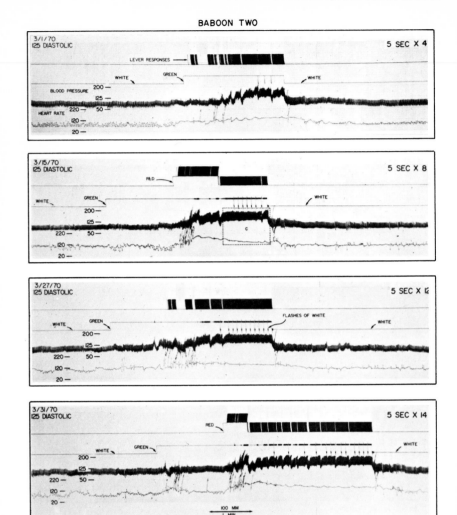

Figure 12. Sample polygraph recordings for $S_2$ showing changes in blood pressure and heart rate in response to four progressively higher contingency unit requirement conditions.

mance similar in virtually all respects to that observed with $S_1$ at a criterion level requiring thirty-two 5-sec. units: the number of "red" periods increased, more frequent shocks occurred, and food intake decreased sharply.

It is perhaps worthy of note that both $S$s emitted relatively high rates of responding on the lever manipulandum in the presence of the green light early in the experiment even though no reinforcement contingencies were programmed. That the physical activity associated with this generalized responding was neither a necessary nor sufficient condition for the recorded blood pressure changes, however, is indicated by two additional observations. One of the baboons $(S_1)$ showed a gradual reduction in this "superstitious" lever pulling with the result that periods of maintained pressure elevation with virtually no associated lever responding (e.g., point C, bottom panel, Figure 11) occurred with increasing frequency as the experiment progressed. Additionally, the second baboon $(S_2)$, trained to obtain food by pulling the lever 150 times for each ten pellets, showed relatively little change in blood pressure despite even vigorous and sustained responding during such separately programmed food periods.

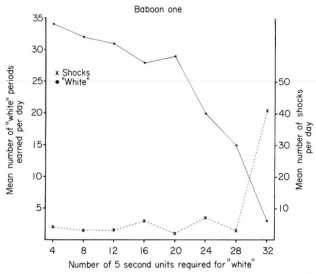

**Figure 13.** Changes in the number of "white" (shock-free, food available) periods earned per day and the number of shocks received each day by $S_1$ as a function of the number of 5-sec. contingency units required.

Figures 13 and 14 summarize the effects of unit number increases upon the number of "white" (shock-free, food available) periods earned per day and upon the number of shocks received each day. As the unit number increased, $S_1$ (Figure 13) maintained a low (2–3 shocks/day) shock rate despite a gradually reducing number of earned "white" periods. When thirty-two 5-sec. units were required to earn a "white" period however, the performance of $S_1$ deteriorated rapidly and shock frequency rose sharply. Similar results were obtained with $S_2$ (Figure 14), although the performance deterioration can be seen to have occurred by the time only fourteen 5-sec. units were required to earn a "white" period with this animal. Possibly, the difference in work schedules (one required unit per 40 min. for 23 hr./day, totaling 35 work units/day for $S_1$; and one required unit per 10 min. for two 6-hr. sessions, totaling 72 work units/day for

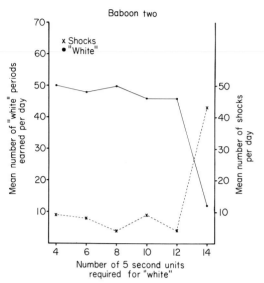

**Figure 14.** Changes in the number of "white" (shock-free) periods earned per day and the number of shocks received each day by $S_2$ as a function of the number of 5-sec. contingency units required.

$S_2$) may account, at least in part, for the difference between the two $S$s in the maximum unit number requirement which could be sustained. Significantly, this 2 to 1 "work ratio" between the performance schedules corresponds closely to the ratio of unit number limits (i.e., 32 for $S_1$ to 14 for $S_2$) reached by the two $S$s.

## VII. CONCLUSIONS

The results of these experiments establish firm relationships between a broad range of autonomic-endocrine system activity and psychopathological models involving emotional interactions. The initial findings emphasizing changes in absolute levels of selected hormones can be viewed as reflecting relatively undifferentiated consequences of arousal states associated with such emotion-inducing situations. The definite temporal course of visceral and steroid changes under such conditions and the quantitative nature of the relationship between degree of behavioral stress and level of physiological response has been well documented. In addition, the critical role of an organism's behavioral history in determining the nature and extent of autonomic-endocrine response to such psychopathological situations has been convincingly demonstrated. Clearly, however, the most meaningful dimension for hormone and visceral analysis in relationship to more chronic psychopathological interactions would appear to be the broader patterning or balance of secretory and visceral change in many interdependent autonomic and endocrine systems which in concert regulate adjustments of the internal milieu. The extensive and prolonged participation of these fundamental systems suggests a relationship between such physiological activity and the more durable consequences of emotional interactions. Indeed, the differentiation and control of such autonomic-endocrine response patterns in relationship to the historical and situational aspects of behavioral events may well provide important leads in the development of useful laboratory models for experimental psychopathological phenomena.

# REFERENCES

Banks, J. H., Miller, R. E., & Ogawa, N. The development of discriminated autonomic and instrumental responses during avoidance conditioning in the rhesus monkey. *Journal of Genetic Psychology*, 1966, **108**, 199-211.

Benson, H., Herd, J. A., Morse, W. H., & Kelleher, R. T. Behavioral inductions of arterial hypertension and its reversal. *American Journal of Physiology*, 1969, **217**, 30-34.

Berlanger, D., & Feldman, S. Effects of water deprivation upon heart rate and instrumental activity in the rat. *Journal of Comparative and Physiological Psychology*, 1962, **55**, 220-225.

Black, A. H. Heart rate changes during avoidance learning in dogs. *Canadian Journal of Psychology*, 1959, **13**, 229-242.

Brady, J. V. Emotion and the sensitivity of the psychoendocrine systems. In D. Glass (Ed.), *Neurophysiology and emotion*. Proceedings of a conference on biology and behavior. New York: The Rockefeller University Press and Russell Sage Foundation, 1967. Pp. 70-95.

Brady, J. V. Endocrine and autonomic correlates of emotional behavior. In P. Black (Ed.), *Physiological Correlates of Emotion*. New York: Academic Press, 1970. Pp. 95-125.

Brady, J. V. Experimental studies of psychophysiological responses to stressful situations. *Symposium on the medical aspects of stress in the military climate*. Washington, D.C.: Government Printing Office, 1965. Pp. 271-289.

Brady, J. V. Operant methodology and the production of altered physiological states. In W. Honig (Ed.), *Operant behavior areas of research and application*. New York: Appleton-Century-Crofts, 1966. Pp. 609-633.

Brady, J. V., Kelly, D., & Plumlee, L. Autonomic and behavioral responses of the rhesus monkey to emotional conditioning. *Annals of the New York Academy of Sciences, Emotional Behavior*, 1969, **159**, Art. 3.

Brady, J. V., Porter, R. W., Conrad, D. G., & Mason, J. W. Avoidance behavior and the development of gastroduodenal ulcers. *Journal of the Experimental Analysis of Behaviour*, 1958, **1**, 69-72.

Brener, J. Heart rate as an avoidance response. *Psychological Record*, 1966, **16**, 329-336.

Cannon, W. B. *Bodily changes in pain, hunger, fear, and rage*. New York: D. Appleton, 1915.

DiCara, L. V., & Miller, N. E. Instrumental learning of systolic blood pressure responses by curarized rats. Dissociation of cardiac and vascular responses. *Psychosomatic Medicine*, 1968, **30**, 489.

DeToledo, L., & Black, A. H. Heart rate: Changes during conditioned suppression in rats. *Science*, 1966, **152**, 1404-1406.

Eldridge, L. Respiration rate change and its relation to avoidance behavior. Unpublished doctoral dissertation, Columbia University, 1954.

Engel, B. T., & Hansen, S. P. Operant conditioning of heart rate slowing. *Psychophysiology*, 1966, **3**, 176-187.

Estes, W. K., & Skinner, B. F. Some quantitative properties of anxiety. *Journal of Experimental Psychology*, 1941, **29**, 390-400.

Ferreira, S. H., Gollub, L. R., & Vane, J. R. The release of catecholamines by shocks and stimuli paired with shocks. *Journal of the Experimental Analysis of Behaviour*, 1969, **12**, 623-631.

Findley, J. D., & Brady, J. V. Blood pressure and heart rate changes in a continuously programmed environment. *Proceedings of the American Psychological Association*, 1969, 77th Annual Convention, 807-808.

Findley, J. D., Robinson, W. W., & Gilliam, W. A restraint system for chronic study of the baboon. *Journal of the Experimental Analysis of Behaviour*, 1971, **15**, 69-71.

Forsyth, R. P. Blood pressure responses to long-term avoidance schedules in the restrained rhesus monkey. *Psychosomatic Medicine*, 1969, **31**, 300-309.

Frazier, T. W. Avoidance conditioning of heart rate in humans. *Psychophysiology*, 1966, **3**, 188-202.

Gantt, W. H. *Experimental basis of neurotic behavior*. New York: Hoeber Company, 1944.

Hahn, W. W., Stern, J. A., & McDonald, D. G. Effects of water deprivation and bar-pressing activity on heart rate of the male albino rat. *Journal of Comparative and Physiological Psychology*, 1962, **55**, 786-790.

Hearst, E., Beer, B., Sheatz, G., & Galambos, R. Some electrophysiological correlates of conditioning in the monkey. *Electroencephalography and Clinical Neurophysiology Journal*, 1960, **12**, 137-152.

Herd, J. A., Morse, W. H., Kelleher, R. T., & Jones, L. G. Arterial hypertension in the squirrel monkey during behavioral experiments. *American Journal of Physiology*, 1969, **217**, 24-29.

John, E. R., & Killam, K. F. Electrophysiological correlates of avoidance conditioning in the cat. *Journal of Pharmacology and Experimental Therapeutics*, 1959, **125**, 252-274.

Lacey, J. I., Kagen, J., Lacey, B. C., & Moss, H. A. Situational determinants and behavioral correlates of autonomic response patterns. In P. J. Knapp (Ed.), *Expression of the Emotions in Man*. New York: International University Press, 1963. Pp. 161-196.

Liddel, H. S. *Emotional hazard in animals and man*. Springfield, Ill.: Charles G. Thomas, 1956.

Mahl, G. F. Effect of chronic fear on gastric secretion of HCL in dogs. *Psychosomatic Medicine*, 1949, **11**, 30.

Malmo, R. B. Experimental studies of mental patients under stress. In M. L. Reymert (Ed.), *Feelings and emotions*. New York: McGraw-Hill, 1950. Pp. 169-180.

Malmo, R. B. Slowing of heart rate after septal self-stimulation in rats. *Science*, 1961, **133**, 1129.

Mason, J. W. Restraining chair for the experimental study of primates. *Journal of Applied Physiology*, 1958, **12**, 130-133.

Mason, J. W., Brady, J. V., Robinson, J. A., Taylor, E. D., Tolson, W. W., & Mougey, E. H. Patterns of thyroid, gonadal and adrenal hormone secretion related to psychological stress in the monkey. *Psychosomatic Medicine*, 1961, **23**, 446.

Mason, J. W., Brady, J. V., & Sidman, M. Plasma 17-hydroxycorticosteroid levels and conditioned behavior in the rhesus monkey. *Endocrinology*, 1957, **60**, 741-752.

Mason, J. W. Organization of psychoendocrine mechanisms. *Psychosomatic Medicine,* 1968, **30**, Part II, 565-808 (monograph).

Mason, J. W., Brady, J. V., & Tolson, W. W. Behavioral adaptations and endocrine activity. In R. Levine (Ed.), *Endocrines and the central nervous system.* Baltimore: Williams and Wilkins Company, 1966, Vol. 43, pp. 227-248.

Mason, J. W., Mangan, G., Brady, J. V., Conrad, D., & Rioch, D. McK. Concurrent plasma epinephrine, norepinephrine and 17-hydroxycorticosteroid levels during conditioned emotional disturbances in monkeys. *Psychosomatic Medicine,* 1961, **23**, 344-353.

Miller, N. E., & DiCara, L. Instrumental learning of heart rate changes in curarized rats: Shaping, and specificity to discriminative stimulus. *Journal of Comparative and Physiological Psychology,* 1967, **63**, 12.

Nathan, M. A., & Smith, O. A. Differential conditional emotional and cardiovascular responses—a training technique for monkeys. *Journal of the Experimental Analysis of Behaviour,* 1968, **11**, 77-82.

Parrish, J. Classical discrimination conditioning of heart rate and bar-press suppression in the rat. *Psychonomic Science,* 1967, **9**, 267-268.

Pavlov, I. P. Uber die normalen blutdruckschwandungen beim hunde. *Archiv für die Gesamte Physiologie des Menschen und der Tiere,* 1879, **20**, 215.

Perez-Cruet, J., Black, W. C., & Brady, J. V. Heart rate: Differential effects of hypothalamic and septal self-stimulation. *Science,* 1963, **140**, 1235-1236.

Perez-Cruet, J., Plumlee, L., & Newton, J. E. O. Chronic basal blood pressure in unanesthetized dogs using the ring-catheter technique. *Proceedings of the Symposium on Biomedical Engineering,* 1966, **1**, 383-386.

Perez-Cruet, J., Tolliver, G., Dunn, G., Marvin, S., & Brady, J. V. Concurrent measurement of heart rate and instrumental avoidance behavior in the rhesus monkey. *Journal of the Experimental Analysis of Behaviour,* 1963, **6**, 61-64.

Polish, E., Brady, J. V., Mason, J. W., Thach, J. S., & Niemeck, W. Gastric contents and the occurrence of duodenal lesions in the rhesus monkey during avoidance behavior. *Gastroenterology,* 1962, **43**, 193-201.

Porter, R. W., Brady, J. V., Conrad, D., Mason, J. W., Galambos, R., & Rioch, D. McK. Some experimental observations on gastrointestinal lesions in behaviorally conditioned monkeys. *Psychosomatic Medicine,* 1958, **20**, 379-394.

Porter, R. W., Conrad, D. G., & Brady, J. V. Some neural and behavioral correlates of electrical self-stimulation of the limbic system. *Journal of the Experimental Analysis of Behaviour,* 1959, **2**, 43-55.

Rice, H. K. The responding—rest ratio in the production of gastric ulcers in the rat. *Psychological Reports,* 1963, **13**, 11-14.

Ross, G. S., Hodos, W., & Brady, J. V. Electroencephalographic correlates of temporally spaced responding and avoidance behavior. *Journal of the Experimental Analysis of Behaviour,* 1962, **5**, 467-472.

Shapiro, A. P., & Horn, P. W. Blood pressure, plasma pepsinogen, and behavior in cats subjected to experimental production of anxiety. *Journal of Nervous and Mental Diseases,* 1955, **122**, 222-231.

Sidman, M. Avoidance conditioning with brief shock and no exteroceptive warning signal. *Science,* 1953, **118**, 157-158.

Sidman, M., Mason, J. W., Brady, J. V., & Thach, J. Quantitative relations between avoidance behavior and pituitary-adrenal cortical activity. *Journal of the Experimental Analysis of Behaviour,* 1962, **5**, 353-362.

Smith, O. A., Jr., & Stebbins, W. C. Conditioned blood flow and heart rate in monkeys. *Journal of Comparative and Physiological Psychology,* 1965, **59**, 432-436.

146        JOSEPH V. BRADY, JACK D. FINDLEY, AND ALAN HARRIS

Snapper, A. G., Schoenfeld, W. N., Ferraro, D. P., & Locke, B. Cardiac rate of the rat under DRL and a non-contingent temporal schedule of reinforcement. *Psychological Reports*, 1965, 17, 543-552.
Stebbins, W. C., & Smith, O. A. Cardiovascular concomitants of the conditioned emotional response in the monkey. *Science*, 1964, 144, 881-883.
Stern, J. A., & Word, T. J. Heart rate changes during avoidance conditioning in the male albino rat. *Journal of Psychosomatic Research*, 1962, 6, 167-175.
Swinnen, M. E. T. Blood pressure digitizer. *21st ACEMB* 1968, p. 184.
Trowill, J. A. Instrumental conditioning of the heart rate in the curarized rat. *Journal of Comparative and Physiological Psychology*, 1967, 63, 7-11.
Webb, R. A., & Obrist, P. A. Heart-rate change during complex operant performance in the dog. *Proceedings of the American Psychological Association*, 1967, 137-138.
Wenzel, B. M. Changes in heart rate associated with responses based on positive and negative reinforcement. *Journal of Comparative and Physiological Psychology*, 1961, 42, 638-644.
Werdegar, D., Johnson, D. G., & Mason, J. W. A technique for continuous measurement of arterial blood pressure in unanesthetized monkeys. *Journal of Applied Physiology*, 1964, 19, 519-521.

# 8

# Schedule-Controlled Modulation of Arterial Blood Pressure in the Squirrel Monkey

W. H. MORSE,
J. ALAN HERD,
R. T. KELLEHER,
and SUSAN A. GROSE

Harvard Medical School
and New England Regional Primate
Research Center

## I. INTRODUCTION

Some 10–15% of the population in the U.S. have chronically high blood pressure (hypertension). Hypertension seriously increases the incidence and progression of coronary artery disease in young and middle-aged American adults. Epidemiological studies have shown that the incidence of coronary artery disease in hypertensive patients is approximately twice as great as in normotensive adults of the same age (Dawber & Kannel, 1966). Patients with coronary artery disease who are hypertensive have approximately twice the likelihood of myocardial infarction as patients with normal blood pressure (Frank *et al.*, 1968). A variety of other cardiovascular diseases, especially cerebrovascular accidents, are accelerated in individuals with chronically high blood pressure.

Despite its common occurrence, the pathogenesis of most hypertension is poorly understood. Long-term studies of patients with hypertension suggest that permanently elevated blood pressures follow periods of transiently elevated blood pressures (Finkielman *et al.*, 1965; Eich *et al.*, 1966; Julius & Conway, 1968). Since individuals in early stages of hypertension are usually young and otherwise healthy, they seldom seek medical attention. Consequently, there has been little opportunity to study the early cardiovascular changes associated with hypertension of unclear origin (essential hypertension).

Systemic mean arterial pressure is a function of both cardiac output and peripheral vascular resistance. While cardiac output and peripheral vascular resistance vary greatly, arterial blood pressure normally is regulated within a narrow range. Regulation of arterial pressure involves compensatory adjustments in cardiac rate and force of contraction, arteriolar tone, and venous tone. Nevertheless, arterial blood pressure can be significantly modulated by a variety of physiological and environmental events. Transient elevations of arterial blood pressure normally occur during exercise (Levv et al., 1967), ingestion of food, and in response to stimuli (Brod et al., 1959). The mean resting blood pressure of a young man may be around 90 mm Hg, but in sleep it may fall 15 to 20 mm Hg, and before and during severe exercise it may rise to 150 mm Hg.

Usually, when increases in blood pressure occur, compensatory reflex regulation of the cardiovascular system tends to restore the blood pressure to a lower value. However, with a continually elevated blood pressure, for whatever reason, cardiovascular regulatory mechanisms become less effective in maintaining the previously normal level of blood pressure. Although the exact sequence of events is poorly understood, the first signs of essential hypertension may be exaggerated pressor responses to various stimuli (Brod et al., 1959; Levy et al., 1967). Eventually an initial phase of reversible, labile hypertension may be followed by episodes of persistent, then permanent hypertension with an irreversible increase in peripheral vascular resistance. Thus, a chronic elevation of arterial blood pressure at rest of 15% above the normal for a particular age group is commonly taken as sufficient indication for initiating medical treatment. The regulatory mechanisms still function, but now regulate the blood pressure at a higher value (McCubbin et al., 1956). In some instances the chronic reduction of arterial blood pressure by continued drug treatment results in the compensatory regulation occurring around a lower value even after drug treatment is stopped.

Because episodic elevations in blood pressure can be experimentally induced, a rational approach would be to attempt to produce a sustained pathological hypertension in experimental animals by repeatedly subjecting them to situations associated with episodic elevations in mean arterial blood pressure. Electrical stimulation of the hypothalamus of unanesthetized animals can increase heart rate and blood pressure in association with behavioral changes (Hess, 1957). Using intermittent electrical stimulation of the brain over long periods of time, Folkow and Rubinstein (1966) have produced significantly increased levels of resting blood pressure in rats. Chronic elevations in blood pressure can also be associated with environmental circumstances. Mice subjected to crowding and other social stimuli have been reported to develop elevations in blood pressure that persisted for long periods of time (Henry et al., 1967). Forsyth (1969) has found sustained elevations of blood pressure in rhesus monkeys maintained for long periods under avoidance schedules of electric shock postponement. Herd *et al.* (1969) found that continued performances under schedules of reinforcement that produced episodic elevations in systemic arterial blood pressure later led to sustained elevations in blood pressure.

We were particularly interested in studying the physiological changes associated with sustained ongoing behavior because we had found that ongoing schedule-controlled behavior powerfully modified both the effects of environmental stimuli and the behavioral effects of drugs (Kelleher & Morse, 1964, 1968a). An individual's own behavior is an exceedingly important part of his environment. His history and his ongoing behavior profoundly affect the way in which environmental events modify subsequent behavior. For example, in a squirrel monkey that is already responding steadily, the scheduled presentation of response-produced electric shocks that would suppress responding under other conditions may enhance and later maintain responding. In general, the effectiveness of consequent events in maintaining responding depends upon the ongoing level of responding. Thus, the rates and patterns of schedule-controlled behavior are not just dependent variables that reveal other behavioral processes; rather, the patterning of responding is itself a powerful determinant of behavior. Ongoing behavior also modifies physiological functioning. We will describe here some of the changes that occur in the blood pressure of the squirrel monkey engaged in schedule-controlled behavior.

Briefly, the rationale for these experiments involves several essential points:

1. Continued excessive elevation in blood pressure (hypertension) leads to pathological cardiovascular disease;

2. Episodic elevations in blood pressure that recur repeatedly can result in chronic elevations in blood pressure;

3. Blood pressure can be significantly changed by environmental circumstances;

4. Strongly controlled behavior is an important aspect of any individual's environment and episodic elevations in blood pressure are associated with ongoing schedule-controlled behavior. Therefore, sustained chronically-elevated blood pressure can be developed by controlling the behavior of an individual in its environment.

## II. METHODS

Systematic observations of cardiovascular changes associated with responding under various schedules of reinforcement have been made in more than 30 squirrel monkeys. While each monkey was anesthetized with mixtures of halothane and oxygen, one end of a small polyvinyl chloride catheter (id .38 mm and od .76 mm) was implanted into the aorta through the right internal iliac artery, the right common iliac artery, or the left common carotid artery. The other end of the catheter was brought out through the skin in the middle of the back and protected by a leather jacket which the monkey wore at all times. Each day the catheter was flushed with saline (.9% NaCl), filled with heparin solution (10mg. Na heparin/ml.) and sealed with a stainless steel obturator.

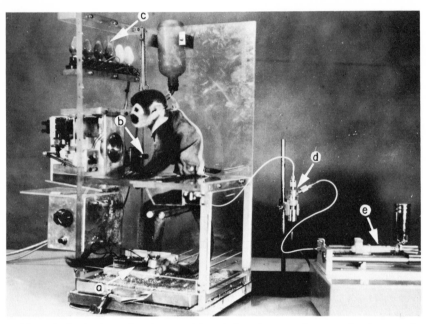

Figure 1. Squirrel monkey in restraining chair and system for recording key-pressing behavior and arterial blood pressure. The monkey is restrained in the seated position by a waist lock and its tail is held firmly by a small stock (a). Electric shocks can be delivered through two hinged metal plates that rest lightly on a shaved portion of the tail; electrode paste ensures good electrical contact. The response key is mounted on the right side of the lucite wall facing the monkey (b); the stimulus lights are mounted behind and near the top of this wall (c). A liquid food dispenser is shown behind a recessed area in the wall. The catheter is led out from the bottom of the monkey's jacket through a small hole in the waist lock and connected to the Statham gauge (d) which is in turn connected to the infusion pump (e).

As previously described (Herd et al., 1969), arterial blood pressure was measured while each monkey sat in a restraining chair (Figure 1) within a sound-attenuating isolation chamber. The implanted catheter of the monkey was connected by Teflon tubing to the fluid-filled chamber of a Statham P23Db strain gauge pressure transducer, which in turn was connected to a Harvard

Apparatus Co. constant-infusion syringe pump. A heparin and saline solution (.08 mg. Na heparin/ml. and .9% NaCl) was infused continuously through the gauge and tubing at a rate of .01 ml./min. to prevent blood from clotting in the tubing. The hydrostatic pressure attributable to the continuous flow of fluid through the gauge, connecting tubing, and the small polyvinyl chloride catheter was found to be <2 mm Hg at .01 ml./min. At low rates of infusion, doubling the flow rate or stopping the flow of fluid through the gauge and catheter had no perceptible effect on the recorded level of mean arterial blood pressure (Figure 2). The Wheatstone bridge connections of the Statham strain gauge were

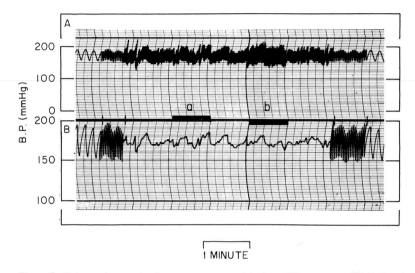

1 MINUTE

Figure 2. Polygraph records of pressure measured during different rates of infusion from a syringe pump through pressure transducer connected to indwelling arterial catheter of a hypertensive squirrel monkey. (A) and (B) were recorded simultaneously from same pressure transducer using different output voltage amplification and different amplifier frequency-response filtering; (A) was recorded with a calibration sensitivity of 5 mm Hg/division and a half amplitude high-frequency response of 75 Hz; (B) was recorded with a calibration sensitivity of 2 mm Hg/division, a half amplitude high-frequency response in middle of record of .1 Hz, and 75 Hz at beginning and end. Paper speed in middle of record was 10 sec./division; at beginning and end of record it was .16 sec./division, and, during transition periods between fastest and slowest recordings, paper speed was .83 sec./division. Upward deflection of event marker (a) indicates time during which rate of infusion from syringe pump was doubled to .02 ml./min. Downward deflection (b) indicates time during which infusion was stopped by turning off pump and clamping tubing between syringe and the pressure transducer. The rest of the time, rate of infusion was .01 ml./min. Note that changing rate of infusion from syringe pump had no perceptible effect on recorded level of mean arterial blood pressure. Clamping tubing between infusion syringe and pressure transducer did affect frequency-response characteristics of recording system seen as an increase in amplitude of change in pressure with each beat of heart during the time tubing was clamped. (From Herd et al., 1969, with permission.)

attached to a Grass Instrument Co. polygraph, model 5 or 7. Because of the distensibility of the chronically implanted catheter and the low frequency response of the system, no attempt was made to measure systolic or diastolic blood pressures. All pressure values reported are mean arterial blood pressure obtained by low-pass filtering in the driver amplifier of the polygraph. Average daily mean blood pressures were calculated, using horizontal lines of best fit drawn through polygraph records. Heart rate was obtained by means of a Lexington Instrument Co. cardiotachometer which sensed the changes in blood pressure recorded in the preamplifier of the polygraph with each heartbeat.

Patency of the arterial catheters was verified by the free flow of blood out of the open end before each experimental session and was assessed during sessions by the amplitude of pressure oscillations synchronous with each beat of the heart. Arterial catheters in these squirrel monkeys functioned well for an average of about 6 months. Since eventually they all broke or became obstructed with endothelial tissue, there were opportunities to study the distortions of pressure measurements caused by failing catheters. When blood did not flow freely from a catheter, the mean arterial pressures recorded were always about 10 mm Hg lower than mean pressures recorded on days when blood refluxed freely. High-frequency recordings showed that the decrease in mean pressure was due to a loss of the upper part of each arterial pressure pulse contour. Apparently flaps of endothelial tissue obstruct an arterial catheter more during systole than diastole. Because the catheters were vigorously flushed with saline solution every day, obstruction of a catheter by endothelial tissue eventually resulted in a false passage from the end of the catheter through the wall of the artery along the track of the catheter and into the connective tissue around the artery. Consequently, when a catheter failed, the mean arterial pressure recorded was 20 or 30 mm Hg lower than it had been when the catheter was functioning properly. The only data reported here were recorded from arterial catheters that gave a free flow of blood from the open end.

## III. BLOOD PRESSURE CHANGES ASSOCIATED WITH DIFFERENT SCHEDULE PERFORMANCES

Although systematic observations have been made under only a limited number of different schedules, it appears that there are characteristic changes in blood pressure associated with different schedule performances. Most monkeys were studied under fixed-ratio schedules in which key pressing terminated a visual stimulus associated with a schedule of electric shock presentation (stimulus-shock termination). Some of these monkeys were then studied under fixed-interval schedules of stimulus-shock termination. Limited observations were also made under schedules of electric shock postponement (3 animals) and under fixed-ratio and fixed-interval schedules of food presentation (7 animals). Under the fixed-ratio schedule of stimulus-shock termination, noxious electric stimuli were delivered periodically in the presence of a green light. Pressing the key a fixed minimum number of times (3, 10, 30 or 100) turned off the green light for a 1-min. time-out period. During the time-out period the experimental chamber was dark, electric shocks were never delivered, and responding had no programmed consequences. When the time-out period ended, the green light came on again and the cycle repeated. As described previously (Morse & Kelleher, 1966; Azrin *et al.*, 1963), appropriate parameter values of this schedule engender sustained high rates of key pressing characteristic of fixed-ratio schedules.

Figure 3 shows the characteristic patterns of blood pressure and heart rate associated with stable performances under this fixed-ratio schedule. When the light came on, the monkey pressed the key rapidly (top tracing), while its blood pressure (bottom tracing) and heart rate increased (middle tracing). When the light went off, each monkey stopped pressing the key and blood pressure and

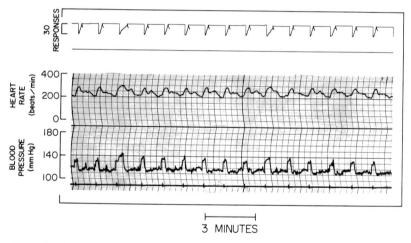

3 MINUTES

**Figure 3.** Characteristic patterns of key pressing (top record) and changes in mean heart rate (middle record) and mean arterial blood pressure (bottom record) for monkey S-110 under a fixed-ratio schedule of stimulus-shock termination. Electric shocks were scheduled to occur every 30 sec. in the presence of a green light; the 30th response turned off the light. The top record shows cumulative recordings of key-pressing responses. The slope of the cumulative record is directly related to the rate of key-pressing. The resetting of the recording pen and strokes across the event record at the bottom of the figure indicate the onset of the green light at the start of a cycle. Downward strokes on the event record indicate key presses. The short diagonal strokes on the cumulative record show where the light was turned off and the 1-min. time-out period began. Heart rate and mean arterial blood pressure were recorded simultaneously. Note the episodic increases in heart rate and blood pressure associated with key pressing.

heart rate decreased. The episodic increases in blood pressure and heart rate shown in Figure 3 tended to become more pronounced as the number requirement under the fixed-ratio schedule was increased and tended to be more pronounced when the blood pressure and heart rate during time-out periods were low. Thus, this close association between fixed-ratio responding and elevated blood pressure and elevated heart rate could be modified quantitatively by the parameters of the schedule and depended, in part, upon the average values of blood pressure and heart rate.

Figure 4 shows the blood pressure and heart rate patterns associated with performances under two parameter values of a fixed-ratio schedule of stimulus-

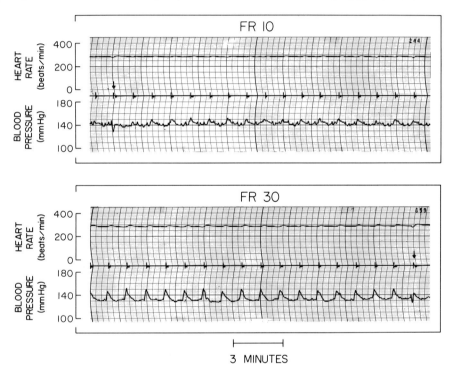

Figure 4. Blood pressure and heart rate changes associated with performances under two parameter values of a fixed-ratio schedule of stimulus-shock termination for monkey S-223. Electric shocks were scheduled to occur every 20 sec. in the presence of the green light and whenever a cumulative time of 5 min. had elapsed in the presence of the green light; the 10th response (FR 10; upper frame) or 30th response (FR 30; lower frame) turned off the light. In the event recording (middle record of each frame), vertical strokes across the line indicate the onset of the green light at the start of a cycle; downward strokes indicate key presses; arrows above the records indicate presentations of 5 mA. electric shocks. Note that the episodic increases in blood pressure are more marked under FR 30 than FR 10 and that electric shocks cause a transient decrease in blood pressure.

shock termination. Although the rises in blood pressure associated with responding are minimal when the requirement is 10 responses, they are of larger magnitude when the requirement is 30 responses. These blood pressure increases occur without any appreciable change in heart rate. At both parameter values, the presentation of the electric shock causes a transient decrease in blood pressure. Figure 5 shows episodic increases in blood pressure and heart rate associated with performances under two parameter values of a fixed-ratio schedule of food presentation. In this monkey, the episodic heart rate changes associated with the schedule performance are more marked. The maximum increase in blood pressure is no greater under the FR 300 schedule than under the FR 100 schedule but is more sustained. When the parameter value was decreased from FR 300 to FR 100, the earlier pattern of episodic blood pressure was obtained again, but changes in heart rate were less marked than previously. As in Figures 3 and 4, the maximum elevations in blood pressure and heart rate occur when the rate of key pressing is greatest. Because the performances shown in Figures 4 and 5 were maintained by different types of events, it seems likely that these particular patterns of blood pressure and heart rate are more dependent upon the schedule-controlled performance than upon the maintenance events themselves. These findings add to the growing body of evidence indicating that schedule-controlled behavior is exceedingly powerful in modifying environmental as well as physiological and pharmacological variables (Kelleher & Morse, 1968a, b; Morse & Kelleher, 1970).

Monkeys originally trained to terminate a stimulus associated with noxious electric shocks under a fixed-ratio schedule were then studied under a fixed-interval schedule of stimulus-shock termination (Herd et al., 1969; Morse & Kelleher, 1966). Under the fixed-interval schedule, noxious stimuli were programmed to occur t sec. after a white light had been on for a fixed minimum interval of time (2 or 4 min.). The first key-press after this minimum interval turned off the white light for a 1-min. time-out period. When the time-out period ended, the white light came on again and the cycle repeated. The pattern of key-pressing under the fixed-interval schedule was characterized by a pause (period of no responding) followed by positively accelerated responding. The episodic blood pressure changes under the fixed-interval schedule were quite different from those under the fixed-ratio schedule (Figure 6). As soon as the light indicating the start of the interval came on, mean arterial blood pressure began to rise and then fell slightly as the rate of responding increased. In intervals in which steady responding was not sustained the blood pressure tended to increase during pauses, and thus oscillated between high and low values when responses were followed by pauses (see also Figure 10A). Since the blood pressure was highest in the absence of responding, the work involved in the key-pressing response probably contributed only minimally to the increased blood pressure under strongly controlled schedule performances.

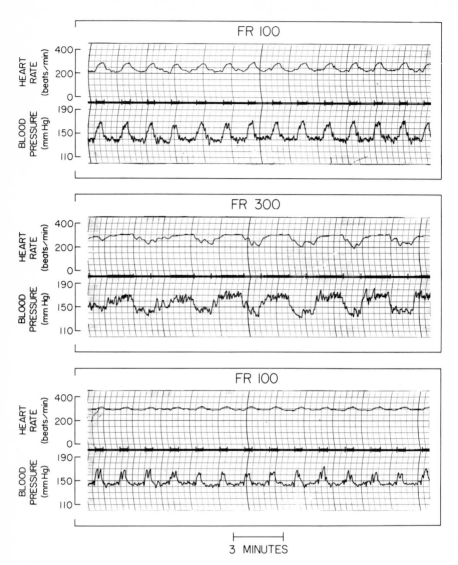

Figure 5. Blood pressure and heart rate changes associated with performances under two parameter values of a fixed-ratio schedule of food presentation for monkey S-139. A 250 mg food pellet was delivered just after every 100th response (FR 100; top and bottom frames) or every 300th response (FR 300; middle frame). In the event-recording (middle record of each frame), vertical strokes across the line indicate the onset of the white light at the start of a cycle and the presentation of food at the end of a cycle; downward strokes indicate key presses. Note that the episodic increases in blood pressure are more prolonged under FR 300 than under FR 100.

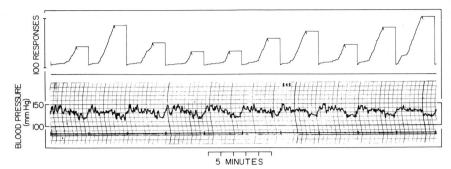

Figure 6. Characteristic patterns of key-pressing (top record) and changes in mean arterial blood pressure (bottom record) for monkey S-83 under a fixed-interval schedule in which electric shocks were scheduled to occur every 3 sec. after 2 min. had elapsed in the presence of a white light; the first key press after 2 min. turned off the light. Key pressing and blood pressure recordings as in Figure 3. Note that the blood pressure was highest at the beginning of each interval and tended to fall as responding increased.

This monkey was later studied under the fixed-ratio schedule and then under a 4-min. fixed-interval schedule. Figure 7 shows the second transition from the fixed-ratio to the fixed-interval schedule. With the onset of the white light associated with the fixed-interval schedule, the blood pressure abruptly increased in association with key-pressing. Although the monkey did not respond steadily, the blood pressure remained high, even during time-out periods. Such transitory increases were often observed following schedule changes. Subsequently, the pattern of blood pressure change shown in Figure 6 developed again.

Limited observations have been made on the blood pressure changes associated with two different schedules of electric shock postponement. Figure 8 shows the pattern of key-pressing and changes in mean arterial blood pressure under an avoidance schedule of shock postponement. The pattern of key-pressing was relatively steady throughout the 1-hr. session, except for the burst

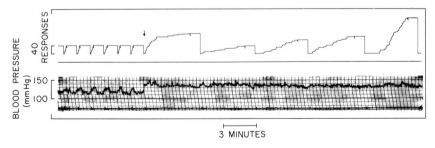

Figure 7. Key-pressing and blood pressure changes during transition from fixed-ratio to fixed-interval schedule in monkey S-83. Recording as in Figure 6. At the arrow, the schedule of stimulus-shock termination was changed from FR 40 (green light) to FI 4-min. (white light). Note the elevated blood pressure associated with the transition.

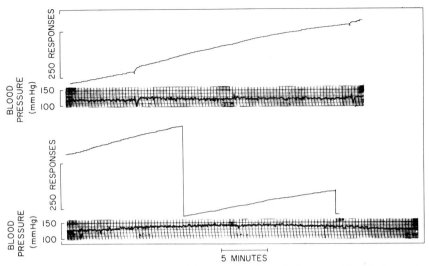

Figure 8. Characteristic patterns of key-pressing (cumulative records) and changes in mean arterial blood pressure (polygraph records) for monkey S-108 under an avoidance schedule of shock postponement. Electric shocks were scheduled to occur every 30 sec. and each response postponed electric shock for 30 sec. The records shown in the lower half of the figure are a continuation of those shown in the upper half. The recording pen reset to the baseline whenever 500 responses had accumulated and at the end of the session. Strokes on the cumulative record and the event pen indicate 5 mA. electric shocks. Note the increase in blood pressure during the session and the transient decrease in blood pressure after each electric shock.

of responses following each of the two shock deliveries. With each shock delivery there was a momentary increase in mean blood pressure followed by a larger transient decrease that persisted during the burst of responses. In addition, the mean blood pressure increased from about 120 mm Hg at the start of the session to a maximum of about 145 mm Hg near the end of the hour. In contrast to the episodic changes in mean arterial blood pressure when schedule components alternate with time-out periods, there are no pronounced cyclical changes in mean blood pressure under the continuously present avoidance schedule.

Under an avoidance schedule of shock postponement no noxious stimuli are delivered if the durations between successive responses are less than the response–shock interval. We have recently studied schedules of shock post-ponement in which relations between interresponse times and shocks could vary over a wide range (Kelleher & Morse, 1969). Under an interlocking fixed-ratio, shock-postponement schedule, successive groups of responses decreased the time by which a response postponed the next scheduled shock until a shock immediately followed the $n$th response. Figure 9 shows the pattern of key-pressing and the changes in mean arterial blood pressure under the

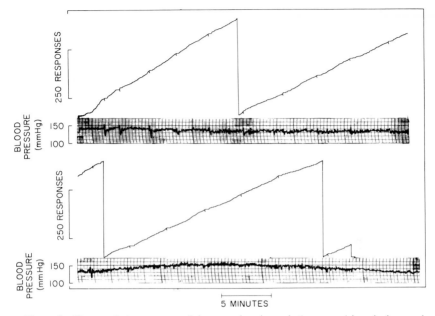

**Figure 9.** Characteristic patterns of key-pressing (cumulative records) and changes in mean arterial blood pressure (polygraph records) for monkey S-105 under an interlocking fixed-ratio, shock-postponement schedule. The fixed-ratio requirement was 100 responses, the response–shock time was 30 sec., and the shock intensity was 5 mA. (see Kelleher & Morse, 1969). Recording as in Figure 8. Note the increase in blood pressure during the session and the transient decrease in blood pressure after electric shock early in the session.

interlocking schedule. In comparison to the performance under the avoidance schedule (Figure 8), the rate of responding is about three times greater and the frequency of shocks about ten times greater. There is some tendency for the rate of responding to increase gradually between shocks. In general, the blood pressure changes associated with this schedule were similar to those seen under the avoidance schedule. During the early part of the session each shock delivery resulted in a momentary increase followed by a larger transient decrease in mean blood pressure; later in the session there is no discernible effect of the shock delivery on the blood pressure. Besides the changes associated with shock delivery, the mean blood pressure slowly increased from about 135 mm Hg to a maximum of 155 mm Hg during the latter part of the session.

In summary, the differences in mean arterial blood pressure under the fixed-ratio, fixed-interval, avoidance, and interlocking schedules indicate that there are characteristic changes in blood pressure related to behavior controlled by these particular schedules. There seems to be no necessary correlation between blood pressure and key pressing. Under fixed-ratio schedules the blood pressure was highest when the monkey was responding; under the fixed-interval schedule the blood pressure was highest when the monkey was not responding. Under the avoidance schedule the blood pressure was lowest during the burst of responses following after a shock. Finally, the blood pressure changes were comparable under the fixed-ratio schedules of presentation of food and termination of a stimulus-shock complex.

## IV. THE DEVELOPMENT OF CHRONIC HYPERTENSION ASSOCIATED WITH SCHEDULE-CONTROLLED PERFORMANCES

Recent experiments indicate that chronic elevations in arterial blood pressure can be associated with ongoing schedule-controlled behavior. Forsyth (1969) found increased levels of arterial pressure in five of six monkeys studied for extended time periods under shock-avoidance schedules. Three of the four experimental monkeys maintained 12 hr./day under a 20-sec. Sidman avoidance schedule showed similar blood pressure elevations; a four- or five-month period of normal or hypertensive pressures was followed by a steady monthly increase in pressure. The two other experimental monkeys, under 5- and 7-sec. avoidance schedules for 16 hr./day, also showed marked elevations in pressure after seven and twelve months. The sixth monkey and three other monkeys studied under various control procedures showed very little change in blood pressure.

Using procedures that produce episodic increases in arterial blood pressure described above, Herd et al. (1969) found persistent elevations in arterial blood pressure in four of six squirrel monkeys studied over four to eleven months. During the early stages of training, characteristic increases in blood pressure developed in association with characteristic patterns of key-pressing. Eventually four of the monkeys had sustained elevations in mean arterial blood pressure during the whole of each experimental session. Further, studies with the continuous measurement of arterial blood pressure 24 hr./day showed that the hypertension in each of these squirrel monkeys persisted even after the monkey had been returned to its home cage.

Figure 10 shows instances of episodic and sustained elevations in blood pressure under the fixed-interval schedule of stimulus-shock termination. In the earlier session (100) the blood pressure changes were those described above; mean arterial pressure began to rise as soon as the light came on and actually fell slightly as the rate of responding increased (Figure 10B). In the later session (326) blood pressure was elevated not only during periods of responding but also during time-out periods (Figure 10D). Thus, the experimental results with this monkey support the view that episodic elevations in blood pressure can indeed proceed to a chronic hypertension.

A summary of the entire experimental history of this hypertensive monkey is shown in Figure 11. The mean blood pressure during the whole of each session,

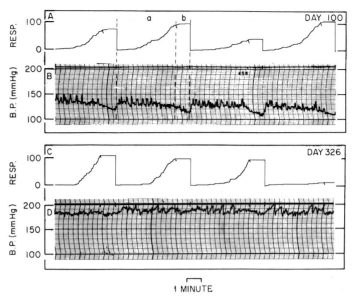

1 MINUTE

Figure 10. Characteristic patterns of key-pressing [(A) and (C)] and changes in mean arterial blood pressure [(B) and (D)] for monkey S-83 from Day 100 [(A) and (B)] and from Day 326 [(C) and (D)] under a fixed-interval schedule in which electric shocks were scheduled to occur every 15 sec. after 4 min. had elapsed in the presence of a white light; the first key-pressing response after 4 min. turned off the light. (A) and (C) show cumulative recordings of key-pressing responses. The recording pen reset to the bottom of the record when the light was turned on automatically (beginning of period a). The short diagonal strokes show where the light was turned off and the 1-min. time-out period began (b). (B) and (D) show polygraph records of mean arterial blood pressure. The pause followed by increasing key-pressing in the presence of the light is characteristic of performance on fixed-interval schedules. No electric shocks were presented during the time shown in these records. Note that on Day 100 the blood pressure was consistently higher when the light was on, but it remained within the control range; on Day 326, the blood pressure remained elevated above control levels. (From Herd et al., 1969, with permission.)

mean rates of key-pressing (R/sec.), and electric shocks delivered (S/hr.) are shown for each day. Before behavioral experiments began, control observations were made for several days. In the blood pressure diagram in Figure 11, the solid horizontal line indicates mean arterial pressure during the control period; the dashed horizontal lines indicate one standard deviation from the mean. These values are similar to those obtained with other squirrel monkeys (Herd et al., 1969). In this monkey, the blood pressure was higher under the fixed-interval schedule than under the fixed-ratio schedule.

In other monkeys, however, there was some relation between the rate at which the monkey pressed a key and the level of its mean arterial blood pressure; squirrel monkeys with a high rate of responding tended to have

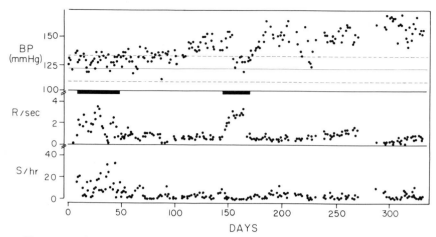

Figure 11. Changes in daily mean arterial blood pressure of monkey S-83 during prolonged training under fixed-ratio (solid bar) and fixed-interval schedules (absence of bar). The scatter diagrams show (from top to bottom) mean arterial blood pressure in mm Hg (BP), rate of key-pressing in responses per sec. (R/sec.), and rate of delivery of electric shocks in shocks per hour (S/hr.). In the blood pressure diagram, the solid horizontal lines indicate mean arterial pressure during the control period and the dashed horizontal lines indicate one standard deviation from the mean. In the late phases of the experiment, the monkey had elevated blood pressure during the whole of each session even though few electric shocks (S/hr.) were delivered.

elevated blood pressure (Herd *et al.*, 1969). Some additional behavioral factors may be important in the production of sustained hypertension. Those elevations in mean arterial blood pressure that were relatively independent of rates of key-pressing or delivery of noxious stimuli seemed to be more closely related to the consistency of the monkey's daily performance. Sustained hypertension occurred only in monkeys whose behavior was continuously and reproducibly controlled by the experimental conditions.

The scheduling of electric shocks also affects the magnitude and duration of hypertension, but there is no simple relation between frequency of their delivery and the level of mean arterial blood pressure. All animals received the greatest number of electric shocks in the early stages of the experiment, but arterial pressures were not elevated at that time. The occasional delivery of electric shocks may not even be a necessary part of these experiments. Comparable temporal patterns of responding in the squirrel monkey can be maintained by appropriately scheduling presentation of either food or electric shock (Kelleher & Morse, 1964). Further, the results shown in Figure 5 indicate that episodic increases in blood pressure can be associated with behavior under fixed-ratio schedules of food presentation.

Behavioral hypertension in the squirrel monkey has many similarities to the clinical course described for patients with essential hypertension. In early phases of training, arterial blood pressures measured through catheters in the abdominal aorta of squirrel monkeys rose transiently during periods in which each monkey pressed a key controlled by delivery of food or noxious stimuli. During time-out periods, blood pressure returned to control values. After several months of daily sessions on certain schedules of reinforcement, mean arterial blood pressure was elevated before, during, and after each session. In some monkeys, mean arterial blood pressure measured continuously was found to be elevated 24 hr./day. This sequence of changes in systemic arterial blood pressure, progressing over a four- to eight-month period, is remarkably similar to that described in some patients with essential hypertension. Normal blood pressure initially was interrupted by transient hypertension and eventually replaced by sustained hypertension. Thus the behavioral induction of hypertension may provide the opportunity to study cardiovascular control mechanisms during the hypertensive state.

### ACKNOWLEDGMENTS
We thank Professors A. C. Barger and P. B. Dews for their advice and encouragement, Mr. Lionel King and Mrs. Carolyn Fishken for technical assistance, and Miss Eleanor Bates for help in preparation of the manuscript. This work was supported by U. S. Public Health Service Grants HE 09154 (CV), HE 13346, MH 02094, MH 07658, and NASA Grant No. 22 007 137. W. H. Morse was the recipient of Research Career Program Award 5-K3-GM-15,530 from the National Institutes of Health. J. Alan Herd was the recipient of Research Career Program Award 1-KO-MH-13,414 from the National Institute of Mental Helath. R. T. Kelleher was the recipient of Research Career Program Award 5-K3-MH-22,589 from the National Institute of Mental Health.

## REFERENCES

Azrin, N. H., Holz, W. C., Hake, D. F., & Allyon, T. Fixed-ratio escape reinforcement. *Journal of the Experimental Analysis of Behavior*, 1963, 6, 449-456.

Brod, J., Fencl, V., Hejl, Z., & Jirka, J. Circulatory changes underlying blood pressure elevation during acute emotional stress (mental arithmetic) in normotensive and hypertensive subjects. *Clinical Science*, 1959, **18**, 269-279.

Dawber, T. R., & Kannel, W. B. Atherosclerosis and you: Pathogenetic implications from epidemiologic observations. *Journal of the American Geriatrics Society*, 1966, 10, 805-821.

Eich, R. H., Cuddy, R. P., Smulyan, H., & Lyons, R. H. Hemodynamics in labile hypertension. A follow-up study. *Circulation*, 1966, 34, 299-307.

Finkielman, S., Worcel, M., & Agrest, A. Hemodynamic patterns in essential hypertension. *Circulation*, 1965, 31, 356-368.

Folkow, B., & Rubinstein, E. H. Cardiovascular effects of acute and chronic stimulations of the hypothalmic defence area in the rat. *Acta Physiologica Scandinavica*, 1966, **68**, 48-67.

164       W. H. MORSE, J. A. HERD, R. T. KELLEHER, AND S. A. GROSE

Forsyth, R. P. Blood pressure responses to long-term avoidance schedules in the restrained rhesus monkey. *Psychosomatic Medicine,* 1969, 31, 300-309.
Frank, C. W., Weinblatt, E., Shapiro, S., & Bager, R. Prognosis of men with coronary heart disease as related to blood pressure. *Circulation,* 1968, 38, 432-437.
Henry, J. P., Meehan, J. P., & Stephens, P. M. The use of psychosocial stimuli to induce prolonged systolic hypertension in mice. *Psychosomatic Medicine,* 1967, 29, 408-432.
Herd, J. A., Morse, W. H., Kelleher, R. T., & Jones, L. G. Arterial hypertension in the squirrel monkey during behavioral experiments. *American Journal of Physiology,* 1969, 217, 24-29.
Hess, W. R. The Functional Organization of the Diencephalon. New York: Grune & Stratton, 1957.
Julius, S., & Conway, J. Hemodynamic studies in patients with borderline blood pressure elevation. *Circulation,* 1968, 38, 282-288.
Kelleher, R. T., & Morse, W. H. Escape behavior and punished behavior. *Federation Proceedings,* 1964, 23, 808-817
Kelleher, R. T., & Morse, W. H. Determinants of the specificity of behavioral effects of drugs. *Ergebnisse der Physiologie,* 1968a, 60, 1-56.
Kelleher, R. T., & Morse, W. H. Schedules using noxious stimuli. III. Responding maintained with response-produced electric shocks. *Journal of the Experimental Analysis of Behavior,* 1968b, 11, 819-838.
Kelleher, R. T., & Morse, W. H. Schedules using noxious stimuli. IV. An interlocking shock-postponement schedule in the squirrel monkey. *Journal of the Experimental Analysis of Behavior,* 1969, 12, 1063-1079.
Levy, A. M., Tabakin, B. S., & Hanson, J. S. Hemodynamic responses to graded treadmill exercise in young untreated labile hypertensive patients. *Circulation,* 1967, 35, 1063-1072.
McCubbin, J. W., Green, J. H., & Page, I. H. Baroceptor functions in chronic renal hypertension. *Circulation Research,* 1956, 4, 205-210.
Morse, W. H., & Kelleher, R. T. Schedules using noxious stimuli. I. Multiple fixed-ratio and fixed-interval termination of schedule complexes. *Journal of the Experimental Analysis of Behavior,* 1966, 9, 267-290.
Morse, W. H., & Kelleher, R. T. Schedules as fundamental determinants of behavior. *In* Theory of Reinforcement Schedules (W. N. Schoenfeld, Ed.). Appleton-Century-Crofts, New York, 1970.

# 9

## Pathological Inhibition
## of Emotional Behavior[1]

### H. D. KIMMEL
University of South Florida

## I. INTRODUCTION

The study of the basic principles and processes of behavior change, or learning, is manifestly the study of normal behavior. The basic laws evolving from this research are, at once, descriptive of the growth and elaboration of all of the nuances of individual, intraspecies, and interspecies behavioral variation and of the general features of commonality and sameness that cut across individuals and species. In this psychology of normal behavioral growth and change there can be no true nomothetic-idiographic distinction, since the general principles purport to and should be able to comprehend *both* the similarities and the differences in behavioral potential which naturally develop. Thus, the law of effect applies to fish as well as men and is a fundamental factor in all chordate and probably subchordate behavioral processes, just as gravity has its influence on and is a property of all matter. Yet, the individual man and the individual raindrop bear idiographic scrutiny since the particular manner in which the behavior of each differs idiosyncratically from that of others of its class is the result of the operation of so great a number and variety of factors including chance.

Behavior pathology, whether defined normatively or in relation to species or individual adaptation, is just as "natural" as any other behavior and exemplifies the same general laws. In infectious disease, for example, the natural defensive processes of the body produce most, if not all, of the symptoms of the "pathology." The local inflammation or swelling of tissue, the concentration of white cells, the elevation of body temperature and general adrenergic action, and the pain and systemic weakness themselves are all manifestations of natural

[1] This work was supported in part by USPHS grant No. MH16839-02.

adaptation to natural events. Usually, these processes have an ultimately adaptive result and the individual throws off the invasion and recovers its "health." Yet, not infrequently, the very process which most often has an adaptive consequence may itself increase the likelihood of death or reduce the likelihood of species propagation. Prolonged elevation of body temperature may lead to brain damage, sterility, or even death; rejection of foreign tissue may prevent recovery from necessary surgical transplantation, etc.

Whether he be Freudian or Skinnerian, the psychologist has assumed that the development of those behavioral adjustments that are said to be psychopathological (a paradoxical use of the term "adjustment") involves the same basic natural processes and exemplifies the same laws as are relevant to the growth of "normal" behavior. An unresolved oedipus conflict may underlie the Texas Tower murders, via projection and displacement, or the nine Beethoven symphonies, via sublimation. Similarly, a healthy avoidance of hot stoves or dangerous snakes may reflect some of the same developmental factors as a phobic inability to go into a kitchen or out of doors.

The primary purpose of this paper is to describe and analyze the seemingly pathological consequences of a common conditioning phenomenon which ordinarily appears to be quite psychobiologically adaptive. The normal process, which has only recently been given systematic experimental attention, has been called "management" of conditioned fear (Kimmel, 1963); its pathological version, if such a differentiation is meaningful, has been studied under the label, "learned helplessness" (Maier, Seligman, & Solomon, 1967).

A second purpose of this paper is to consider the general proposition that the critical factor which determines whether or not a normally adaptive process generates maladaptive consequences is extrinsic to the basic process, itself. It may be either extra- or intraorganismic, but is essentially adventitious as regards its coincidence with the original process.

## II. MANAGEMENT OF CONDITIONED FEAR

There are few behavioral characteristics of living organisms more patently adaptive than their capacity to learn to fear formerly indifferent stimuli which are associated with painful events. Simple fear conditioning is both rapid and ubiquitous and its basic principles have been generally known to man for some time, certainly since long before Pavlov first began the formal study of classical salivary conditioning in dogs.

Yet, as adaptively urgent as it may be for the organism to learn to react with emotion to events signaling impending danger and, thus, to differentiate them from those other stimuli of safer significance, fear reactions, themselves, do little or nothing to prevent harm or to prepare the organism for its occurrence. In fact, since proprioceptive feedback from the fear reaction is itself aversive to the organism, the persistence of learned fear reactions in unavoidable-inescapable pain situations would be biologically wasteful, if not downright self-punitive. The only circumstances in which conditioned fear reactions should be expected to persist through repeated elicitations are those in which an adaptive instrumental response is both available and utilized by the organism to prevent or attenuate the painful event. From this point of view, there is nothing "paradoxical" about the "avoidance paradox." Rather, its opposite is what would be paradoxical.

As reasonable as the foregoing argument may appear, its utilization to explain a number of known conditioning phenomena is relatively recent (Kimmel, 1963; 1965). It has been known for many years that the classically conditioned galvanic skin response (GSR) in humans is both easily extinguishable and subject to diminution even during continued acquisition trials (e.g., Grings, 1960). A typical example of the course of conditioned GSR magnitude over repeated paired presentations of a previously indifferent stimulus and a painful electric shock is shown in Figure 1.

Two curves of GSR magnitude are shown in Figure 1, one depicting the average response of a group of Ss receiving paired presentations of tone and shock and the other from a group of Ss receiving unsystematically ordered, unpaired tones and shocks. The tone was 4.0 sec. in duration and quite mild in intensity. The shock was set at an intensity reported by the S to be definitely annoying. As is shown in Figure 1, the paired condition brings about very rapid acquisition of the tendency to make a GSR to the tone, prior to the time of delivery of the shock, but this tendency begins to fade dramatically after about eight conditioning trials. By the time the Ss had received twenty paired trials

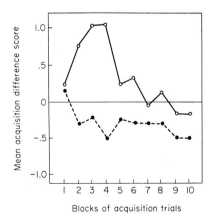

Figure 1. Magnitude of anticipatory GSR in Ss receiving paired (O) or unpaired (●) acquisition trials, averaged in two-trial blocks.

they were no longer making reliably larger GSRs to the tone than were the unpaired controls.

Data of this type do not mean that the subjects who have been receiving paired tones and shocks begin to "forget" the learned association between tone and shock. In the present context, this tendency for the rapidly acquired fear reaction to disappear (in the sense that the tone loses its ability to elicit a large anticipatory GSR), is interpretable as a manifestation of the organism's adaptive adjustment to the inescapability and unavoidability of the shock. Although there is more for the S to fear in this situation than fear itself, at least his anticipatory fear can be managed and inhibited. The relationship between this kind of inhibitory phenomenon and Pavlovian "inhibition of delay" is far more than superficial since the latency of the conditioned response has been shown to increase at the same time that its magnitude decreases, and also since the phenomenon of diminution of the conditioned response occurs in fewer trials under longer interstimulus intervals than under shorter ones.

As has already been noted, once the rapid inhibition of the ineffective and intrinsically aversive conditioned fear reaction is viewed in the context of the organism's adaptive economy, the "avoidance paradox" becomes unparadoxical. When the initially conditioned fear reaction is given instrumental consequences, e.g., if the subject is able to prevent the electric shock by making an anticipatory GSR to the tone, diminution of the conditioned fear reaction is no longer found (Baxter & Kimmel, 1964). Nor is it observed if the electric shock is omitted and the tone presented alone as soon as the peak of the GSR magnitude function is reliably identified (Silver & Kimmel, 1969; Schramm & Kimmel, 1970). As has been observed by Solomon and Wynne (1954), the remarkable persistence of skeletal avoidance behavior in the absence of primary aversive stimuli presupposes the preservation of the conditioned fear which motivates the skeletal avoidance response. The only "new" dimension added in the present discussion is the possibility that the fear response itself resists inhibition if *it* is made instrumental in the prevention of shock.

The possibility exists, also, that inhibition of the conditioned fear reaction in unavoidable-inescapable shock situations may have additional adaptive benefits to the organism. Paired presentations of conditioned and unconditioned stimuli in eyelid, GSR, and cardiac conditioning situations have been shown to result in marked diminution of the unconditioned responses also (Kimble & Ost, 1961; Kimmel & Pennypacker, 1962; Fitzgerald, 1966). Although the evidence on whether this reduction in the magnitude of the unconditioned response is accompanied by a reduction in its experienced aversiveness is equivocal (Kimmel, 1967), aversion associated with proprioception from the unconditioned response itself must surely be attenuated as a consequence of diminution of the response.

The notion that unconditioned response diminution results from the same adaptive adjustment to inevitable pain as does conditioned response diminution and is closely tied to the futility of the situation gains strong support from the observation (Kimmel, 1965) that unconditioned response diminution is not found in a conditioning situation in which the occurrence of the anticipatory fear reaction has the instrumental consequence of preventing the electric shock, i.e., in a GSR avoidance conditioning procedure. In the study in question, one group of Ss received paired tones and shocks only on those trials on which an anticipatory conditioned GSR failed to occur. If the fear reaction indexed by the conditioned GSR occurred during the interstimulus interval, no shock was delivered on that trial. Yoked control Ss were run who received paired tones and shocks and unpaired tones on appropriate trials as determined by the behavior of the avoidance Ss with whom they were yoked. In spite of the fact that unconditioned response diminution has been shown to be reduced under partial reinforcement conditions (Fitzgerald, 1966), the partially reinforced yoked control Ss in this human GSR experiment showed some diminution of the unconditioned response while the avoidance Ss showed none at all. Presumably, the adaptive inhibitory process which develops in unavoidable-inescapable shock circumstances, resulting in attenuation of both the conditioned and unconditioned reactions, does not occur when the performance of the conditioned response is given instrumental consequences, as in avoidance or escape situations.

That complex organisms are able to adjust effectively and rather rapidly to the double jeopardy of persistent fear under conditions of unavoidable-inescapable pain, and to inhibit both the learned anticipatory fear reaction and the unlearned reaction to the painful stimulus, is in no way maladaptive. Rather, it exemplifies the remarkable docility of the nervous system in adjusting to the unusually hostile environmental conditions. But, as is shown below, adaptive adjustments of the type in question may have quite maladaptive consequences under certain circumstances.

## III. PATHOLOGICAL INHIBITION

The potential pathology inherent in the tendency to inhibit conditioned and unconditioned responses in classical conditioning, oddly enough, was first noted in appetitive salivary conditioning in dogs (Kupalov, 1961). Under conditions of long temporal intervals between the conditioned and unconditioned stimuli, with the conditioned stimulus remaining on during the long delay, the anticipatory secretion of saliva begins to occur later and later following the onset of the conditioned stimulus and the magnitude of the response is attenuated. With protracted training of this type, the S may eventually cease responding entirely, both to the conditioned stimulus and, of greater significance, even to the food unconditioned stimulus. In an extreme case of this type, Kupalov found that the S did not salivate even when eating in its home cage. Apparently, no evidence of response diminution is shown in salivary conditioning when the conditioned response is instrumental in producing reward (Miller & Carmona, 1967), up to 30 days of such training, with a slight reduction in responding beyond that point.


IV. LEARNED HELPLESSNESS

Research on the effects of unavoidable-inescapable shock using subhuman subjects, because of the higher intensities and numbers of shocks that may be employed, has been most clear in illustrating the maladaptive consequences of initially adaptive response-inhibition. In a study comparing the effects of escapable and inescapable shock, Seligman and Maier (1967) ran one group of dogs in a Pavlovian harness which permitted the S to terminate shock by pressing a panel with its head or nose. The shock was unsignaled. Another group of Ss served as yoked controls, receiving exactly the same number and duration of shocks as the Ss in the first group, but with no opportunity to perform instrumentally with respect to shock duration. A third group of Ss received no shocks at all in this stage of the experiment. The Ss which were able to make the panel press to escape the shock demonstrated efficient acquisition of this response option. Their reaction latencies became minimal and the response itself was finally a single, precise head movement.

The yoked control Ss, in contrast, obviously could not acquire the panel press response. Moreover, after about 30 trials of inescapable shock, these Ss typically assumed a motionless, supine posture in which they seemed to accept their plight passively and "take" the shock. Under the circumstances, this behavioral adjustment to unavoidable and inescapable shock ("uncontrollable," in the language of Maier, Seligman, & Solomon, 1967) is quite analogous to the management of conditioned fear shown in the GSRs of classically conditioned human Ss. And, it too must be considered to be the most adaptive option available to the organism in this difficult situation. The unconditioned skeletal reaction to the shock is likely to be minimal under conditions of completely passive relaxation. In fact, the animal jerked and whimpered, but ceased to howl and jump about when the shock was delivered. Furthermore, the anticipatory condtioned fear, which might be expected to increase steadily from an immediately postshock minimum to an immediately preshock maximum (Brown, Meryman, & Marzocco, 1956) is also apparently inhibited. In a manner of speaking, the S's learned helplessness adjustment to an unavoidable-inescapable shock situation is somewhat like self-taught Wolpian desensitization, in the sense that the probability of anxiety (fear) is inversely related to the extent that relaxation is accomplished by the S.

The same kind of helplessness is displayed by dogs given repeated paired presentations of an indifferent stimulus and an intense electric shock (Overmier & Seligman, 1967). In addition, the effect does not depend upon shock frequency or duration parameters.

As adaptive as the learned helplessness pattern may be in a situation of inevitable and inescapable shock, a single session containing 64 such trials may render the S totally unable subsequently to acquire an instrumental or avoidance response when such an option is made available. The Ss given preliminary presentations of unavoidable-inescapable shock, either signaled or unsignaled, do not acquire a shuttlebox avoidance response (Seligman & Maier, 1967; Overmier & Seligman, 1967). In fact, of 87 dogs studied in Solomon's laboratory, two-thirds do not even escape from the shock during its entire 50-sec. duration (Maier, Seligman, & Solomon, 1967). Instead, these Ss persist in their previously acquired helplessness pattern, now a decidely maladaptive state of affairs.

There are a number of important related findings regarding this phenomenon of interference with the acquisition of shuttlebox avoidance learning (or, even, learning to escape the 50-sec. shock). It does not appear to be due to simple adaptation to shock, since escapable shock does not produce an interference effect, nor does an abrupt increase in shock intensity from 4.5 to 6.5 mA. (Overmier & Seligman, 1967). Furthermore, the failure to escape may be overcome by dragging the dog over the barrier and, thus, exposing it repeatedly to the escape and avoidance contingencies (Seligman, Maier, & Geer, 1968). Peculiarly, a dog which has first been given the inescapable shocks and then placed in the avoidance shuttlebox, and which *occasionally* jumps over the barrier on its own in time to escape or avoid, does not then learn to adopt the adaptive option of continued escape or avoidance. This difference may be due to the number and distribution of trials of this type.

Since the possibility exists that the learned helplessness response and the subsequent interference with the acquisition of an adaptive avoidance response may be due to the S's having learned a competing skeletal response pattern during the preliminary shock session which is incompatible with the performance of the barrier-jumping response, Overmier and Seligman (1967) attempted to produce the interference effect in curarized dogs. During the preliminary session of inescapable shock, their Ss were completely paralyzed by d-Tubocurarine. The Ss, thus, could neither move nor change their muscular tonus during the inescapable shock presentations. Obviously, there was no way to determine during this period whether helplessness was developing since the Ss were already completely immobilized due to the curarization. When these Ss were placed subsequently in the shuttlebox, in an uncurarized state, they were no different from Ss given preliminary inescapable shocks without being curarized. In other words, even though the S was unable to perform any particular muscular adjustments during the inescable shock session, it displayed learned helplessness when uncurarized and placed in the shuttlebox and this resulted in interference with either escape or avoidance behavior. Control Ss which were curarized and kept in the Pavlov harness, but not preshocked, showed no impairment of their ability to acquire escape and avoidance behavior. As Maier, Seligman, and Solomon (1967) have pointed out in discussing this finding, ". . . the unknown mechanism for this must be central to the myoneural junction."

The relationship between the phenomena of learned helplessness and fear-inhibition seems quite clear to this writer. The only adaptive response option available to a dog which is forced to receive a series of signaled or unsignaled inescapable-unavoidable shocks is to *relax*, or to *inhibit* the aversive fear response. It must be emphasized that *relaxing* and *inhibiting fear* are operationally identical descriptions of the same observable behavior, as well as reflecting the same neurophysiological state. Neither precedes nor causes the other since the reciprocal inhibition which characterizes autonomic nervous system functioning directly implies that relaxation and inhibition of fear are manifestations of one and the same autonomic state.


## V. INTERFERENCE IN GSR AVOIDANCE CONDITIONING

The work of Solomon and his colleagues on learned helplessness and the interference it generates in the acquisition of avoidance conditioning has helped to clarify recent findings in studies of autonomic avoidance conditioning. Soon after Baxter and Kimmel (1964) reported their finding that human Ss whose anticipatory GSRs are made instrumental in preventing electric shock show significantly larger responses than were found in a group of yoked controls, Church (1964) presented a critical analysis of the yoked control design they used. His main argument was that random differences between the members of a yoked pair of Ss in responsiveness, sensitivity, classical conditionability, etc. could have the net effect of artifactually favoring the avoidance condition over the yoked control condition, thus leading to the spurious conclusion that the effect was due to instrumental conditioning. His recommendation was that either yoked control designs not be used at all or that their use be restricted to studies in which the yoked pairs of Ss could be matched in these critical and potentially contaminating variables.

In order to match subjects in classical conditionability, it is, of course, necessary to present at least a few classical conditioning trials, so that a measure of acquisition is available for each subject. We have tried to accomplish this goal in two different ways. In one study (Kimmel & Sternthal, 1967) each subject was given two preliminary classical conditioning trials prior to the initiation of the avoidance contingency, following three initial exposures to the shock (unpaired) and ten presentations of the tone (unpaired). The Ss were matched in both *responsiveness* (magnitude of the GSR to the unpaired tone prior to the classical pairing) and *conditionability* (change in the magnitude of the GSR to the tone resulting from classical pairing), following which one member of each pair was run in an avoidance procedure while the other served as his yoked control. Since the matching procedure was done during actual data-collection, i.e., in real time, some of the pairs turned out to be less well matched than others. When the magnitude of the GSRs of the 19 best-matched pairs of subjects were examined, it was clear that the difference between avoidance and yoked control Ss was considerably smaller than had previously been found by Baxter and Kimmel (1964) and Kimmel, Sternthal, and Strub (1966), although it was in the same direction as in the earlier studies. As was noted by Kimmel and Sternthal, ". . . the manner in which it was necessary to conduct the experiment to obtain acceptable measures of responsivity and conditionability (especially the latter) probably reduced the possiblity of achieving avoidance conditioning . . .." "The Ss could not avoid the shock until the third acquisition trial in this experiment. The inability to avoid on the first two acquisition trials may have *interfered*[2] with the development of an avoidance response, especially since Ss may demonstrate attentuation of the CR very early in classical GSR conditioning" (1967, pp. 145-146, italics not in original).

Because it seemed possible that very rapid development of an adaptive inhibitory adjustment to inescapable-unavoidable shock might have been responsible for the reduced avoidance conditioning found by Kimmel and Sternthal (1967), a different approach to dealing with the criticism raised by Church (1964) was undertaken in a subsequent experiment on GSR avoidance conditioning (Kimmel, Kimmel, & Silver, 1969). In this study, 72 Ss were run in a classical conditioning procedure involving paired presentations of light and shock and were next run in an avoidance procedure, the latter occurring some two months after the conclusion of the classical conditioning session. In the initial session two different shock intensities were used with subgroups of 36 Ss each, and the classical conditioning acquisition was followed immediately by eight extinction trials. The Ss were run with the same shock intensity in both sessions and the avoidance contingency was implemented throughout the second session from the very first trial.

It was reasoned that the use of an extinction procedure following the classical acquisition of the first session would "wipe out" any learned inhibition of fear that might have developed. Thus, it was assumed, we would be able to obtain the measures of classical conditionability that were needed to match Ss for the subsequent avoidance session, but would still be able to study the acquisition of avoidance responding uncontaminated by any inhibition resulting from the

[2] We were quite unaware of the work then underway in Solomon's laboratory when this statement was written. Our use of the term "interfered" is obviously quite the same as Solomon's.

classical acquisition. As is shown in Figure 2, however, this reasoning must have been faulty. Neither the strong nor the weak UCS conditions produced superiority of the avoidance group as compared with their yoked classical controls, in contrast with what had previously been found in avoidance studies which did not involve preliminary classical pairing (Baxter & Kimmel, 1964; Kimmel, Sternthal, & Strub, 1966). In fact, the present use of a complete

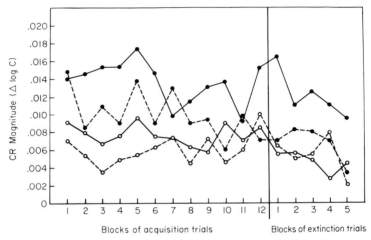

Figure 2. Magnitude of anticipatory GSR during acquisition and extinction in avoidance and yoked control conditions. Classical: strong (●──●), weak (○──○); avoidance: strong (● ─ ─ ─ ●), weak (○ ─ ─ ─ ○).

classical acquisition and extinction procedure resulted in even greater reduction of the magnitude of the avoidance groups' responses than had occurred in Kimmel and Sternthal's (1967) study. Inspection of Figure 2 shows that, if anything, the yoked classical controls made larger responses than the avoidance Ss did.

Even with a two-month interval between sessions and in spite of the use of an extinction procedure following the initial classical acquisition, the Ss showed significant spontaneous recovery on the first two trials of the second session (none of the Ss received a shock on the first trial of the second session since all of the avoidance subjects made criterion responses on that trial and thus prevented the shock). Additionally, the Ss who had been run in the first session with the strong shock showed significantly greater spontaneous recovery than those run with the weak shock. Thus, it seemed likely that our hope that the extinction procedure would be effective in eliminating the consequences of the preliminary classical procedure was not realized. It may be that the human adults who have served as Ss in our studies develop inhibition of fear in inescapable-unavoidable shock situations so rapidly that even a single classical conditioning trial will interfere with the acquisition of an avoidance response.

A recent study by Lucas (1971) provides further illustration of the futility of attempts to achieve instrumental reinforcement effects following even highly controlled and brief preliminary classical GSR conditioning. On the assumption that the best early objective sign of inhibition of conditioned fear is diminution of the conditioned response, Lucas gave his human Ss classical conditioning trials only until it could be determined reliably that the magnitude of the anticipatory GSR had reached its peak value, i.e., two trials past the peak response, a procedure which has been shown to produce maximal resistance to extinction (Silver & Kimmel, 1969; Schramm & Kimmel, 1970). The Ss were then divided into subgroups to receive one of three different procedures:

1. an instrumental procedure in which the anticipatory GSR resulted in immediate termination of the conditioned stimulus;

2. a yoked control procedure in which each S received varying durations of the conditioned stimulus determined by the performance of the instrumental S with whom he was yoked; and

3. a regular extinction procedure, with the full 8.0-sec. duration of the conditioned stimulus that had been used for all three groups during classical conditioning acquisition.

None of the Ss received shock during the second phase of the experiment.

It was assumed that the Ss in the first condition described above would display greater resistance to extinction, because of the instrumental reinforcement expected to result from the contingency relationship between their performance of an anticipatory fear reaction and the termination of the conditioned fear stimulus. The yoked control Ss were receiving what may be described as an extinction procedure with varying durations of the conditioned stimulus. The Ss in the third condition were expected to display a standard extinction curve. No reliable differences were found among the three groups of Ss, either in average number of trials to a criterion of two consecutive nonresponses or in average magnitude of the anticipatory GSR. No evidence whatsoever for an instrumental response-maintenance effect was obtained. In the present context, these results may be viewed as still another manifestation of the way in which preliminary inescapable shock interferes with the later adoption of an instrumental response option, even, as in Lucas' study, when an effort was made to minimize the development of inhibition during the initial classical procedure. If the present line of reasoning is correct, it must be assumed that inhibition of fear develops sufficiently rapidly to produce interference with subsequent instrumental responding even without being manifested in much fear-inhibition as seen in the anticipatory GSR. Using the criterion of two trials past the peak GSR is, obviously, not adequate to prevent the interference effect.

In accord with the foregoing argument, a possible additional complication associated with Lucas' study, which remains to be examined experimentally should be noted. Lucas used an interval of 8 sec. between the onsets of the conditioned and unconditioned stimuli. The prior studies which identified two trials past the peak as the most effective index of the beginning of inhibition of fear used a 5-sec. interval. Since related research has shown that inhibition develops more rapidly with longer temporal intervals between the conditioned and unconditioned stimuli (Kimmel, 1966; Morrow & Keough, 1968), it may be that fewer classical acquisition trials would have produced less interference with the expected instrumental effect.


## VI. MALADAPTIVE CONSEQUENCES OF ADAPTIVE PROCESSES

Approaches to the study and understanding of psychopathology which have emerged from the experimental and theoretical learning literature have been criticized on the grounds that what they offer are, at most, general principles, in scientific-sounding terminology, but with little more than "allegorical and superficial" relevance (Millon, 1969). It does not suffice simply to state that psychopathology is no more than a composite of learned response tendencies, based upon the reinforcement (or conditioning) history of the individual, according to this criticism. The main thrust of this negative evaluation may be exemplified by considering the following quotation from Eysenck (1960): "How, then, does modern learning theory look upon neurosis? In the first place, it would claim that neurotic symptoms are learned patterns of behavior *which for some reason or other are inadaptive*" (italics not in original). Without some suggestion of the etiological differentiation of those learned patterns of behavior which are adaptive and those which are not, a proposition such as Eysenck's is more irksome than it is illuminating.[3]

Much the same criticism may be leveled at the basic presupposition of the present paper, that "somehow" a psychobiologically adaptive process results in maladaptive behavior patterns. To be sure, the simple-minded preachment that pathology, after all, is the result of "natural" processes is of little value in comprehending the particular etiological factors resulting in bacterial infection in one exposed individual but not in another, no less in extending its mellifluous moral to psychopathogenesis as well. If the inhibition of fear in

---

[3] In fairness to Eysenck, it should be pointed out that he does go on to observe that "chance" and "environmental hazzards" must be assigned a significant role in establishing this differentiation since, he asserts, the mechanism of acquisition of, say, a healthy fear of dangerous snakes, is identical to that of a phobia for harmless furry animals. His choice of fear of snakes to illustrate an adaptive learned response tendency, nevertheless, is inept since it readily brings to mind the obvious difference between a "healthy" fear of snakes and "phobic" anxiety for the same stimulus. How now does "chance" or "environmental hazzard" play its critical role in establishing this difference?

inescapable-unavoidable shock situations is adaptive, as has been asserted above, if it interferes with the subsequent acquisition of future adaptive behavioral options, and if the environment is sufficiently fickle as to soon require such behavioral modifications, how can we argue that fear-inhibition is "adaptive"? How, indeed, can we use the term "adaptive" at all?

To eat is adaptive. But not to gorge; nor to eat paper. To sleep is adaptive. But not to sleep while driving an automobile. To love is adaptive, but not to love cloyingly, nor possessively, nor, even, too blindly. What is adaptive in one situation, on one occasion, to a certain degree, or in a particular way may be quite maladaptive otherwise. There is a critical contextual relativity involved in the meaning of "adaptive," a relativity which makes both the present suggestion that adaptive fear-inhibition interferes with adaptive avoidance learning and the Freudian notion that neurotic symptoms are adaptive in preventing anxiety but also may prevent adaptive happiness both seem somewhat foolish.

How, then, can this *neurotic paradox* be resolved? If behavior is to be viewed as a manifestation of the finely tuned adjustment of the nervous system, always tending toward the most adaptive behavioral alternative available in a particular situation, how is it that the self-punitive patterns of reaction which characterize psychopathology are maintained? Why don't they extinguish or otherwise become suppressed?

It has been implied above that simply asserting that psychopathological behavior is the result of the individual's previous learning history is no more adequate an answer to these questions than is the more traditional, pious proposal that the pathological symptoms are themselves adaptive mechanisms which stand protectively between the individual and personal disaster. Accepting the behavioristic presupposition that an individual organism behaves as it does because it has learned to behave that way and, additionally, assuming that at least some of the laws of behavior acquisition and maintenance *are* known and *do* apply to pathological as well as normal behavior, we must nevertheless ask, both generally and in particular cases, how behavior as blatantly maladaptive as that which is called psychopathological could "adaptively" come into existence and "adaptively" be maintained.

In the introduction of this paper, it was indicated that one of its purposes was to evaluate the proposition that the critical factor which determines whether or not a normally adaptive process results in maladaptive consequences is *extrinsic* to the basic process, itself. Most often, this factor may be found in the capriciousness of the organism's environment, if not its out and out conspiratorial hostility. But, sometimes, coincidental arousal of competing and incompatible behavior processes, themselves "adaptively" functioning in the organism, may be critically involved.

Experimenters are no more ingenious than nature in arranging situations which conspire against the organism's well-being. The development of a phobia is not, as some have argued, merely an instance of fear conditioning, since conditioned fear as it is known in the laboratory is so unlike phobic panic and tends to be so easily extinguishable. Phobic fear is defined, in part, by its great persistence. Furthermore, phobic fear tends to be irrational, while conditioned fear is obviously based upon an objectively painful recent history, although the mechanism of its acquisition is probably not in any way cognitive. The adaptive acquisition of conditioned fear must *somehow* interact with external or other internal factors, if it is to provide the model for the development of phobias. The use of the word "somehow," clearly puts us into the same potential blind alley as Eysenck's "in some way," which was quoted above. The path out of this cul de sac, it is proposed, is not to be found in the fear acquisition itself. Rather, attention should be directed to the possibility that a changing environment may create a "trap," *at some critical point* in fear acquisition, in which the performance of the fear reaction is followed closely in time by abrupt termination or removal of the conditioned aversive stimulus. If the performance of the conditioned fear response has the fortuitous effect of providing safety, and if this instrumental consequence occurs at a critical time in relation to the development of the fear reaction and prior to the development of fear inhibition, the stage may have been set for a persistent phobia. This, it may be argued, is what has recently been demonstrated, in microcosm, by Silver and Kimmel (1969), Bishop and Kimmel (1969), and Schramm and Kimmel (1970). In particular, Bishop and Kimmel found that half of their $S_3$, who had been given paired conditioning trials up to the peak GSR and then had the shock removed, did not reach an extinction criterion of two nonresponses in 50 extinction trials, even when a six-month interval occurred between acquisition and extinction and no shock at all was given in the second session.

The removal of the shock at the appropriate time is, of course, essentially adventitious in relation to the $S$'s trial-by-trial behavior. On one trial, the fear reaction is made and the shock is delivered. On the next trial, the reaction is made and the shock is absent. Except in the most subtle way, there is little in this situation which would ordinarily be called differential reinforcement, although it should be obvious that a reinforcement interpretation is what this discussion is about.

What has happened is that something in the situation has changed and the change has occurred just in time to perpetrate a positive feedback loop upon the $S$'s nervous system. The same type of entrapment is discernible in "vicious-circle" experiments and in other self-punishment research, and in Solomon's work on learned helplessness. It is significant to note, regarding the vicious circle effect (Brown, Martin, & Morrow, 1964) that it is only obtained if the transition from escape training to punished extinction occurs after a small number of escape trials and is camouflaged by beginning the punished extinction in the middle of a daily escape session. Similar observations may be made with respect to the response-potentiating effects of superimposed shock in free operant avoidance experiments (Powell & Morris, 1969) and, probably, to other situations involving appropriately-timed changes in experimental procedure.

Emotional responses are not ordinarily instrumental, as has already been noted, in the sense that they do not themselves either prevent or attenuate the punishment which was responsible for their acquisition. This is, of course, merely a special case of the broader proposition, first stated by Miller and Konorski (1928) and repeated by many others, e.g., Skinner (1938), that autonomically mediated responses are not ordinarily[4] instrumental in any way. An individual does not ordinarily modify his external environment by performing glandular, cardiac, or smooth muscle responses, although, as Miller (1969) has pointed out, emotional-circulatory or emotional-digestive patterns of reaction may be strengthened in *extraordinary* circumstances, such as in families with particular sensitivity to and fear of these types of symptoms.

What is ordinarily the case, however, is not always so. While it may be adaptive to inhibit fear in an inescapable-unavoidable shock situation, it remains adaptive to do so only as long as the circumstances are unchanged. If the change is an ordinary change, e.g., if the shock is eliminated, or if the organism is removed from the situation, no maladaptive consequences result. The adaptive process results in maladaptive consequences only when an extraordinary coupling of situational conditions occurs, and even then, as Maier, Seligman, and Solomon (1967) have shown, only when the interval between conditions is appropriately chosen.

The contextual relativity of the meaning of the word "ordinarily" is unquestionably the crux of the present approach to understanding maladaptive emotional behavior. In each individual learning history, where did the *extraordinary* transition in conditions occur? Which types of transitions are significant in which initial processes? And at what critical developmental point in the initial process must the transition occur? These are questions for future research. For the present, it is appropriate to conclude by noting that there is nothing inherently illogical in this emphasis on the extraordinary in the etiology of psychopathology, since psychopathology is itself not ordinary.

## REFERENCES

Baxter, R., & Kimmel, H. D. Avoidance conditioning of the GSR. *Journal of Experimental Psychology*, 1964, 68, 482-485.

Bishop, P. D., & Kimmel, H. D. Retention of habituation and conditioning. *Journal of Experimental Psychology*, 1969, 81, 317-321.

[4] Miller and Konorski (1928) said "naturally" instead of the more accurate "ordinarily."

Brown, J. S., Martin, R. C., & Morrow, M. C. Self-punitive behavior in the rat: Facilitative effects of punishment on resistance to extinction. *Journal of Comparative and Physiological Psychology*, 1964, 57, 127-133.

Brown, J. S., Meryman, J. W., & Marzocco, F. N. Sound-induced startle response as a function of time since shock. *Journal of Comparative and Physiological Psychology*, 1956, 49, 190-194.

Church, R. M. Systematic effect of random error in the yoked control design. *Psychological Bulletin*, 1946, 62, 122-131.

Eysenck, H. J. *Behavior therapy and the neuroses*. London: Pergamon Press, 1960.

Fitzgerald, R. D. Some effects of partial reinforcement with shock on classically conditioned heart-rate in dogs. *American Journal of Psychology*, 1966, 79, 242-249.

Grings, W. W. Preparatory set variables related to the classical conditioning of autonomic responses. *Psychological Review*, 1960, 67, 243-252.

Kimble, G. A., & Ost, J. W. P. A conditioned inhibitory process in eyelid conditioning. *Journal of Experimental Psychology*, 1961, 61, 150-156.

Kimmel, Ellen. Judgments of UCS intensity and diminution of the UCR in classical GSR conditioning. *Journal of Experimental Psychology*, 1967, 73, 532-543.

Kimmel, H. D. Management of conditioned fear. *Psychological Reports*, 1963, 12, 313-314.

Kimmel, H. D. Instrumental inhibitory factors in classical conditioning. In W. F. Prokasy (Ed.), *Classical conditioning: A symposium*. New York: Appleton-Century-Crofts, 1965. Pp. 148-171.

Kimmel, H. D. Inhibition of the unconditioned response in classical conditioning. *Psychological Review*, 1966, 73, 232-240.

Kimmel, H. D., & Pennypacker, H. S. Conditioned diminution of the unconditioned response as a function of the number of reinforcements. *Journal of Experimental Psychology*, 1962, 64, 20-23.

Kimmel, H. D., & Sternthal, H. S. Replication of GSR avoidance conditioning with concomitant EMG measurement and Ss matched in responsivity and conditionability. *Journal of Experimental Psychology*, 1967, 74, 144-146.

Kimmel, H. D., Kimmel, E. B., & Silver, A. I. The effect of UCS intensity in classical and avoidance GSR conditioning. *Conditional Reflex*, 1969, 4, 32-51.

Kimmel, H. D., Sternthal, H. S., & Strub, H. Two replications of avoidance conditioning of the GSR. *Journal of Experimental Psychology*, 1966, 72, 151-152.

Kupalov, P. S. Some normal and pathological properties of nervous processes in the brain. *Annals of the New York Academy of Sciences*, 1961, 92, 1046-1053.

Lucas, M. E. *Escape conditioning of the galvanic skin response*. Unpublished M.A. Thesis, Univ. of South Florida, 1971.

Maier, S. F., Seligman, M. E. P., & Solomon, R. L. Pavlovian fear conditioning and learned helplessness: Effects on escape and avoidance behavior of (a) the CS-US contigency and (b) the independence of US and instrumental responding. In B. A. Campbell and R. M. Church (Eds.), *Punishment and aversive behavior*. New York: Appleton-Century-Crofts, 1967. Pp. 299-342.

Miller, N. E. Learning of visceral and glandular responses. *Science*, 1969, 163, 434-445.

Miller, N. E., & Carmona, A. Modification of a visceral response, salivation in thirsty dogs, by instrumental training with water reward. *Journal of Comparative and Physiological Psychology*, 1967, 63, 1-6.

Miller, S., & Konorski, J. Sur une forme particuliere des reflexes conditionels. *Proceedings of the Biological Society* (Polish). Paris, 1928, 99, 1155-1157.

Millon, T. *Modern Psychopathology*. Philadelphia: Saunders, 1969.

Morrow, M. C., & Keough, T. E., III. GSR conditioning with long interstimulus intervals. *Journal of Experimental Psychology*, 1968, 77, 460-467.

Overmier, J. B., & Seligman, M. E. P. Effects of inescapable shock upon subsequent escape and avoidance responding. *Journal of Comparative and Physiological Psychology*, 1967, 63, 28-33.

Powell, R. W., & Morris, G. Continuous punishment of free operant avoidance in the rat. *Journal of the Experimental Analysis of Behavior*, 1969, 12, 149-157.

Schramm, C, F., & Kimmel, H. D. Resistance to extinction in GSR conditioning following different numbers of postpeak acquisition trials. *Journal of Experimental Psychology*, 1970, 84, 239-243.

Seligman, M. E. P., & Maier, S. F. Failure to escape traumatic shock. *Journal of Experimental Psychology*, 1967, 74, 1-9.

Seligman, M. E. P., Maier, S. F., & Geer, J. The alleviation of learned helplessness in dogs. *Journal of Abnormal and Social Psychology*, 1968, 73, 256-262.

Silver, A. I., & Kimmel, H. D. Resistance to extinction in classical GSR conditioning as a function of acquisition trials beyond peak CR size. *Psychonomic Science*, 1969, 14, 53-54.

Skinner, B. F. *The behavior of organisms: An experimental analysis.* New York: Appleton-Century-Crofts, 1938.

Solomon, R. L., & Wynne, L. C. Traumatic avoidance learning: The principles of anxiety conservation and partial irreversability. *Psychological Review*, 1954, 61, 353-385.

# PART 4

Psychopathology is manifested both in the individual's own self-punitive and maladaptive psychophysiology, behavior, and experience and in a breakdown in his social interactions with others. Frequently, in human psychopathology, attention is first drawn to the existence of maladjustment because of the noticeable deterioration of the social behavior of the individual concerned. Whether or not the social manifestations of pathology are what are noticed first, their significance and seriousness are undeniably great.

The three chapters in the final section of this book describe research programs in which the major manifestation of the psychopathology studied is in the social realm of the organism's behavior. Each of these research efforts also involves, as part of its experimental strategy, interventions which are distinctively of a social type. In the research described in Chapter 10, by Frank A. Logan, social manipulations are introduced following an earlier experimental stage in which individual subjects receive separate training, exemplifying the strategy described in Chapter 1. In Chpater 11, by Harry F. and Margaret K. Harlow, the basic social manipulation, partial or complete isolation, is shown to occur in the beginning of the experimental procedure or at varying times later. In Chapter 12, by Joseph B. Sidowski, an experimental social intervention referred to as "restraint" is evaluated. This procedure also is introduced in the first stage of the research, but at different ages of the animal.

Logan's first entry into the field of experimental psychopathology, although beginning somewhat accidentally, nevertheless was built on a long research history in the area of animal motivation. The peculiar breakdown in the performance of earlier learned adaptive response tendencies, shown by Logan to occur when the situation is changed from an individual one to a social one, along with the violent aggressive behavior which occurs, are both fascinating and potentially illuminating. The role of social dominance in these situations suggests a new connection between social and animal psychology, since the experimental Ss in Logan's experiments are laboratory rats.

The chapter written by the Harlows (Chapter 11) contains descriptions of social and individual behavior pathology, produced by varying degrees of social isolation, which may be as close to human psychosis as the behavior of the monkey can come. As was true of his earlier work on the development of mother-love in monkeys, the present work will probably be seen in the future as marking a new and important direction for research in experimental psychopathology.

The work described by Sidowski in Chapter 12 was also done at Harlow's

Wisconsin Regional Primate Research Center where Sidowski spent one year as a senior research scientist. Using the novel social intervention of permitting an unrestrained young monkey to explore and interact with a completely restrained one, Sidowski found a variety of potentially important social psychopathological behavioral consequences. Just as his pioneer work on the minimal social situation opened new research doors in experimental social psychology, the present work in experimental psychopathology may provide an important impetus for new experimental efforts to understand social psychological maladjustment.

# 10

# Dominance
# and Aggression[1]

## FRANK A. LOGAN

University of New Mexico

## I. INTRODUCTION

One of the basic, albeit often implicit, assumptions of experimental psychology is that the fundamental principles derived from the experimental analysis of simple learning situations will apply equally to more complex situations. This is not to deny that new principles will be discovered in the latter situations, but only to emphasize that the fundamental ones will still be relevant. Indeed, it is this assumption which justifies the strategy of first studying the simpler situations in order to have those principles available to help understand behavior in the more complex ones.

This strategy was epitomized in the work of C. Hull. The two published books of his projected trilogy, *Principles of behavior* (1943), and *A behavior system* (1952), were intended to present first the most basic principles of behavior, revealed in classical and instrumental conditioning, and then to apply these principles to more complex instances of individual behavior such as discrimination learning, avoidance conditioning, and conflict. The third book was to have extended these principles further, into the realm of social interaction, thus presumably encompassing the entire domain of mammalian behavior.

Consider in the foregoing image the familiar paradigm of avoidance conditioning. A rat is placed in a small enclosure, the grid floor of which may periodically be electrified. Preceding the shock, however, is a warning light and, if the rat responds soon enough by turning a wheel protruding into the chamber,

[1] Supported by a grant from the National Science Foundation. The author is indebted to David Governski, Barbara Lerman, Wesley Lynch, and George Taylor for assistance in running the subjects.

the light goes out and the shock is prevented. Failing that, the rat must turn the wheel to terminate (escape) the shock. Rats typically learn to avoid the impending shock, presumably on the basis of the principle of secondary negative reinforcement. That is to say, the warning light acquires secondary aversive properties as a result of being paired with the primarily aversive shock, and hence the termination of the light is reinforcing.

To be sure, this description is an oversimplification of many experimental results. Few rats learn to avoid all of the signaled shocks, and some fail to learn to avoid at all. Still more perplexing are those rats who do learn to avoid to a reasonably high level but then gradually stop avoiding (Coons, Anderson & Myers, 1960). Thus, it should not be inferred that our understanding of even the simple avoidance conditioning situation is yet even approximately complete.

Nevertheless, we may ask what should happen if two naive rats are placed in the avoidance situation together. The simplest expectation is that they would learn to avoid shock according to some combination of what each might have done individually. Although we cannot be confident of what any individual rat might have done in the chamber alone, on the average, two rats should do better than one.

But the fact is that we have never observed a pair of rats to learn to avoid shock by turning the wheel in response to the warning light! One reason for this is the fact that electric shock applied simultaneously to two rats tends to cause them to aggress against each other (Ulrich & Azrin, 1962). However, this does not prevent them from learning to turn the wheel to escape the electric shock nor does it prevent them from learning the significance of the warning signal. Apparently, whatever new principles are invoked by the presence of another rat in an avoidance context, they counteract the principle of secondary negative reinforcement.

As a beginning toward an experimental analysis of the finding that two naive rats never learn to avoid a signaled electric shock, we (Logan & Boice, 1969) paired rats that had been pretrained individually to turn the wheel in order to avoid the shock. Our principal observation was that a decrement in their avoidance behavior occurred, coupled with aggression. The present paper considers further extension of research into this phenomenon.

## II. AVOIDANCE DECREMENT AND AGGRESSION

When two rats, individually pretrained to avoid shock by turning a wheel in response to a warning light, are placed in the apparatus together, they continue to show distinct orienting responses to the onset of the warning light, accompanied by conspicuous signs of fear such as freezing, defecating, and sometimes teeth-chattering and anticipatory sqealing. However, they do not make the avoidance response that each has separately learned. With the eventual and inevitable onset of the shock, the animal independently judged to be the submissive member of the pair makes the wheel-turn response to escape the shock for both of them. If this escape response is not immediate, the shock may elicit threat and aggressive responses by the dominant S; in any event, aggression often appears following termination of the shock. These aggressive responses may be subtle, such as muzzling and crawling over-and-under, although frequently open sparring, biting, and pushing occur. One dramatic form of aggression involves mounting with pelvic thrusts mimicking sexual assault, behaviors which occur equally if both members of the pair are of the same sex, male or female, or opposite sex independent of the oestrous state of the female.

Substantially, the same phenomenon was observed in a number of pairs of rats of different species and regardless of their prior experimental history. Specifically, for example, pairing an S that had been trained to avoid the shock with a naive S did not result in continued avoidance by the trained S; instead, the submissive naive S learned and performed the escape response during the paired sessions.

It is not obvious how such a phenomenon could be derived from any simple combination of principles based on individual behavior. For example, one might attempt to account for the avoidance decrement by appeal to the principle of external inhibition. The presence of another S changes the situation from that in which pretraining occurred, possibly resulting in a stimulus generalization decrement. But subsequent tests with toys, even mechanical ones which move and make noise, produce at most a temporary decrement, whereas the decrement in question persists for as long as testing continues, up to 90 sessions. Indeed, on some occasions the decrement does not occur immediately when the Ss are first paired, but develops gradually over several paired sessions. Accordingly, external inhibition is probably involved in the phenomenon but is insufficient alone to account for it.

A similar phenomenon has been reported by Davis (1969) in a nondiscriminated avoidance context, but it is important to note that this outcome is not indigenous to all avoidance learning situations. Specifically, if rats are first trained to jump a hurdle in a one-way avoidance procedure, their subsequent pairing leads to neither avoidance decrement nor aggression. What appears to be the critical feature of this second situation is the fact that both Ss can and must make the avoidance response even when paired. That is to say, if one S fails to jump the hurdle, it receives shock until it does so. In contrast, the wheel situation presents a single manipulandum which one S may turn to avoid or escape shock for both Ss. Although this distinction requires further systematic experimental analysis, our attention was diverted from it by subsequent informal observations.

In the course of training and testing additional pairs of animals, both for demonstration and pilot purposes, it became apparent that the complete phenomenon did not always occur even in the situation employing a single manipulandum. Some pairs showed little or no avoidance decrement, even cooperating in the sense that their combined performance equaled their individual performance. Other pairs, while showing some avoidance decrement, managed to maintain a reasonable level of performance with little aggression. It is thus apparent that the effect of pairing two Ss in an avoidance context may vary from complete avoidance decrement coupled with postescape aggression, through intermediate stages, all the way to quite adaptive combined performance. The principal purpose of the series of experiments reported in this paper, therefore, was to provide at least preliminary data on the circumstances which determine the effect of pairing rodents in an avoidance context.

Our principal focus of attention was on the dominance relationship between the two paired rats. It will be recalled that it was almost invariably the submissive S that made the wheel-turn response. If this response occurred too late to avoid the shock, escape was often followed by aggression by the dominant S. The intensity of this aggression could then "feed back" further to inhibit subsequent avoidance responding and result in additional aggression. Accordingly, the phenomenon of avoidance decrement and aggression may depend not simply upon the *presence* of any two Ss in the situation, but upon their relative social dominance.

## III. EXPERIMENTAL PROCEDURES

The Ss employed in these studies were rats bred in the colony maintained at the University of New Mexico. Both hooded and albino rats, and males and females were included as available and appropriate for the various pairing conditions. They were maintained throughout the research on ad lib food and water.

Two variations of the basic avoidance apparatus were employed. One was a semicircular chamber, 48 x 18 x 20 in, the back wall of which was plywood and the circular perimeter was Plexiglas. The floor was constructed of ¼-in. stainless steel rods set ¾ in. apart. Shock was provided by a Grason–Stadler scrambler, typically set at 1 mA. A bank of six 6-W. white lights and 10 green indicator lights combined to form the warning signal against a dim background illumination. A 6-in. diameter wheel mounted on the back wall of the apparatus provided the manipulandum, a rotation of about 1 in. breaking a microswitch and terminating shock and/or lights. Programming was accomplished with commercial timing and relay circuitry activated by a paper-tape reader.

The other apparatus was a two-compartment shuttlebox with a glass front and the remaining sides plywood. It was 18 in. high and 4 in. wide. The start chamber was 24in. long with a floor of $\frac{1}{8}$ in. stainless steel grids set $\frac{3}{8}$ in. apart. The goal chamber was 12 in. long and had a solid floor. Separating these chambers was a partition containing a 1½-in. diameter hole set 2 in. above the floor through which the $S$ had to jump to avoid or escape shock. A plywood door covering this hole prevented intertrial responses and its opening served as the warning signal. Shock was provided by a Grason–Stadler shock source set at 1 mA., the CS–US interval timed by a Hunter timer. Opening the door and other timing operations were done by the experimenter.

Dominance was determined by confining two $Ss$ in a small enclosure (9 x 3½ x 7½ in.) and applying brief pulses of electric shock until one animal made distinct attack gestures with the other animal in a defensive position. A typical posture was for the dominant animal to be physically on top of the submissive animal, with the latter partially on its back and its forepaws fending off blows. In the present research, such testing was done immediately before the first paired session and hence after any individual avoidance training.

For the main experiments, a group of 45 male $Ss$ was tested for dominance by a progressive paired-comparisons procedure. After dominance of the first two $Ss$ was determined, the third $S$ was tested first against the submissive of the original pair. If this $S$ was submissive in that pairing, it was placed lower on the scale; if not, it was tested against the dominant $S$ to determine whether it was intermediate or the most dominant. Then the fourth $S$ was tested against the intermediate $S$ and then, depending on the outcome of that test, against the dominant or submissive for further placement on the scale. This process continued until all $Ss$ had been approximately ordered on a dominance-submissive scale, after which three groups of nine $Ss$ each were formed from the top, middle, and bottom of the scale. Thus, the two intermediate groups of nine $Ss$ separating these three groups were discarded. Of course, there was variation within each group, but a second test indicated there was no overlap between the groups. The $Ss$ in these groups will be referred to as A (dominant), B (intermediate), or C (submissive).

In the wheel-turn procedure, $Ss$ were placed directly from their home cage, either individually or in pairs, in the apparatus. They were given 50 trials a day with a CS–US interval of 5 sec. and an intertrial interval of 40 sec. Avoidance responding was cumulated on electromechanical counters, but performance when paired was also monitored by the experimenter to record which animal turned the wheel and what, if any, aggression occurred. Varied amounts of training were given, as indicated below.

In the shuttle procedure, $Ss$ were placed manually into the start chamber for an average intertrial interval of 30 sec. During individual pretraining, the CS–US interval was initially 5 sec. to facilitate learning the avoidance response, and then reduced to 3 sec. before pairing. The $S$ remained in the safe compartment for 10 sec. and then was manually removed and replaced into the start chamber for the next trial. They were given 25 such trials a day, all performance scores being recorded directly by the experimenter. The procedure was the same for the first seven paired sessions, except that each S was moved first from the safe to the start compartment on alternate trials and second on the remaining trials. During four additional sessions, the door was not opened until 3 sec. after shock onset, thus requiring escape but precluding avoidance.

Avoidance and escape responses are defined as those which preceded or followed the scheduled shock. In those few cases where both Ss appeared to address the wheel, the response was credited to the one that initiated movement. For purposes of reliability, aggressive responses were scored only when one S made physical attack upon the other. Since more subtle forms of aggression such as stalking, muzzling, and looking away were not scored, the actual incidence of aggression was higher than that reported.

## IV. RESULTS

### A. Preliminary Results in the Wheel-Turn Apparatus

The performance of fifteen pairs of Ss is displayed in Table I to give some indication of the range of phenomena observed in the paired avoidance situation.

TABLE I  Data from Fifteen Pairs Run during Preliminary Research

| Pair number | Sex | Number days indiv. | Percent avoid indiv. | Number days paired | Percent avoid paired | Percent escape paired | Percent aggression by (nature) |
|---|---|---|---|---|---|---|---|
| 1 | M | 0 | — | 7 | 2 | 98 | |
|   | M | 0 | — | | | | |
| 2 | M | 0 | — | 7 | 4 | 96 | |
|   | M | 0 | — | | | | |
| 3 | M[a] | 0 | — | 5 | 0 | 0 | 7 (mounting) |
|   | F | 9 | 85 | | 80 | 20 | 0 |
| 4 | M[a] | 0 | — | 5 | 0 | 0 | 19 (mounting) |
|   | F | 9 | 60 | | 62 | 38 | 0 |
| 5 | M[a] | 30 | 78 | 3 | 26 | 74 | 2 (sparring) |
|   | F | 0 | — | | 0 | 0 | 0 |
| 6 | M[a] | 3 | 85 | 3 | 7 | 3 | 0 |
|   | M | 3 | 100 | | 73 | 17 | 0 |

TABLE I—*continued*

| Pair number | Sex | Number days indiv. | Percent avoid indiv. | Number days paired | Percent avoid paired | Percent escape paired | Percent aggression by (nature) |
|---|---|---|---|---|---|---|---|
| 7 | F[a] | 2 | 85 | 7 | 6 | 4 | 12 (mounting) |
|   | F | 2 | 60 |   | 70 | 20 | 0 |
| 8 | M[a] | 7 | 90 | 7 | 0 | 4 | 26 (mounting) |
|   | M | 7 | 85 |   | 62 | 34 | 0 |
| 9 | M[a] | 23 | 48 | 8 | 15 | 20 | 38 (sparring) |
|   | M | 8 | 40 |   | 15 | 5ſ | 0 |
| 10 | M[a] | 6 | 78 | 2 | 5 | 15 | 28 (fighting) |
|   | M | 9 | 78 |   | 25 | 55 | 27 (fighting) |
| 11 | M[a] | 4 | 88 | 3 | 0 | 25 | 13 (fighting) |
|   | M | 5 | 75 |   | 35 | 40 | 0 |
| 12 | M[a] | 7 | 23 | 7 | 0 | 7 | 10 (sparring) |
|   | M | 9 | 78 |   | 3 | 90 | 0 |
| 13 | M[a] | 3 | 85 | 3 | 7 | 17 | 30 (fighting) |
|   | M | 5 | 65 |   | 6 | 70 | 8 (fighting) |
| 14 | M[a] | 9 | 65 | 2 | 0 | 15 | 68 (mounting and |
|   | M | 7 | 23 |   | 0 | 85 | 0   fighting) |
| 15 | M[a] | 9 | 65 | 7 | 0 | 10 | 70 (fighting and |
|   | M | 6 | 78 |   | 5 | 85 | 0   mounting) |
| 6 thru | [a] | 7 | 71 | 5 | 4 | 12 | 27 |
| 15 |   | 5 | 68 |   | 29 | 55 | 7 |

[a] The dominant member of the pair.

The first two pairs received no individual pretraining and are included to illustrate the contention made earlier that naive $S$s do not learn to avoid a signaled shock. After 6 days of training, their level of avoidance was only 2% and 4% respectively the 23 $S$s given a comparable amount of *individual* training averaged over 70% avoidance. Pairs of $S$s readily learn to escape the shock, but rarely does this response become anticipatory so as to prevent the shock.

The next two pairs are included to illustrate that if the submissive member of the pair is pretrained to avoid while the dominant $S$ is naive, avoidance responding may be maintained with little or no decrement. The fifth pair, however, in which the dominant $S$ was pretrained while the submissive $S$ was naive, displayed a substantial decrement in avoidance. Hence, the effect of pretraining of one member of the pair depends on which $S$ has learned the avoidance response before pairing. More broadly, the effect depends upon the dominance relationship of the two $S$s.

The remaining ten pairs involved $S$s each of which had received some degree of individual pretraining in the avoidance response. Their data are averaged in the bottom two rows to summarize the overall effect of pairing $S$s in an avoidance context. After five to seven days of individual training, they were averaging about 70% avoidance. But after five additional days, involving pairing, their combined avoidance was only 33% coupled with clear signs of aggressive behavior on or after 34% of the trials. Hence, some avoidance decrement with aggression is the typical result of pairing $S$s in an avoidance context.

However, more detailed examination of the data indicates the range of effects that can be observed. The pairs have been ordered in the table beginning with those which showed the greatest degree of adaptive combination of their prior training down to those which showed the greatest decrement. It may be observed that in no pair did the combined avoidance performance equal the level attained by the better of the $S$s individually, and in only one pair did that performance exceed the poorer of the $S$s individually. Hence, some degree of decrement from the level that might be expected from combining their individual performances is the ubiquitous finding. It may also be observed that, regardless of the size of the decrement resulting from the pairing, it was almost invariably the case that the submissive member of the pair turned the wheel, whether performing an avoidance or an escape response. It was also mainly the dominant $S$ that initiated the overt aggressive behaviors observed.

These preliminary results thus confirm and extend earlier findings and may be summarized as follows:

1. A pair of naive $S$s do not learn to avoid when given paired training.

2. If one of the pair has been pretrained to avoid, avoidance continues if the pretrained animal is the submissive $S$ but is disrupted if it is the dominant $S$.

3. If both of the $S$s have been pretrained to avoid, the avoidance performance of the pair is invariably below the level that might be expected by simply combining the individual performances.

4. The size of the avoidance decrement and the amount of resulting aggression varies among pairs, for reasons not clearly revealed in these data.

5. The submissive $S$ makes the vast majority of the avoidance and/or escape responses.

6. The dominant $S$ initiates the vast majority of the aggressive responses elicited in the situation.

## B. Effect of Dominance on Avoidance, Escape, and Aggression

Each of four A, four B, and four C Ss was paired with each of the other eleven Ss in randomized order. The average performance of the various combinations of A, B, and C Ss is shown in Table II. It will be suggested in the next section that the effect of pairing may depend on prior pairing experience, and since the present procedure necessarily involved testing each S a number of times, the effects are probably attenuated and possibly complicated. Nevertheless, the trends are sufficiently clear to permit several conclusions. Most conspicuously, there was a substantial avoidance decrement in all pairs. The overall average of the individual avoidance levels of the twelve Ss was about 60% before the pairing tests began, which may be compared with the first column of data in Table II.

The overall effect of dominance on participation in the avoidance–escape responding may be seen in the third column of Table II. Consider, for example, the dominant (A) Ss. When two such Ss were paired together, the more dominant member of that pair made 41.6% of the total responses; when an A S

TABLE II   The Averaged Results of Pairing each of Four Dominant (A), Four Intermediate (B), and Four Submissive (C) Rats with Each of the Other Rats Following Individual Pretraining

|        | Percent avoidance | Percent escape | Percent response | Percent aggression[a] |
|--------|-------------------|----------------|------------------|------------------------|
| A*     | 5.8               | 35.8           | 41.6             | 25.2                   |
| A      | 4.2               | 54.2           | 58.4             | 10.0                   |
| B*     | 28.3              | 32.5           | 60.8             | 23.3                   |
| B      | 5.8               | 33.3           | 39.1             | 3.3                    |
| C*     | 6.6               | 52.5           | 59.1             | 15.8                   |
| C      | 1.7               | 39.2           | 40.9             | 10.8                   |
| A**    | 3.1               | 30.9           | 34.0             | 31.3                   |
| B      | 7.5               | 58.4           | 65.9             | 5.0                    |
| B**    | 6.9               | 43.1           | 50.0             | 31.3                   |
| C      | 5.3               | 44.7           | 50.0             | 2.2                    |
| A***   | 4.7               | 23.1           | 27.8             | 36.6                   |
| C      | 6.3               | 65.9           | 72.2             | 1.3                    |

[a] The predominant form of aggression in each case was sparring followed by the dominant rat assuming a position on top of the submissive rat, occasionally in the form of a sexual mount.

was paired with a B *S*, the average participation dropped to 34.0%; and when paired with a C *S*, only 27.8% of the responses were made by the A *S*s. Conversely, looking at the more submissive C *S*s, we find they made 72.2% of the total responses when paired with an A *S*, 50.0% of the responses when paired with a B *S*, and 40.9% of the responses when paired with a less submissive C *S*. It is therefore clear that the extent of responding by any one *S* in the paired avoidance context depends on its degree of dominance/submission to its partner.

It is also clear that the initiation of aggression varies with dominance. Over all pairings, the A *S*s attack their partners on 28% of the occasions, the B *S*s on 17%, and the C *S*s on 5%. More interestingly, these aggressive attacks are inversely related to the extent to which the animal participates in the avoidance–escape responding. Specifically, the dominant A *S*s attack another A *S* on 25.2% of the trials, but attack a B *S* on 31.3% of the trails and a C *S* on 36.6% of the trials. And the submissive C *S*s rarely attack an A or a B *S* (1.3% and 2.2% respectively) but attack a dominant C *S* on 10.8% of the trials.

Accordingly, we may now extend and refine the previous conclusions as follows:

7. The participation of a rat in avoidance–escape responding in the paired avoidance context depends on the relative degree of dominance–submission between the members of the pair: the greater one *S*'s dominance over the other, the less he participates in the instrumental response.

8. The initiation of aggression also depends on the relative degree of dominance–submission between the pair: more aggressive attacks occur by the dominant *S* the greater his dominance, and more aggressive attacks occur by the submissive *S* the less his submissiveness.

## C. Effects of Prior Pairings on Paired Avoidance Behavior

Three B *S*s were repeatedly paired with an A and a C *S*, and their performance is displayed in Table III. As a basis for evaluation of these data, it will be recalled from the previous table that, on the average, the B *S*s make about 50% of the responses when paired with a C *S* and 66% of the responses when paired with an A *S*.

In the first trio, the B *S* was paired with the A and the C *S* each day. As a result of his exposure to the dominance and aggression by the A *S*, his responding with the C *S* was greater than typical (66% versus 50%). A similar but more extreme result occurred in the second trio where the B *S* was first run six sessions with the A *S* before being paired with the C *S*. In this case, his responding accounted for 95% of the total avoidance–escape responses even though he was the dominant *S* and initiated many aggressive attacks. An effect in the opposite direction can be seen in the third trio, where the B *S* was first

TABLE III  The Effect of One Pairing on Performance in Another Paired Avoidance Situation[a]

| | Individual avoidance | Paired avoidance | | Paired escape | | Percent aggression | |
|---|---|---|---|---|---|---|---|
| A** | 60 | 6 | | 12 | | 48 | |
| B* | 64 | 10 | 0 | 72 | 66 | 0 | 12 |
| C | 38 | | 26 | | 8 | | 12 |
| | | | | | | | |
| A** | 60 | 10 | | 30 | | 45 | |
| B* | 75 | 5 | 20 | 55 | 75 | 15 | 40 |
| C | 35 | | 0 | | 5 | | 0 |
| | | | | | | | |
| A** | 35 | | 5 | | 40 | | 45 |
| B* | 65 | 0 | 0 | 20 | 55 | 55 | 35 |
| C | 35 | 10 | | 70 | | 0 | |

[a] In the first set, $S$ B* was given two sessions each day, one with A** and one with C, alternating which was first. In the second set, $S$ B* was first given six sessions daily with $S$ A**, and then an additional six daily sessions with $S$ C. In the third set, $S$ B* was first given six sessions daily with $S$ C, and then an additional six daily sessions with $S$ A**. The performance of the B* $S$ with each partner is shown in the columns corresponding to their data.

given six sessions with a C $S$ before being paired with an A $S$. In the latter pairing, he made 55% of the avoidance–escape responses and initiated substantially more aggressive attacks (35%) than customary for a B $S$ paired with an A $S$ (5%).

These effects are small in absolute size but are suggestive of the following additional conclusion:

9. The performance of an $S$ in the paired avoidance context can, to some extent, be modified by prior experience as the dominant or submissive member of a prior pairing, affecting his performance appropriately in relation to that experience.

## D. Paired One-Way Shuttle Behavior

Six $S$s were paired in A-B, B-C, and A-C combinations in the one-way shuttle situation where only one $S$ could cross the hurdle at one time and the CS–US interval was too short for both to effectively avoid the shock. Their performance is shown in Table IV. Interestingly enough, the dominant $S$ did not force his way into position at the hurdle during the intertrial interval. Instead, whichever $S$ was introduced to the start chamber nearest the hurdle remained in the position and typically responded in time to avoid the shock. This, however, did result in a

**TABLE IV**   Performance of Paired Rats in a One-Way Shuttle Apparatus Initially with Avoidance Possible and Then with an Escape Procedure

|     | Individual avoidance | Paired avoidance | Paired escape | Escape first | Avoidance aggression | Escape aggression |
| --- | --- | --- | --- | --- | --- | --- |
| A*  | 90 | 45 | 55 | 90 | 45 | 45 |
| B   | 90 | 45 | 55 | 10 | 0  | 5  |
|     |    |    |    |    |    |    |
| A*  | 45 | 30 | 70 | 70 | 30 | 40 |
| C   | 90 | 50 | 50 | 30 | 0  | 5  |
|     |    |    |    |    |    |    |
| B*  | 70 | 55 | 45 | 80 | 40 | 25 |
| C   | 85 | 10 | 90 | 20 | 0  | 20 |

substantial incidence of aggression in the safe compartment after both had completed the hurdle response. Such aggression was confined to those trials in which the submissive S had initially been placed closer to the hurdle and, hence, the dominant S received some shock before getting into the safe compartment. On such trials, aggression in the form of hitting, climbing on top of, and sexual mounting typically occurred.

When the procedure was changed to permit escape only, the effect of dominance appeared prior to crossing the hurdle. Specifically, the shock-elicited aggressive behaviors resulted in the dominant S being the most likely to cross the hurdle first. Comparable postresponse aggression was also quite common, especially on those trials where the submissive S managed to be first to escape the shock.

## V. DISCUSSION

The phenomenon of paired–avoidance decrement coupled with agression is certainly not adaptive. If a dominant S "knows" the avoidance response that is required, it would be reasonable to expect him to "take charge" and protect both itself and the submissive animal. Or even if the submissive S is required to make the response, it might reasonably do it in time to avoid the shock rather than waiting to escape it. Yet the consistency with which these expectations fail to be realized strongly suggests that fundamentally contradictory principles are operating.

Maladaptive phenomena are not easy to explain theoretically. For one committed to an evolutionary conceptualization, at least, the expectation would be that only adaptive principles would be selectively bred into any existing species. Accordingly, it would appear that several principles, each individually adaptive, are combined in unusual situations when the outcome appears maladaptive. At least, that is my basic premise.

First, let us assume that it is adaptive for organisms in a social situation to establish a "pecking order," a scale of dominance–submission. The fact that such orders are widespread among most mammalian species would indicate their survival value. The function appears to be protection of the social group. Once an order is established, it is typically no longer necessary for conflicts to occur that might result in self-destruction. In general, the dominant animal behaves as he wishes and the submissive animal behaves as he must.

Granting the adaptive value of establishing a pecking order, assume further that *maintaining dominance at all costs* is a basic principle of social interaction. We may hope that mature humans can overcome this inherent tendency, but there is no reason to believe they fully escape it. Nor is it necessary to postulate peculiarly human personality traits to account for displaying dominance; it is as natural in rats as in man. An unambiguously dominant organism tends not to respond in a way that would adulterate its dominance, even if its behavior results in exposing itself to pain. The dominant rat cannot turn the wheel; the submissive rat must do it.

Nor need the behavior of the submissive rat in not avoiding the shock require the assumption of any peculiarly human frailties such as "getting even" with the dominant rat. Instead, it can be seen to reflect the operation of two basic but conflicting anticipatory response tendencies. First, fear has been conditioned to the warning signal by association with shock, setting the occasion for secondary negative reinforcement for turning the wheel to prevent the shock. But in the paired avoidance context, shock may also elicit aggression from the dominant rat, and the unlearned anticipatory response to the threat of attack is to freeze. Freezing is incompatible with an active avoidance response, and the outcome thus depends on the relative strengths of these two anticipatory tendencies.

Specifically, for example, when both Ss are relatively equal in dominance, and especially if both are generally submissive, the severity of the ensuing attack would reasonably be low. Hence, the anticipatory tendency to freeze would be weak, enabling the avoidance response to occur. Further, since there is no clear dominance relationship within the pair, both are free to turn the wheel, reducing the incidence of shock and any ensuing aggressive behaviors. When, however, there is a clearout difference in dominance, and apparently even when they are fairly equal but both highly dominant rats, the anticipatory freezing tendency successfully competes with the avoidance tendency, leading to the extreme instance of avoidance decrement coupled with shock-induced aggression. The response of two Ss paired in an avoidance context thus depends importantly on their status in a dominance-submissive hierarchy.

It also appears that dominance is not entirely determined by genetic constitution but is modifiable as a function of social interactions. An *S*'s prior experience as the dominant or submissive member of one pair can, to some extent, affect his subsequent behavior when paired with a new *S*. How extreme and prolonged such changes may become is still a matter of conjecture, but a *S* might become more dominant or more submissive as a result of playing that role in an aversive situation. It would thus appear possible experimentally to manipulate dominance rather than treating it primarily as an *a priori* subject variable.

The range of situations that may lead to aggressive behaviors remains to be determined empirically. An early analysis of this question linked aggression with frustration (Dollard, Miller, Doob, Mowrer, & Sears, 1939). Their hypothesis was that blocking of goal-directed behavior resulted in frustration which contributed motivation to further potentiate responding. Furthermore, since the resulting aggressive behaviors were, in many instances, likely to remove the source of frustration, the initial tendency toward aggression would be enhanced by its association with reinforcement. This analysis assumes that the aggression would be directed predominantly at the frustrating agent, although the authors realized that a threat of counteraggression might lead to the displacement of aggression onto a similar object via stimulus generalization.

The present data suggest that aggression is a much more common result of aversive control. Aggression occurs in both avoidance and escape situations. More importantly, perhaps, the object of aggression need not be the agent responsible for the pain. And while it is true that the dominant organism tends to initiate most of the aggressive attacks, and is more likely to do so the greater his relative dominance over his partner, the aggressive tendency is also evident in the submissive organism. While it (wisely) does not attack a highly dominant organism, its tendency to aggress becomes manifest when paired with a more equal partner.

It is also possible that the extent of aggression is related to the number of organisms involved in the aversive situation. We put three *S*s (the trio listed first in Table III) all together in the wheel-turn apparatus. Collectively, they made no avoidance responses and aggression of some form occurred on virtually every trial. In some cases, all three *S*s would engage in a "free-for-all." On other occasions, the C *S* was trapped in a corner and pounded by the A and B *S*s. And on other occasions, the A *S* attacked the C *S* while the B *S* maneuvered for position to turn the wheel to terminate shock. Accordingly, the extent of the phenomenon of avoidance decrement coupled with aggression may depend not only on the range and pattern of dominance displayed within the group, but also on the size of the group.

## VI. POSSIBLE APPLICATIONS

There is always danger in extrapolating observations made on lower animals to the complex situations of human behavior. Nevertheless, with that disclaimer in mind, it seems appropriate to provide some illustrations of situations in which the phenomenon herein described seems analogous to ones familiar in everyday life. The generalization on which these illustrations are based is this: *If a single avoidance response is required of two or more organisms in which a clear dominance relationship exists, avoidance may not occur and aggression may follow the escape behavior.*

With that principle in mind, consider a group of soldiers informed that their barracks will soon be inspected. Each dutifully goes to his own area of the barracks to make his bed tightly, polish his shoes, and get it into shape. These are his individual avoidance responses. But there are areas of the barracks which are shared by all, such as the latrine, which also require cleaning. Unless responsibility for such areas has been designated, they are likely to go unattended. When the aversive event of not passing inspection occurs, the submissive (lower-rank) soldiers are likely to clean the latrine but then there is also likely to be dissention in the ranks. Morale problems in group situations may thus reflect, in part, the same phenomenon we have observed in rats paired in an avoidance context.

Next consider a more homey example. A mother, noticing that the garbage can is full as she is leaving for the store, calls out, "Will one of you children please empty the garbage while I'm gone?" The children are otherwise engaged, to be sure, and fail to make this avoidance task right away and then forget about it. When the mother returns, she scolds them and one (the younger) is likely to make the escape response after which they bicker. Sibling rivalry may thus reflect, in part, this same phenomenon.

It would be appropriate to recall in this context that sexual attack may be a form of aggression, even between members of the same sex. The incidence of homosexual mounting observed in our rats suggests that a similar result might occur among people subjected to a paired avoidance context. At least this possibility cannot be dismissed.

As a final example, consider a class run as a discussion seminar. Not infrequently, the instructor will begin the class meeting with a general but easy question to get discussion started. So he throws it out to the group: "Will someone please tell the class . . .". Everyone familiar with this scene knows the likely result. No one volunteers an answer, and all studiously turn to their notes and appear involved so as not to have to make this avoidance response. Now perhaps the context is not intended to be aversive, but if no one talks, the silence is oppressive and the instructor finally has to challenge the class. Subsequently, the students may grumble. Low esprit-de-corps in class may reflect the same phenomenon.

Each of these examples is admittedly far-fetched and undoubtedly more complicated than described here. But the important point remains: there appears to be a basic principle (or combination of principles) of behavior tending to prevent an organism from making an adaptive avoidance response when it is in the company of other organisms. This appears to be most likely true when there is some basis for identifying a clear dominance relationship within the group, and the failure of avoidance culminates in aggressive interactions following the escape behavior.

In this connection, it is important to recognize that the aggression need not be directed at the responsible agent. None of the rats in these studies showed an unusual proclivity toward biting the experimenter or even resisting being placed in the apparatus. Instead, aggression is directed against any organism over which the individual is physically dominant. If this fact can be extended to include the tendency for oppressed people to form into groups and to respond in relation to their collective strength, one fundamental basis for violence may be uncovered. Specifically, the apparent mystery of sheer, wanton destruction may have been provoked by the nature of the aversive control procedures employed.

This would suggest the following dictum: do not assign indiscriminately to two or more people a task that only one can do and need do. If there is but a single task, designate the individual responsible for doing it. The soldiers should have a latrine duty schedule; the mother should identify which child is to empty the garbage; the instructor should call on a specified student. Or alternatively, ensure that everyone has a task to perform and time to perform it. In short, the widespread practice of "leaving it to the troops" may be very poor strategy indeed.

There is even greater reason to attend to this dictum than simply that the avoidance response will not be made and aggression will ensue. If animals that have shown the phenomenon of paired avoidance decrement and aggression are returned to the situation alone, they may no longer avoid. Even if they previously acquired and demonstrated the avoidance response, their individual behavior is disrupted by the pairing situation. This is analogous to the housewife who, after having a maid do her cleaning for a while, finds it difficult to do the work herself when the maid is not around. Whatever the theoretical mechanism for the phenomenon, it appears to be a widespread source of maladaptive behavior.

## REFERENCES

Coons, E. E., Anderson, N. H., & Myers, A. K. Disappearance of avoidance responding during continued training. *Journal of Comparative and Physiological Psychology*, 1960, 53, 290-292.
Davis, H. Social interaction and Sidman avoidance performance. *Psychological Record*, 1969, 19, 433-442.
Dollard, J., Miller, N. E., Doob, L., Mowrer, O. H., & Sears, R. R. *Frustration and aggression.* New Haven: Yale Univ. Press, 1939.
Hull, C. L. *Principles of behavior.* New York: Appleton-Century, 1943.
Hull, C. L. *A behavior system.* New Haven: Yale Univ. Press, 1952.

Logan, F. A., & Boice, R. Aggressive behaviors of paired rodents in an avoidance context. *Behavior*, 1969, in press.

Ulrich, R., & Azrin, N. H. Reflexive fighting in response to aversive stimulation. *Journal of the Experimental Analysis of Behavior*, 1962, 5, 511-521.

# 11

# Psychopathology
# in Monkeys

HARRY F. HARLOW and
MARGARET K. HARLOW
University of Wisconsin

Our deliberate entry into the field of psychopathology came about in this manner: We started by creating an animal which had no trace of abnormality and absolutely no capabilities of ever becoming abnormal. This "organism" was the cloth surrogate mother, and it had, as a control, a wire surrogate. Both cloth and wire surrogates were built in lactating and nonlactating models. A typical nonlactating cloth mother is shown in Figure 1. It was this form that allayed forever the Freudian concept of the cupboard theory of mother love, the theory that hunger satisfaction was the primary variable binding the infant to the mother. Because infant rhesus monkeys showed almost equal attachments for lactating and nonlactating cloth surrogates, as described by Harlow (1958), we have known ever since that although one may hunger for love, one does not love from hunger or its satisfaction.

On the basis of even limited previous experience we were not surprised particularly that the infant clung to the nonlactating cloth mother most of the time. Nor were we surprised that the infant showed distress, at least mild distress, when it was separated from the cloth mother. Actually the effects of experimental separation would probably have been even greater had it not been for the fact that for purposes of cleanliness we had separated the infants from their cloth mothers an hour a day from birth onward and then brought back a freshly laundered terry-cloth mother.

## I. SURROGATE SECURITY

Although we were not surprised that infant monkeys became firmly attached to cloth surrogate mothers, we were quite surprised to find that the infant

Figure 1. Infant rhesus with cloth surrogate.

monkeys gained a deep sense of security from the presence of their inanimate mothers just as human and monkey infants gain security from the presence of their real mothers. The human literature reports studies demonstrating that in the second half of the first year of life, infants seek their mothers in a strange situation and are comforted by them. Spitz (1950) has properly labeled this stage the period of "eight-month anxiety."

If a surrogate-reared infant monkey is placed in a strange room with a cloth mother, it clings tightly to the maternal figure and then apparently feels sufficiently secure in this strange situation to go out and explore it and to contact and play with inanimate objects or toys. Of even more importance, the infant feels free to leave the mother and play, at an appropriate developmental age, with animate objects, particularly age-mates or peers, and thereby forms the essential age-mate or peer affectional relationships. Since it is age-mate or peer affection even more than maternal affection that is basic to the success or failure of a monkey's or human's subsequent social and sexual life (Harlow & Harlow, 1962), one can defend the position that the mother's primary personal–social function is to aid and abet the infant in making age-mate adjustments. The mother's role in this regard is twofold: that of imparting security to the infant so that it will explore and play, and, if necessary, abetting the infant's exploratory tendencies by persuasive separating behavior.

Basic trust is the first human social–emotional achievement described by the psychoanalyst Erik Erikson (1951). It is the task of his first developmental stage, and its antecedent is a sensitive, loving mother. Basic trust or security, as we have labeled it, appears also to be the first monkey social–emotional achievement, and its antecedent is also effective mothering, in this instance either animate or inanimate. Acceptance of the infant and good instincts are apparently sufficient to impart security to an infant monkey, but they are not sufficient to encourage a reluctant infant to explore its world. It is at this point that the cloth mother fails but a *good* live mother succeeds. Some mothers, monkey and human, do fail, however, in this second task, for they overprotect and overindulge and may even interfere actively with the developing infant's efforts to contact its peers. "Smother love" is no misnomer.

## II. INANIMATE MATERNAL PSYCHOPATHOLOGY

When we had established that the love of the monkey infant for the cloth surrogate was lasting, we felt we were ready to study the psychopathology of maternal rejection by creating evil cloth surrogate mothers that would upon schedule or command engage in acts of hostility or bestiality toward their trusting babies. The first of these evil mothers had embedded in its deep nylon pile body a metal frame that would spring forward and hurl the infant to the floor. The displaced babies were always deeply disturbed, cried piteously, clasped their arms to their bodies, and rocked, but as soon as the iron undergarments were returned to their proper position, the babies rushed back to the ventral surface of their mothers' bodies and clung tightly again. In retrospect we asked the question, Where else can the frightened baby go?

On the basis of earlier data (Rosenblum & Harlow, 1963) we knew that air blasts were enormously noxious stimuli to monkeys. We had seen a monkey once driven to what could be called experimental neurosis by being air-blasted for errors on a difficult learning problem. With this in mind we built our air-blast surrogate. Whenever the mother vented from her body streams of compressed air at high pressure, the babies were distraught. Their hair was blown flat to their cranium and away from their body; they closed their eyes and they screamed. Nevertheless, they never left the mother's body but instead clung to the mother with frenzied zeal while the ordeal was in progress.

Determined not to give up, we next built our shaking mother, which upon command or schedule would vibrate so violently that one could hear the infant's teeth chatter and watch the infant's body shake convulsively. Again during the ordeal the baby clung more tenaciously to the mother than before, and for all practical purposes, instead of producing experimental neurosis we had achieved a technique for enhancing maternal attachment. It can be said in self-defense that we had come very close to creating experimental neurosis, not in monkey babies, but in ourselves. Our last and final desperate attempt to unseat infant sanity lay in the creation of the porcupine surrogate mother which could suddenly extrude brass spikes through her ventral surface. When the spikes struck forward, the infants were clearly unhappy and abandoned the mother's ventral surface. They cried and they engaged in distressed posturing, huddling, self-clasping, and rocking, but the infants also watched from the corners of their eyes for the spikes to be retracted, and as soon as that happened they rushed forward desperately and determinedly and clung to the mother's ventral area. The findings are certainly in keeping with the human data that children of mothers who punish for dependency are more dependent than children of accepting mothers.

Perhaps we gave up too soon on our mechanical mother monsters. Had we persisted more ingeniously for longer periods of time, we might have induced anaclitic depression in infants rejected by malicious surrogate mothers. Sometime we may try again, but a critical instance had occurred at the time that we stopped. We had by then produced our so-called "motherless mothers," real monkey mothers that had never known any antecedent love, either maternal or peer. The behaviors of these unloved mothers were so evil toward their own infants and sometimes so lethal that we despaired of producing inanimate paradigms that could match them in their violence, vindictiveness, and unpredictability. We shall say more about the motherless mothers later.

## III. EFFECTS OF SOCIAL ISOLATION

Our actual but unplanned entry into the production of abnormal infants antedated the accepting and rejecting surrogate models and the motherless mothers by some six years, and the motherless mothers were only a few of the larger population of abnormal monkeys we had created. During the first two decades of the Wisconsin Primate Laboratory, we worked with feral animals. Pregnancies were unwanted and rare and resulted only when animals escaped temporarily from their individual cages. In the 1950's, when the promise came of enlarged facilities, we began a breeding program to produce infant monkeys for research into the development of learning abilities and, we hoped, for the start of a sturdy breeding group free of the diseases endemic to rhesus imported from India. We carefully separated each new infant from its mother at birth, housed it in an individual cage, and nurtured it by hand. Accommodations of this type are shown in Figure 2. This system permitted us to study the infant without having to pry it away from its mother each day, a hazardous procedure for experimenters, and it freed the mother for return to the basic breeding colony.

Figure 2. Rhesus infants in the partial social isolation rearing condition.

## A. Partial Social Isolation

The infants thrived, and though we noted their high orality, their self-clasping, and their huddling and rocking behavior, we assumed it was normal for rhesus infants. As the animals matured, we paired them and awaited the healthy offspring we had so confidently expected them to produce. A year passed, then two years, without a pregnancy. In fact, we did not even observe a single mount. It was then we realized we had a laboratory full of abnormal monkeys and that the longer we kept them, the more abnormal they became. We have since referred to this rearing condition as *partial social isolation*—partial because the monkeys from the start can see other monkeys in adjoining cages and in the racks opposite them and they can hear the other occupants of the room, but social isolation because they cannot contact each other, a condition we have discovered is essential for normal social and sexual development.

Observation of monkeys housed alone from birth or the first four to six weeks of life until one to ten years of age has shown that the frequency and severity of aberrant behaviors increases with time spent in partial isolation (Cross & Harlow, 1965). Early in life they show an abnormal amount of oral activity as compared with mother-raised animals, mouthing fingers, toes, penis, and the wire on their cages. Mother- and peer-raised infants also engage in oral behavior, but to a lesser extent. The partial isolates frequently clasp their hands about their bodies and rock back and forth or extend their arms upward or behind their head and bend their neck backward against the corner of the cage and sit with their ventral surface fully exposed in a gesture normal infants show when disturbed following parental rejection or when presenting for grooming. A frequent variation combining finger-sucking and abnormal posturing is shown in

Figure 3. Partial-social-isolate infant showing abnormal posturing and simultaneous finger-sucking.

Figure 3. In addition, many animals develop repetitive stereotypic movements, usually in the second year or later, jumping up and down, shaking their cages, or circling from top to bottom of the cage. These stereotyped movements, like the other behaviors described, are not confined to isolates but also occur in milder degrees in feral animals confined to cages. Perhaps their equivalent may occur even in the wild where various species of monkeys have been observed to engage in stereotyped tree-shaking.

An interesting and usually late-appearing behavior is one which we call the schizophrenic stare. The animal goes to the front of the cage and puts its face against the mesh, not fixating on other monkeys nor objects, as shown in Figure 4. If it looks to the left, its right arm may gradually rise, and as the arm rises the wrist and fingers go into a tight flexion pattern which is unnervingly

Figure 4. Partial social isolate displaying "vacant stare."

like the pattern of *cerea flexibilitas* or waxy flexibility of the human catatonic. This is preceded developmentally by frequent periods of passivity to events in the environment.

Another late-appearing abnormal activity is that of self-aggression in which the animals, as seen in Figure 5, bite at their arm, hand, foot or leg. Ordinarily

Figure 5. Self-biting behavior in a partial social isolate.

they do not break the skin, but under conditions of stress or threat they may literally tear their limb to pieces. In a considerable number of instances, injury has been so severe that the animals had to be sacrificed. An occasional feral animal housed alone or in social groups shows mild or abortive self-biting, but none of our feral monkeys has ever broken the skin.

We know that aggression is a late-developing, normal response in monkeys, and ordinarily we do not see it at all in the socially adjusted infant or even the maladjusted monkey infant during the first year of life. Externally directed aggression typically starts early in the second year of life and steadily increases in frequency and intensity in that and subsequent years. Under normal environmental conditions aggression postdates the affectional attachment to mother and age-mates. Provided at least one or both these forms of affection have been established, the aggression of animals toward age-mate associates is relatively benign, but the intensity of aggression directed toward any outgroup member is far from benign, and this outgroup member is often a caretaker or experimenter. Cross & Harlow (1965) studied aggression of partial social isolates toward experimenters and found a sharp increase in males in the second year and thereafter and a later and more attenuated increase in females. They found self-directed aggression to be infrequent until after the third year of life in males and the fourth year in females. Aggression, it is interesting to note, regardless of form or rearing conditions, appears earlier in the male than in the female though eventually it is a prevalent behavior regardless of sex.

Recently Suomi and Harlow initiated a systematic observational study of the disturbances shown by animals subjected to the partial social isolation of the home cage situation. Data thus far collected on five classes of behavior for three age groups are shown in Figure 6. Each of approximately one hundred rhesus was observed a total of 15 min. on three separate days between 8:30 a.m. and 4:30 p.m. The categories are not mutually exclusive. A monkey might rock and huddle and self-mouth simultaneously, although the only behavior compatible with passivity is having a body part in the mouth without mouth movements. It is apparent that rocking and huddling and self-mouthing are early

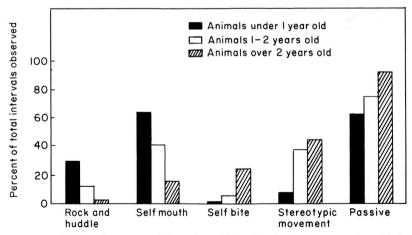

Figure 6. Relative frequency of five selected behaviors in three groups of partial social isolates.

behaviors that decrease with age and that self-biting and stereotypic movements are infrequent early but increase with age. Passivity is the predominant state during the observations at each age level and tends to increase progressively. This latter finding may in whole or in part reflect the decreasing activity level observed in many mammalian species as they progress from infancy to maturity.

Our animals raised in partial social isolation have for the most part been separated from their mothers a few hours after birth and placed immediately in individual cages, thus being denied any chance to form maternal or peer ties. Their assignment to partial isolation precedes the emergence of specific fears, an event Harlow and Zimmermann (1959) ascribe to the third month of life, and continues through and beyond the period at about one year of age when normal social aggression emerges. It may be that the symptoms of social isolation can be accounted for as an exaggeration of normally developing behaviors through restriction of physical activity alone, but it seems more likely that restraints and interference with normal emotional development and expression are at least part, perhaps the major part, of the etiology. Thus, fear, when it appears, may be abnormally strong because it is not alleviated by the security imparted by a mother or even by peers, nor is there safe opportunity to interact with feared objects to extinguish inappropriate fears. Similarly, much later, when aggression appears, it may be abnormally violent because it is not attenuated by antecedent affection nor is there opportunity to interact with the objects of aggression, other than the self, to acquire adaptive habits in the presence of strangers. Lacking the mechanisms to reduce or inhibit emotional expression toward social objects or to substitute environmental outlets, the animals turn to themselves and self-clutch, rock, mouth, and chew their own bodies. The inescapable outcome is disturbed social, sexual, and maternal behavior in monkeys subjected early in life to partial social isolation.

The infants initially raised on cloth surrogate mothers fared little if any better than the infants raised in bare wire cages. At maturity their sexual responses were inadequate or nonexistent, and in an effort to rehabilitate them, we placed eighteen of them on a monkey island in the Madison zoo (see Harlow, 1962). There were nine of each sex, and they were three to four years of age when placed on the island in June. One was injured and drowned the second day and another was injured and removed. Fighting was intense during the first few days, but it subsided as social ordering developed. Friendship pairs formed and grooming began, but no copulation was observed. Even the most experienced and competent of our breeding colony males, when released on the island a month later, was unable to impregnate the females, and when September arrived there were to our knowledge only a colony of still virgin monkeys and a frustrated king of the island. Some females did show an adequate present but failed to maintain a rigid posture when mounted by our feral male. To our knowledge none of the surrogate-raised males even attempted a mount, but they showed various forms of inadequate behavior.

Preliminary studies of the effects of partial social isolation on the sex behavior of monkeys under controlled conditions have already been published (Harlow, Joslyn, Senko, & Dopp, 1966), and a major study by Senko nears completion. Sexual inadequacy likely results from the unwillingness of the monkeys to maintain bodily contact, inappropriate fear and aggressiveness, and lack of skills in sexual posturing. Although the females' sex behavior more nearly approached the normal than did that of the males, there was a tendency for the female to sit down when the male approached or to rebuff his physical encounters. Frequently the male showed signs of strong biological sex drive, but more often than not he would approach and grasp the female from the side and engage in pelvic thrusting, an activity which left him working at cross purposes with reality. On one occasion we had a male approach the female dorsally and place both feet on one of her limbs, clasp her body, and then fall ignominiously to the floor, never to try again. This was as close to sexual normality as any partial social isolate male attained.

Many cage-reared and surrogate-reared females from our laboratory have become mothers owing to repeated exposure to breeding stock males or, that failing, to restraint in a rack that positioned them for insemination. We call these females "motherless mothers" because they grew up without live mothering; it should be stressed, however, that they were also deprived in the first year or two of life of all association with peers. Some of these females were indifferent to their young, ignoring them when they cried at a distance and pushing them from their bodies when the neonates managed to gain contact. Others were abusive, seeking the infant out to bite or crush it. A number of mothers even killed or maimed their infants. Some, however, have produced second and third infants and in general have improved in their treatment of the later born, apparently having been socialized somewhat by the persistence of the first infants in attaining and maintaining body contact and nursing.

## B. Total Social Isolation

Even greater negative effects on the social–sexual behavior of monkeys have been obtained through *total social isolation.* The monkey was placed at birth or after some predetermined period of time in the social isolation chamber pictured in Figure 7. The inside is cubic with linear dimensions of 28 in. It is sound-dampered, not soundproof, and illuminated so that the animal has minimal sensory deprivation and maximal limitation of perceptual variation. The panel at the front is lowered when the animal is placed in it and not again raised

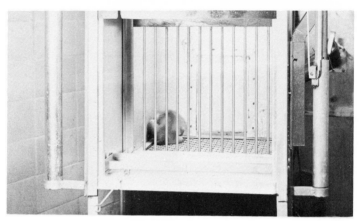

**Figure 7.** A three-month-old infant crouches in the corner of the total social isolation apparatus when the door is raised for the first time.

until the animal is released after three, six, nine, twelve, or more months. Details of apparatus and procedure have been reported elsewhere (Harlow, Rowland, & Griffin, 1964; Griffin & Harlow, 1966).

Progressively devastating effects on social–emotional behavior have been obtained with increasing time spent in the social isolation chamber. Three months of isolation produces a terror response, at the time of release, so severe in one instance that the infant refused to eat and died of starvation. Another infant released at three months of age was force-fed when it refused to eat and soon responded normally. The others have shown only transient severe fear and have rapidly adjusted to the nursery and to peers in a playroom situation, approximating them in play and social behavior, and generally appearing to show no deficits as a result of their privation.

Total social isolation lasting from birth to six months of age produced very different sequellae. These monkeys showed enormous and persisting social deficits when exposed in the playroom regularly to another isolate and a pair of equal-aged controls raised in partial social isolation. Social play was absent in the first eight weeks and was confined to the isolate partner when play eventually began after eight weeks in the playroom (Rowland, 1964). Similar results were obtained for measures of exploration, threat, and sex behavior. Figure 8 shows one of these total isolates in a helpless, self-clutch pattern in the playroom while a control explores him.

Long-term follow-up data on exposure at three years of age to juveniles, peers and adults, indicate continuing social deficits: these animals showed infantile heterosexual behavior or none at all, and they alternately threatened and cowered before monkeys of all ages. Socially reared animals showed no aggression, but the six-month isolates even aggressed against adults and juveniles

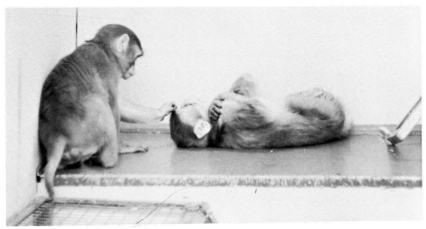

**Figure 8.** A total social isolate lies passively on a platform in the playroom while being explored by a control animal.

(Mitchell, Raymond, Ruppenthal, & Harlow, 1966). These animals have no positive ties to any of their kind and no control over fear or aggression. The principal change since their playroom experience, which ended when they were 14 months old, is the display of aggressive behavior, which was inhibitable by fear during the second year but continued to increase in strength, as it does in normal animals, until it no longer was checked by fear and could not be ameliorated by affection. That aggressive responses were available even in the second year, but inhibited, is evident from a test session at that time with more socially handicapped animals, a test which will be described in the following.

The social devastation imposed by six months of total social isolation is so great that it hardly seems possible any further deficit can accrue during social privation enforced for longer periods of time such as nine months or twelve months. However, three different studies (Rowland, 1964; Clark, 1968; Pratt, 1969) have all indicated that increasing periods of privation beyond six months exaggerate the social deficit. In the twelve-month isolates even the very primitive activity play pattern was essentially absent and sexual behavior was so inhibited that even onanism was never seen. These one-year-old isolates made no attempts whatsoever to interact with each other or with their control play partners, and they rapidly became social objects which their more normal associates attacked and aggressed. This is reflected in the measures of biting in the two groups. Actually, biting was so severe in the control animals that we concluded the experiment after ten weeks of testing to preclude fatal injury to the total isolates.

When our six-month and twelve-month total isolates had completed their playroom experience at a little more than a year of age, we put pairs of each together in the playroom. To our surprise, the six-month isolates, until then nonaggressive, promptly attacked the even more incompetent twelve-month isolates. It is quite obvious that the six-month isolates in their second year had aggressive tendencies, and all they required to display them was more defenseless animals as social objects. Subsequently, two of the twelve-month isolates were tested at three years of age with strange juveniles, peers, and adults and were found, in contrast with socially reared animals, to show no social play, essentially no sex behavior, and a high frequency of fear and threat (Mitchell, Raymond, Ruppenthal, & Harlow, 1966). Only in the complete absence of physical aggression did they resemble the controls. In all other behaviors they were more extreme in their deviance than were the six-month isolates.

In the previous section of the paper we have described our failures, if failures they were, to produce psychopathological traits in macaque monkeys by the use of a dummy monster mother. We have also described abnormal behavior induced in monkeys by raising them for periods of time under conditions of partial or total social isolation. It is obvious that such experimental conditions may destroy the monkey as an effective social animal throughout its lifetime. During and after social isolation, these monkeys exhibit grossly abnormal behavior, but they are of limited value for the study of psychopathological traits because of the totality of their deviations. Consequently, we are turning to a research program designed to produce more limited disorders through creating situations in which development proceeds relatively normally and then is interrupted or distrupted in some constant, specific manner.

## IV. INDUCED ANACLITIC DEPRESSION

We assume that multiple forces operate in the production of major behavioral disturbances, and we expect to assess the role of various factors alone or in combination that might predispose to or precipitate disorders. One condition that is known to lead to behavioral pathology in monkeys is maternal separation during infancy.

### A. Mother–Infant Separation

Some years ago we conducted two investigations of the effects of maternal separation on six-month-old monkeys reared by their mothers and with peers from birth (Seay, Hansen, & Harlow, 1962; Seay & Harlow, 1965). In the first study, two sets of two mothers and their infants lived in two-unit playpens until separation. The wire panel that regularly divided living unit from play area was replaced with a clear Plexiglas panel for three weeks, isolating the infants from physical contact with their mothers but not from the peer. The initial response of the infants was one of intense disturbance, characterized by cooing, screeching, disoriented scampering, attempts to pass through the barrier, and huddling against the panel close to the mothers. The mothers were also disturbed, but less so than their infants. During separation, scores for visual contact with the mother and crying were high, and complex infant–infant social behaviors were extremely infrequent. Following reunion with their mothers, three of the infants and mothers showed elevated scores for cradling, clinging, and ventral contact as compared with scores preceding separation, but the fourth infant showed less mother-directed behavior than before separation. Complex infant–infant social behaviors also resumed in the postseparation period.

The second study separated two sets of four infants each and their mothers which had lived since birth of the infants in four-unit playpens. The mothers in this study were removed from the room and housed beyond hearing range of the infants for a two-week period. In this study the infants had time-limited contact with their peers before, during, and after separation. As in the earlier study, the infants were initially hyperactive and vocal after separation and then settled into a stage of low activity but with crying. Play and other complex social interactions were greatly reduced. Following reunion with their mothers, the infants showed sharply increased mother-directed behaviors as compared with the preseparation period, and their play with peers resumed.

A few years before, Bowlby (1960) had analyzed the sequences of responses exhibited by human infants following maternal separation and identified a stage of protest followed by a stage of despair, and these stages or phases were observed in our maternal separation studies. Bowlby's third stage, detachment from the mother when the human infant and mother are reunited, has not been commonly reported for monkeys. In our twelve mother-infant separations reported above, only one infant showed any detachment, as indicated by less contact with mother after separation as compared with the period before separation. There was no indication of a qualitative change in the infant's relationship with its mother.

Other studies of mother–infant separation in monkeys have also reported Bowlby's protest and despair stages for rhesus (Spencer-Booth & Hinde, 1967) and pig-tail monkeys (Kaufman & Rosenblum, 1967; Jensen & Tolman, 1962), but Rosenblum and Kaufman (1968) failed to observe the despair stage in bonnet macaques. They separated five bonnet infants two to four months of age by removing the mothers for a month from the heterogenous living group. All five infants showed some agitation and increased vocalization and self-directed orality, but not profound depression. Four of the five readily found adoptive mothers and spent as much time in ventral contact with them as they had on their real mothers. The fifth infant had limited ventral contact with other adults. Following reunion, one never regained ventral contact with its real mother and a second did not attain such contact during the first week of reunion. This seems not to be a demonstration of Bowlby's detachment stage, however, but, rather, an instance of a new mother's permanently replacing the old in one case and temporarily in the other.

There appear to be marked individual intraspecies as well as interspecies differences in the severity of the trauma suffered by monkeys during separation and in the duration of symptoms after reunion with the mothers. One infant in the Seay *et al.* (1962) study suffered severely from anorexia and sleeplessness but recovered. In an exploratory study conducted subsequently on a three-month-old rhesus monkey to adapt it to WGTA testing, the infant was separated daily from its mother for a period of about three weeks and then permanently separated and placed in a single cage in the infant animal room. During this time the infant displayed the typical Bowlby syndrome of separation anxiety, complicated by anorexia and failure to respond to forced feeding. After six days the infant died of self-induced starvation. As we have indicated before, three months of age may be a critical period for the rhesus infant since this is the time when fear of strangeness seems to take on overwhelming catastrophic properties for the monkey. Still another indication of individual differences is the finding of Spencer–Booth and Hinde (1967) that two of four seven-month-old rhesus infants, whose mothers were removed from the heterogenous group living situation for six days, recovered from most of the severe effects of the experience in a few days, but in two infants the effects persisted for at least some months.

Fundamental difficulties exist in the utilization of mother–infant separation as a model for studying psychopathology in subhuman depression. Although most separated rhesus infants exhibit depression, the state is not as profound or prolonged as would be desirable for effective research in this area. Moreover, the act of separating the infant from the mother can itself be traumatic, necessitating use of a net and force to pry the infant from the mother.

## B. Peer Separation

In the hope of eventually overcoming some of these problems we are conducting exploratory studies on the effect of separating monkeys that have been raised from birth onward without mothers but with peers. These monkeys, whether raised with a single peer or multiple peers, have been described by us as "together–together" monkeys, and they develop strong physical attachments and presumably strong emotional attachments. Typical positioning of a pair of together–together monkeys is shown in Figure 9 and the characteristic "choo-choo" pattern of groups of four and six together–together monkeys are illustrated in Figures 10 and 11.

**Figure 9.** Two young infants in a ventral–ventral clasp characteristic for a pair raised together.

In a formal exploratory study, a group of four together–together monkeys three months of age were all separated for periods of four successive days each week for twelve weeks. Then, after six weeks of communal living, they were again subjected to a second series of eight such weekly separations, a total of twenty separation periods. Records of the average duration of selected behaviors obtained for the monkeys during the first 24 hr. of the first twelve separations indicate high levels of locomotion and vocalization, typical protest behavior. Measures during the last 48 hr. of these twelve separations show greatly enhanced self-clasping and rocking and huddling responses, indicators of despair. All these responses drop to a low level when the four infants are together, and during this time the frequency of ventral cling is extremely high. Figure 12 shows the protest response of one of these infants when temporarily withheld from its peer group by a wire partition following one of the formal separation periods.

During the period covered by the series of twenty separations, the infants spent more time together than apart. While the treatment did not produce

Figure 10. Modified "choo-choo" clinging pattern of four "together–together" animals.

Figure 11. Six "together–together" monkeys in "choo-choo" pattern characteristic for this rearing condition.

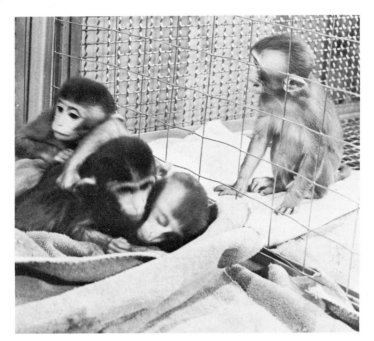

Figure 12. An infant cooing in protest while restrained from rejoining its peers after separation.

devastating depressive states, there is abundant evidence that it drastically interfered with normal personal–social development. Observations of behavior were made during communal living periods at three months, prior to the first separation; at six months, after twelve separations, and at nine months, following the last separation. Figure 13 shows the results at these three times for four behaviors. It can be seen that two very early behaviors, ventral cling and self-mouthing, which normally are high in the first months and then decrease with age, remained at a high level each period, even at nine months. Self-clasp, which develops a little later but is infrequent in together–together animals, actually increased over the three consecutive measurement periods. Most important, play remained at a very low level throughout. Under continuous together–together rearing, play increases steadily and reaches a high level by nine months. The nine-month-old infants in this experiment thus resembled three-month-olds in the maturity of their personal and social behavior.

These monkeys have since been housed individually in wire cages adjacent to four monkeys of the same age recently returned from an early lifetime of total social isolation. An experienced investigator correctly identified the two groups on the basis of greater passivity in the isolates and greater disturbance in the infants repetitively separated. It seems obvious that the multiple separations,

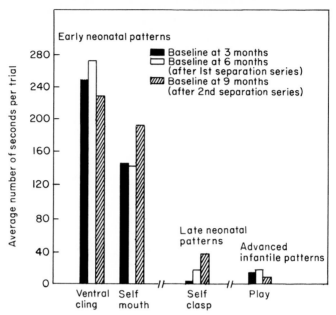

Figure 13. Relative duration measures for various behaviors before separation and after each of two series of separations.

which were not as drastic as they could have been, produced behavioral deviations which are prolonged and possibly profound.

We have stated our belief that truly psychopathological disorders are usually produced by a multiplicity of variables. Consequently we have explored other procedures than separation to determine their effects and to determine whether or not they might be incorporated as a component part of a constellation of treatments which might or might not involve separation. We have already found that social isolation, either partial or complete, frequently gives rise over a period of time to bizarre abnormal behaviors one of which may be depression or a state similar to depression. Following this lead, we have created a partial-isolation chamber which also restricts bodily activities in the hope that this device would produce depressive-type behaviors more rapidly, more permanently, and more invariantly than did the total isolation chambers. We call this new chamber the "pit," and we have produced it in two sizes to accommodate monkeys of different ages.

## C. Pit-Produced Depression

Figure 14 presents an inside view of a small pit with an infant huddled on the floor. A full description has been published elsewhere (Suomi & Harlow, 1969),

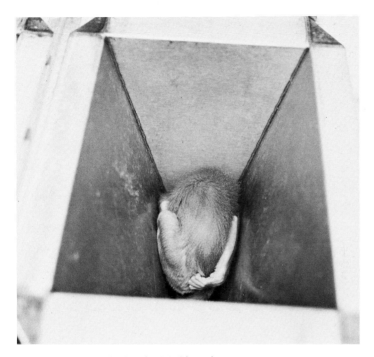

**Figure 14.** Photograph of infant huddled in a pit.

but a few details here will elucidate the animal's environmental situation during confinement in the pit. The pits are of stainless steel sheets that slope to a rounded bottom covered by a wire mesh floor. Solid wastes collect below the floor, and liquid wastes drain to a drip pan below the pit. Milk, solid food, and water are provided through openings in the walls slightly above floor level. The smooth, sloping sides of the apparatus discourage climbing, although it has proved necessary to cover the tops with wire mesh or Plexiglas because some infants become adept at escaping. The floor provides adequate space even for juvenile or older animals to sit up or lie with the limbs extended. Every effort has been made to avoid physical discomfort to the animal during its confinement.

An exploratory study was carried out to test the usefulness of the pits in producing psychopathology in four wire-cage-raised monkeys six months to thirteen months old when placed in the pits for twenty days. At the end of this period they were removed for seven days and kept in their home cages, then returned to the pits for ten additional days, after which they were returned to their home cages. Measures of selected behaviors before pitting and after each period of confinement are presented in Figure 15. The behavioral changes were

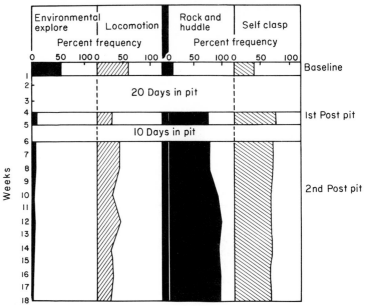

**Figure 15.** Percent frequency of four behaviors before pitting and after each of two series of confinements to the pit.

marked and in the direction of increasing autistic behaviors, including self-clasping and rocking and huddling, and decreasing behaviors oriented to the environment, such as exploration and locomotion. The monkeys' behavior was at least as deviant twelve weeks after the last pitting as it had been in the first week after the last pitting. Figure 16 shows these animals in their individualized postures during the period following the second pitting sequence.

To assay the effects of pit incarceration on the neonatal monkey, we placed four infants in the pits at fifteen days of age. The normal infantile resting posture at this time bears a resemblance to fetal posturing, but the effect of pit living induced total prostration in these infants within a few days, and as a result the babies allowed their limbs and tail to dangle through the openings of the hardware-cloth. Three of the infants developed serious infections from contact with the waste materials before the problem was recognized. All four were removed and treated in the nursery, recovered fully, and were replaced in the baby pits at forty days with a folded gauze diaper. The diaper was removed after five days and the animals after thirty-six days. Obviously we cannot evaluate the long-term effects of pit placement on neonatal monkeys at the present time. We are observing these animals in the playroom three days a week and have found that the two that had been most seriously ill (and therefore handled intensively during their treatment) are least disturbed and the other two show moderate disturbance.

**Figure 16.** Characteristic posturing of four infants after the second series of pit treatments.

Using a larger pit we have been able to demonstrate that extremely limited pit experience may have drastic behavioral consequences for socially experienced monkeys. A group of four older infants that had had social experience an hour a day for the first six months of life and continuous group social experience for most of the following two months showed dramatic behavioral degradation when the animals were subsequently placed in the pits two days a week for ten weeks, a total of only twenty days of pit incarceration. Between pittings, they lived in pairs. During this period of time the animals showed progressive increases in self-clinging and clasping behaviors when out of the pits. Much to our surprise, all showed self-aggression, and two engaged in violent aggression against their partners. These are totally abnormal patterns; externally directed aggression is infrequent in monkeys under a year of age, and self-directed aggression appears even later, but in isolated animals, not socially reared ones. All four monkeys showed disturbances, but there were marked individual differences in rate of induction. Two infants went into fits of autistic posturing in less than one month, a third started three weeks later, and the fourth showed little until after eight weeks of the pit treatment. In the tenth week one infant, while suffering aggression from its partner, suddenly developed an extreme prolapse of the colon, temporarily halting the research on this pair.

We look at the pit data not in terms of what has been achieved in the past but what we hope to achieve in the future. The pits were so designed that the "pitting" treatment can be simultaneously combined with peer separation, a technique already described, and with anxiety-inducing situations as well.

## V. EARLIER SUBHUMAN PSYCHOPATHOLOGY

That anxiety-inducing situations can produce emotional disorders in subhuman animals is amply documented, beginning with the conditioning experiments reported by Pavlov (1928). The first successful technique for producing neurosis in his laboratory was one in which a dog was simultaneously shocked and fed, with application of the shock to a different part of the body on each trial, thereby preventing avoidance behavior. The second technique by which breakdown was achieved involved facing a dog with an increasingly more difficult circle–elipse discrimination. Pavlov interpreted the neuroses in both situations as being the outcome of simultaneous arousal of the opposing processes of excitation and inhibition.

In most studies designed to produce experimental neurosis in subhuman animals, stress has been induced by placing the subjects in an approach-avoidance experimental paradigm in which approach toward food carriers with it the threat of pain. Liddell's (1954) classical experiments were dominated by this conflict paradigm: A learned response which was initially always rewarded by food was subsequently punished frequently by electric shock. Individual and species differences were disclosed, but some subjects became quite disturbed. Masserman (1950) conducted a long series of successful studies on experimental neurosis in cats, also using, for the most part, the conflict paradigm of Pavlov's partial, unpredictable positive and negative reinforcers in performance of a learned response.

In these conditioning studies the conflict is within the animal, and it is a conflict devoid of any component of social stress. A possible exception is the research reported by Brady (1958), who maintained two monkeys in restraining chairs in a manner that provided simultaneous shocking for both contingent on the behavior of one of them. The "executive" monkey was presented with a light signal that remained on for 6 hr. and was accompanied by shock administered to the feet of both animals at 20-sec. intervals. Avoidance was accomplished by the executive monkey's pressing a lever at least once every 20 sec. Work and rest periods alternated every 6 hr. until the executive animal collapsed and died after twenty-three days. Autopsy revealed a perforated duodenum in the executive animal and no abnormality in the partner. A replication on another pair resulted in stomach and duodenal ulcers in the executive and no abnormality in the control monkey. The social component of this design seems not to be crucial, however, for executives separated from partners by isolation in soundproof booths still developed ulcers and their partners did not.

It is apparent that induction of anxiety in subhuman animals is reasonably predictable if one uses an approach–avoidance conflict situation in a classical conditioning situation or, possibly, as in the Brady operant conditioning model, an avoidance–avoidance conflict. The Brady results are somewhat unclear in that various schedules other than 6-hr. avoidance and 6-hr. rest did not produce ulcers. Doubtless other nonsocial techniques will also succeed.

## VI. THE FACE OF THE FUTURE

It is our expectation that we can utilize stimuli with characteristics inherently threatening to monkeys and present them on irregular schedules to produce anxiety. In combination with separation or pitting or both, we hope to induce deeper and more enduring psychopathological states than by any one of the techniques used alone. Hopefully, we shall not pay the price of too total a deviation, as obtained with long-term total social isolation, or too much diversity in symptomatology to be useful. If the addition of anxiety can add endogenous features to the strictly exogenous depression produced by separation, we might be closer to our goal than we presently are. This is especially attractive in view of the additional disadvantages of separation, including the total relief of the depression by return of the loved object or the dissipation with time and/or new relationships. If the monkey is capable of free-floating anxiety, we hope to induce it, and we are convinced that separation alone is not sufficient.

The exploratory researches which we have presented look hopeful, and we are confident that more pervading psychopathic states can be produced in monkeys than have been produced heretofore. There are obviously many ways in which psychopathic disorders can be achieved in subhuman organisms, including stress conditioning, social isolation, social privation, affectional separation, and possibly even disruption of day–night cycles. Few if any major human psychopathic states result from the operation of a single variable, either an intraorganic or extraorganic deficit. There is every reason to believe that the same basic phenomenon holds true for subhuman animals, and the thesis merits detailed investigation.

## REFERENCES

Bowlby, J. Separation anxiety. *International Journal of Psychoanalysis,* 1960, **41,** 89-113.

Brady, J. V. Ulcers in "executive" monkeys. *Scientific American,* 1958, **119** (4), 95-100.

Clark, D. L. Immediate and late effects of early, intermediate and late social isolation in the rhesus monkey. Unpublished doctoral dissertation, Univ. of Wisconsin, 1968.

Cross, H. A., & Harlow, H. F. Prolonged and progressive effects of partial isolation on the behavior of macaque monkeys. *Journal of Experimental Research in Personality,* 1965, **1,** 39-49.

Erikson, E. H. A healthy personality for every child: A fact finding report: A digest. Midcentury White House Conference on Children and Youth. Raleigh, N. C.: Health Publications Institute, 1951. Pp. 8-25.

Griffin, G. A., & Harlow, H. F. Effects of three months of total social deprivation on social adjustment and learning in the rhesus monkey. *Child Development,* 1966, **37,** 533-547.

Harlow, H. F. The nature of love. *American Psychologist,* 1958, **13,** 673-685.

Harlow, H. F. The heterosexual affectional system in monkeys. *American Psychologist,* 1962, **17,** 1-9.

Harlow, H. F., & Harlow, M. K. Social deprivation in monkeys. *Scientific American,* 1962, **207** (5), 136-146.

Harlow, H. F., Joslyn, W. D., Senko, M., & Dopp, A. Behavioral aspects of reproduction in primates. *Journal of Animal Science,* 1966, **25,** 49-67.

Harlow, H. F., Rowland, G. L., & Griffin, G. A. The effect of total social deprivation on the development of monkey behavior. *Psychiatric Research Reports,* 1964, **19,** 116-135.

Harlow, H. F., & Zimmermann, R. E. Affectional patterns in the infant monkeys. *Science,* 1959, **130,** 421-432.

Jensen, G. D., & Tolman, C. W. Mother-infant relationship in the monkey, *Macaca nemestrina:* The effect of brief separation and mother-infant specificity. *Journal of Comparative and Physiological Psychology,* 1962, **55,** 131-136.

Kaufman, I. C., & Rosenblum, L. A. The reaction to separation in infant monkeys: Anaclitic depression and conservation-withdrawal. *Psychosomatic Medicine,* 1967, **29,** 648-675.

Liddell, H. S. Conditioning and emotions. *Scientific American,* 1954, **190** (1), 48-57.

Masserman, J. H. Experimental neuroses. *Scientific American,* 1950, **200** (3), 38-43.

Mitchell, G. D., Raymond, E. J., Ruppenthal, G. C., & Harlow, H. F. Long-term effects of total social isolation upon behavior of rhesus monkeys. *Psychological Reports,* 1966, **18,** 567-580.

Pavlov, I. P. Lectures on conditional reflexes: Twenty-five years of objective study of the higher nervous activity (behavior) of animals. (Tr. by W. H. Gantt.) New York: Liveright, 1928.

Pratt, C. L. Effect of different degrees of early stimulation on social development. Unpublished doctoral dissertation, Univ. of Wisconsin, 1969.

Rosenblum, L. A., & Harlow, H. F. Approach-avoidance conflict in the mother-surrogate situation. *Psychological Reports,* 1963, **12,** 83-85.

Rosenblum, L. A., & Kaufman, I. C. Variation in infant development and response to maternal loss in monkeys. *American Journal of Orthopsychiatry,* 1968, **38,** 418-426.

Rowland, G. The effects of total social isolation upon learning and social behavior in rhesus monkeys. Unpublished doctoral dissertation, Univ. of Wisconsin, 1964.

Seay, B., Hansen, E., & Harlow, H. F. Mother-infant separation in monkeys. *Journal of Child Psychology and Psychiatry and Allied Disciplines*, 1962, 3, 123-132.

Seay, B., & Harlow, H. F. Maternal separation in the rhesus monkey. *Journal of Nervous and Mental Disease*, 1965, 140, 434-441.

Spencer-Booth, Y., & Hinde, R. A. The effects of separating rhesus monkey infants from their mothers for six days. *Journal of Child Psychology and Psychiatry and Allied Disciplines*, 1967, 7, 179-197.

Spitz, R. A. Anxiety in infancy: A study of its manifestations in the first year of life. *International Journal of Psycho-Analysis*, 1950, 31, 138-143.

Suomi, S. J., & Harlow, H. F. Apparatus conceptualization for psychopathological research in monkeys. *Behavior Research Methods and Instrumentation*, 1969, 1, 247-250.

# 12

# Psychopathological Consequences of Induced Social Helplessness during Infancy[1]

**JOSEPH B. SIDOWSKI**

University of South Florida

## I. INTRODUCTION

The purpose of this paper is to describe the development of psychopathological behaviors resulting from the physical restraint of infant monkeys in dyadic social situations. I am referring here to the reactions of an animal immobilized, helpless, and without protection in all social interactions with an unrestrained peer.

Of course neither the use nor the study of physical restraint are novel, because immobilization in one form or another has been used for years. Bundling was a common practice in Europe in the sixteenth and seventeenth centuries; restraining stocks served as punishing devices during the American Colonial period; and, until recently, some American Indian tribes practiced infantile movement restriction with swaddling clothes and cradle boards (Dennis, 1940a). J. B. Watson (1924) went so far as to propose that restriction of physical movement provided the source of arousal for a series of responses defined as "rage," one of three basic emotions. Restraint, in this case, involved

[1] This research was carried out during the author's tenure as Visiting Research Scientist at the Wisconsin Regional Primate Research Center. I am indebted to Prof. H. F. Harlow, Director, for extending the invitation and for providing the facilities for the research. Support was provided in part by USPHS Grant FR–0167 from the National Institutes of Health to the University of Wisconsin Regional Primate Research Center. I wish to express my appreciation to Drs. Gene Sackett and Harry F. Harlow without whose stimulation, advice and help this project would not have evolved.

holding the infant's nose or restricting movement of the limbs. Subjecting the theory to test, Dennis (1940b) and others found little support for Watson's notions, but physical constraint continued to be an object of interest and inquiry.

A series of confinement studies by Hebb's group at McGill University (e.g., Bexton, Heron, & Scott, 1954) stimulated a great deal of sensory deprivation research, much of which continues today. The fact that some subjects exhibited psychopathological behaviors is now well known. The effects included hallucinations, delusions, altered EEG patterns, and a general inability to adjust to the conditions of confinement. Mendelson and Foley (1956) report the same types of responses for poliomyelitis patients during treatment in respirators. Apparently children subjected to various periods of immobilizations in plaster casts, splints, and other restraining devices become hyperactive, stubborn, and/or difficult to reach (Friedman, cited by Prescott, 1967). Phenylketonuria (PKU) children with a history of restraint or some sort of sensory deprivation are reported as either hyperactive–destructive or passive–apathetic.

A more drastic effect is reported for captive mammals closely confined in shipping crates. Many of the animals go into a condition resembling hypoglycemic shock and die as a result of an inability to adapt to the emotionally traumatic situation (Christian & Ratcliffe, 1952). Nissen, Chow, and Semmes (1951), on the other hand, indicate few severe effects resulting from the restriction of tactual, kinesthetic, and manipulatory experiences for an infant chimpanzee (Rob) through the first thirty months of life.

There most certainly are psychophysiological and biochemical effects. Ader (1964), Brodie and Hanson (1960), and Sawrey and Sawrey (1968) induced psychogenic ulcers by encapsulating animals in cylindrical confinement devices. And, after tying the rear limbs of rabbits to the sides of cages for periods of 24–72 hr., Brown–Grant, Harris, and Reichlin (1954) found that the associated emotional stress induced a prompt inhibition of one to two days duration in the release of $^{131}$I-labeled hormone from the thyroid gland. Lavenda, Bartlett, and Kennedy (1956) found that encapsulation in cylinders resulted in lymphopenia in mice with a reduction in polymorphonuclear elements; rats developed lymphopenia with a slight increase in polymorphonuclear leucocytes. Finally, in a series of psychoendocrinological studies concerned with the stressful effects of confinement in primate restraining chairs, Mason (1959) and Mason, et al. (1968) report twofold increases in adrenocortical activity for monkeys so immobilized. Plasma 17-OH-CS showed elevation for the first few days of confinement but declined and stabilized by the end of the week. Not all animals, however, showed the effect.

From this brief review, then, it is obvious that experimental investigations of immobilization effects are not novel and that the deleterious effects of restraint are often drastic. Yet, on the whole, we have been dealing with situations in which subjects have been exposed to little more than the conditions of confinement. In the research to be reported here, inquiries were directed to the influence of constraint on social and toy-play behaviors.

The manner in which the experiment began was relatively simple: twelve newborn infant monkeys were removed from their mothers at birth, isolated individually, and then subjected only to the experimenter's manipulations throughout the first six months of life. In the critical experimental condition, one infant was bound physically to a restrainer in the presence of a same aged peer. The latter animal was mobile, unrestricted, and allowed to respond to the thwarted monkey as he wished—sexually, benevolently, sadistically, or otherwise. Thus, incorporating restraint into a minimal social situation (Sidowski, 1957) allowed not only for the study of simple immobilization effects, but it also permitted us to investigate behaviors of current social interest: namely, helplessness and altruism.

Supporters for the inherently altruistic nature of man or beast are not hard to find. Lorenz (1966), for example, postulates for some animals an innate social inhibition against harming others, an inhibition oftentimes elicited by cries of distress. And, on the basis of primate observations and anecdotes, Hebb and Thompson (1954) suggest an innate motivated concern for others. In *The reproductive beginnings of altruism*, Holmes (1945) argues in support of the instinctive nature of helping behavior and for its place in the preservation of species. In the same vein, Campbell (1965) discusses the survival value of being social, and contends that the innate nature of altruism falls into the scheme of things, coexisting with selfishness.

Altruistic type responses have received attention in the laboratory also. Church (1959) conditioned "helping" behavior in rats by subjecting one group of animals to shock experiences and then affording the same subjects the opportunity to turn off the aversive stimulus for other shocked rodents emitting cries of distress. Rice (1965) developed aiding responses in rats (animals pressed a bar to lift another rat out of a water tank) but not in guinea pigs, although there is some question concerning the effect of aversive squeals being no different than that of other noxious auditory stimuli (Lavery & Foley, 1963). That is, the effect may have been simple avoidance. In one of a series of studies, Miller, Caul, and Mirsky (1967) showed that feral monkeys who had been subjected to shock turned off an aversive stimulus for another animal who showed recognizable signs of distress. Monkeys raised in isolation failed the test.

There are, of course, other laboratory experiments, but little firm evidence is provided in any of these operations to indicate an innate predisposition to help another animal in distress. The research merely demonstrates the importance of conditioning and/or experience in the development of such responses. Kreb (1970) injects the proper words of caution when he states that "Although the existence of genetic or biochemical determinants of altruism are a fascinating possibility, it must remain only that until further evidence appears" (p. 262).


II. THE EXPERIMENT

The restrainer used in this study was of clear ¾-in. sheet Plexiglas, 23-in. from top to bottom with an 18-in. crosspiece attached at shoulder level. These measurements allowed for the expected maximum height and girth growth of animals over the six-month period. The device was cruciform in design and precut for easy attachment of the animal's limbs. Subjects were immobilized merely by attaching 2-in. Dermicel surgical tape (Johnson & Johnson Co.) over each of the extended joints of the arms and legs, and by covering the hands and feet; one strip was wrapped around the abdomen. The Dermicel was easily removed with little or no hair adhesion or subsequent subject discomfort. The Plexiglas unit was attached to a metal baseplate enabling speedy attachment by bolts to the floor of the isolation chamber. Thus, the restrainer and subject were kept in an upright position. The front and sides of the infant's body were uncovered and easily accessible to another animal.

Observers viewed the animals through one-way door peepers embedded into the side and front of the Plexiglas enclosed cages. Defined response categories were scored by pressing coded switches connected to banks of counters and electric clocks.

As noted, the subjects were twelve rhesus monkeys (*Macaca mulatta mulatta*) removed from their mothers at birth and, after a few days of nursery care in partial isolation, placed into individual cages enclosed with reflectionless, black Plexiglas. Each S was raised in an isolation chamber through the first six months of life. The conditions were such that the other infants could be heard but not seen. All Ss were reared in a separate experimental room away from the rest of the laboratory colony.

Because of laboratory breeding practices, Ss were committed to the experiment in squads of six. The first six infants were born in July; the second batch was born in February. All experimental conditions were filled with the first squad of Ss. The second six Ss merely served as a replication group counterbalanced for sex. All infants within a squad were born within a few days of each other.

Two of the Ss, the Isolated–Isolates, were raised in isolation during the entire six months. Two additional newborns were similarly reared in individual isolation except that each was bound to a restrainer for 1 hr./day, the Restrained–Isolate condition. Thus, for the four control Ss noted here, the first six months of life were devoid of contact with any other animal. The two Restrained–Isolates, of course, were handled by the experimenter for approximately 3–4 min. daily for purposes of attachment to and removal from the restrainer. For all of these controls, the first social contact with other monkeys was made during social criterion tests given at the conclusion of the six-month isolation period.

The remaining eight Ss were segregated in individual cages for 23 hr. per day. During the 24th hour, pairs of animals were placed together in a minimal social situation. The same two infants were paired each day for the entire half year.

For two of the four pairs, the one hour of social interaction was free and unrestrained. One member of each pair, however, was physically immobilized alone for one hour prior to being introduced to the social period. This treatment, Unrestrained–Social, served as an added control for the major condition of interest. In addition, the dyadic play allowed for a collection of data covering the early development of social responses for isolated twosomes.

In the experimental condition of primary interest (the Restrained–Socials), one infant was bound physically to the restrainer for one hour each day in the presence of his social partner. The unbound member of the dyad was free to roam the cage and to respond to the helpless infant as he wished. One pair of the Restrained–Socials was male and the other was female.

These, then, were the only animal social experiences for eight of the Ss, and they occurred 1 hr./day throughout the first six months of life. The remainder of each day was spent in individual isolation where toy-play and control observations were made daily. The experimental treatments are detailed in Table I. The Ss serving in the restraint conditions were first subjected to immobilization approximately fourteen days after birth.

Toy-play consisted of daily 10-min. sessions in which a colored plastic chain was introduced into the isolation cage of each animal beginning at birth. The toy stimulus was provided to test for possible generalization effects resulting from the constraint conditions. Use of the chain also allowed for the collection of normative data, unavailable at the time for isolated infant Ss, reflecting the early development of toy-play and object manipulation.

Conditions of restraint and toy-play were counterbalanced over parts of the day, 8–12 a.m. or 12–4 p.m. Assignment to a particular order was randomized with the restriction that each condition be represented an equal number of half days over the six-month period.

Control observations were made with the same bias control restrictions and were carried out during those times of the afternoon or morning involving neither restraint nor play. The scored control categories are noted in Table II.

Within either part of the day, the order in which the different Ss in the counterbalanced morning and afternoon periods were subjected to control or toy-play observations was random. Control observations were 15-min. in duration; the plastic chain session lasted 10 min. each day. The experimental periods of restraint and/or social interaction were scored for 1 hr./day.

Well over 1000 hr. of scored behaviors were recorded on coded clocks and

**TABLE I**  First Six Months of $S$'s Life

|  | Daily conditions | | |
|---|---|---|---|
| Experimental treatment | 23 hr./day | 1 hr./day | Social experiences (1 hr./day) |
| Restrained– social dyads | $S_1$ isolated $S_2$ isolated | $S_1$ restrained during social interaction ($S_2$ nonrestrained) | $S_1$ restrained in presence of $S_2$ who is free to behave at will. |
| Nonrestrained– social dyads | $S_1$ isolated $S_2$ isolated | $S_1$ restrained in isolation ($S_2$ nonrestrained) | $S_1$ restrained alone for one hour immediately prior to social experience. Following restraint $S_1$ and $S_2$ placed together for free social interaction. |
| Restrained– isolates | Isolated | $S$ restrained for one hour daily in isolation | None |
| Isolated– isolates | Isolated (24 hr.) | — | None |

**TABLE II**  General Response Categories Scored during Various Phases of the Experiment[a]

| Restrained–social dyads | |
|---|---|
| Responses of restrained $S_1$ | Responses of nonrestrained $S_2$[b] |
| Sleep | Other oral (e.g., biting) |
| Struggle | Tape biting |
| Coo | Self oral |
| Screech | Touch or grabbing other $S$ |
| Rest | Climbing restrainer |
| Looking at other $S$ | Autoerotic |
| Disturbed | Oral–genital stimulation of other $S$ |
| Threat | Looking at restrained $S$ |
|  | Self-sex |
|  | Convulsions |
|  | Vocalization |

TABLE II—*continued*

| All animals—toy sessions (each *S* in isolation) | |
|---|---|
| Mouth toy | Huddle |
| Manipulate | Convulsions |
| Look at toy | Vocalization |
| Touch | Sex |
| Eye to eye (no touch) | Stereotype |
| Carry toy | Motorpathic |
| Thumbsuck | |

| Unrestrained—social dyads[c] (responses scored for both *S*s in dyad) | | |
|---|---|---|
| Disturbed | Vocalization | Approach |
| Touch | Ventral/ventral cling | Flee |
| Look | Ventral/dorsal cling | Aggress |
| Huddle | Sexual thrusting | Play |
| Convulsions | Self-sex | Grooming other *S* |

| Restraint control sessions (*S*₁ restrained alone) | Control observations (during nonexperimental part of day) | Social criterion tests (all *S*s) |
|---|---|---|
| Sleep | Huddle | Activity (moving) |
| Struggle | Vocalizations | Social contact (and with whom) |
| Coo | Thumbsuck | Passivity |
| Screech | Convulsions | Play |
| Rest | Visual explore | Sex |
| | Scratch | Fear |
| | Locomotion | Disturbance |
| | Sex | Stereotype |
| | | Convulsions |
| | | Threat |
| | | Vocalizations |

[a] As behaviors changed with age and experience, other response categories were scored also.
[b] Subjects in this condition were subjected to occasional control sessions in which reactions were scored to the restrainer *per se*, i.e., without a mounted animal.
[c] Categories changed over the six months as animals developed social play behaviors.

counters during the fourteen months covered by this study. Personal comments of each experimenter were logged also, following individual *S* observation sessions.

Two experimenters scored each social interaction session and the social criterion tests carried out at the conclusion of the six-month isolation period.

One observer was used for all other recordings. The same persons were used to score throughout, and, when necessary, the experimenters were counterbalanced over Ss and sessions. After initial training, interobserver reliability was .80 or better for the various response categories.

Table II shows the behavioral categories scored for the various conditions of animal observation. The primary response measures were frequency and duration of event occurrence.

At the conclusion of the six-month isolation period, all Ss were introduced to a series of social criterion tests. Prior to each test, the Ss were adapted individually to the situation (dual cage or playroom) on each of several days. Care was taken that handling by the experimenters was minimal and that no other S was seen until the specific test period.

In the first test, a socially experienced laboratory S of approximately the same age was placed into one side of a dual cage separated by a divider; one of the experimental Ss was placed into the other half. After preadaptation, the cage divider was removed and the two monkeys allowed social contact for 10 min. For the Isolated– and Restrained–Isolates, this social experience was a first; no other animal had ever been seen. For the dyad experienced experimentals, it was the first and only contact with a monkey other than their 1 hr./day experimental partner, as noted in Table I. Over four different days, each experimental S experienced two separate social tests with the same male stranger monkey and two with a nonexperimental female monkey from the laboratory colony.

During the following week, the same sort of social tests were carried out with paired experimental Ss (peer tests). Each infant in the squad of six was paired separately in the dual cage with each of his peers. The procedure was identical with that of the socially experienced stranger tests noted above.

In the final criterion interaction noted in this report, all experimental Ss of the squad were placed in a playroom and scored for social contacts and individual reactions. The playroom was a large well-lit enclosure containing a wall-mounted shelf, gymnastic type chairs and bars, and a one-way observational window. The group interaction was introduced only after the Ss had been adapted to the room separately for 20 min. on each of two days. Following the 40-min. individual preadaptation phase, the six Ss were placed together for over 2 hr./day, on two successive days, in a situation that became endearingly known as the "Snake Pit."

## III. THE BEHAVIORS

Before proceeding with the results, I would like to comment briefly on the manner in which Ss responded to being attached to the restrainer. During the early phases of the experiment, resistance was minimal and fixing the animals was relatively simple. As the infants grew in size, the job became more difficult because of added strength. But the reactions of these Ss were no different than those usually encountered when one normally fetches, holds, transfers, or handles monkeys of the same age. Control observations were made to determine the number of vocalizations, the amount of struggle, etc. emitted under the conditions of solitary constraint. Seven of the Ss so treated spent most of their hourly sessions looking around. Generally, more time was spent dozing in the upright position than struggling. Vocalizations were fairly frequent with coos making up over 80% of the total emitted; the remainder were screeches. The eighth animal (Restrained–Isolate), with or without constraint, was a loud and frequent screecher—a female, of course.

During the six months of isolation, all Ss developed the typical behaviors described by Harlow and Griffin (1965), namely, rocking, huddling, thumbsucking, anal-picking, and sexual self-stimulation. Self-mutilation, i.e., hair-pulling, arm-biting, and striking the head against the side of the cage, as well as catatonictype motorpathic responses (see Figure 1), were noted for the Isolated–Isolates and Restrained–Social infants. The latter Ss, without exception, exhibited the most intense psychopathological responses. And they showed the behaviors much earlier.

Interactions of the two Restrained–Social pairs were most interesting. Initially the restrained Ss of each dyad showed signs of distress by vocalizing, straining against the binding tape, and orienting visually toward the other animal. The vocalizations appeared to be distressful attention-getting devices directed toward the unrestrained infant. The initial reaction of the latter S was to scurry to the corner of the cage, screech, huddle, and rock with an occasional peek over the shoulder at the constrained S. As the days passed, withdrawal gave way to cautious exploration of the cage and of the restrainer metal base, followed by a period of climbing onto the device and over and around the constrained animal with an apparent air of "detachment." A week of cautious exploration gave way to aggressive manipulations of the restricted animal's body which increased steadily in intensity. The behaviors verged on the sadistic and included eye-gouging, forcing the restrainee's mouth open, sexual thrusting, hair and skin pulling, and oral–genital stimulation, all of which became extremely distressful to the helpless infant S. At approximately the tenth week, the latter S suddenly showed a threatening facial grimace, the appearance of which caused the aggressor to flee into a corner of the cage and rock. The appearance of the grimace was instinctive. There had been no opportunity for the animal to observe or to learn such a reaction. Only after a few days of subsequent cautious investigative activity with slight aggression followed by rapid retreat did the mobile infant learn that the frequent grimaces were accompanied by no overt retaliatory activity. The sadistictype behaviors subsequently increased in intensity. Like human youngsters, the aggressor animals learned rapidly that within their restricted environments "Sticks and stones may break my bones but grimaces can never hurt me."

After two to three months of stressful vocalizing and active struggle against the bonds when approached by the self-serving S, the restrained S's emotional reactivity slowly declined and appeared to give way to a hopeless acceptance. Grimaces and screeches were presented but ignored and no advantage was taken of numerous opportunities to bite the oppressor which thrust fingers or sex organs against or into its mouth.

It is interesting to note also that the socially thwarted male S failed to exhibit a penile erection at any time during the experiment, including toy-play, control observations, dual social or post six-month criterion testing. No other male showed this particular inhibitory reaction regardless of experimental condition.

The mobile female S of the Restrained–Social pairs was neither as aggressive nor as sadistic as the male, and during the first three months spent a great deal of the daily dyadic sessions huddling, rocking, and thumbsucking in the presence of the restrainee. At the end of about twelve weeks, however, the female escalated aggressive activity and increased the intensity of sadistic responding. But the female never quite matched the aggressive tempo set by the male.

Behaviors defined as helpful were seldom noticed in the Restrained–Social interactions, although there were occasions when the aggressor would stop manipulatory and exploratory activities because of the severity of the bound S's distress reactions and scurry to the corner of the cage to huddle and rock—a much more frequent occurrence for the female. During the last eight weeks, however, little or no attention was paid to the pained reactions of the helpless subject regardless of intensity of the responses. Yet, assuming an intrinsic motive to aid or empathize, what might the mobile animal do to help? The most obvious reaction would be to not injure, or at least to not repeat behaviors which distress the thwarted infant. A "concerned" organism might even attempt to free the restrained animal by attempting to loosen the binding tapes. But there was little supportive evidence for either hypothesis. The tape was touched, bitten, and manipulated, but less often than during a control condition when the restrainer was available with tape but no helpless infant attached. If we assume that the "observer" primate empathized or sympathized with the distressed restrainee, we might expect some effect to show itself during the toy or control sessions. None occurred. There was a period of several days, at about three months of age, when the socially aggressive female appeared to show a generalized fearful aversion to the toy, a popular plaything prior to and following that time. However, the developmental data indicated a general tendency for change in emotional responsivity at two or four months of age for most of the experimental Ss, suggesting a maturational period of greater susceptibility to emotional stimulation. The direction of change, of course, was a function of the particular animal involved. Infant rhesus monkeys, like human offspring, show distinct individual differences. The more aggressive and active infants, in whatever the measured activity, showed a short-term reactional depression during this transitory period; the more shy animals responded with increased emotional excitation.

Certainly the effects of social restraint were most noticeable in solitary toy-play. The animals constrained and helpless in the presence of another for one social hour a day appeared to develop a "look but do not touch" attitude toward the toy even though it was their only other source of available outside stimulation for six months. This was not the case for the other animals, including the kookiest Isolated–Isolate controls, all of whom developed some sort of playful interaction with the plastic chain. They touched, manipulated, mouthed, and eventually carried the toy in a very spirited manner. Indeed, in some cases subjects showed an unwillingness to give up the object at the conclusion of the daily 10-min. sessions.

Figure 1 shows the amount of toy contact and play for one of the constrained Ss of the Restrained–Social pairs compared to a Restrained–Isolate control. The lack of play activity for the former animal is indicative of that shown by both social restrainees. The male and female were cautious during all early play periods, circling, smelling, and reaching toward the object frequently but seldom touching it. As these Ss grew older, their responses to the toy became more bizarre. Merely placing the stimulus into the cage sent the infant into a huddle, rock, screech, convulsion, or catatonictype reaction. Figure 2 shows a typical motorpathic response; the toy is in the background. Both arms are extended fully at the sides and slowly closed in a circle with the hands eventually meeting above the head (as shown) or in front of the face, with the subject staring constantly at the paws as though they were newly discovered parts of the body or belonged elsewhere.

Now the Social Treatment pairs, all of whom enjoyed a daily hour of free play dyadic interaction, also developed most of the behavior characteristics associated with isolation. In dual and group social criterion tests at the end of six months, however, these infants proved the most aggressive in movement and social contacts, and thus the least abnormal of the Ss. The solitary hour of restraint applied to one member of the pair prior to the daily social interaction appeared to influence its behavior enough to lead to submissiveness in the Social Treatment pair interactions.

In the post six-month dual social criterion tests, the Ss with an hour of daily social play proved to be the least maladjusted of the groups. But their reactions could hardly be categorized as "normal."

For all of the Ss, being introduced to a strange monkey had an initial frightening effect. The Isolated–Isolates and those previously restrained in the presence of another, however, were the most maladjusted. The Isolate Ss

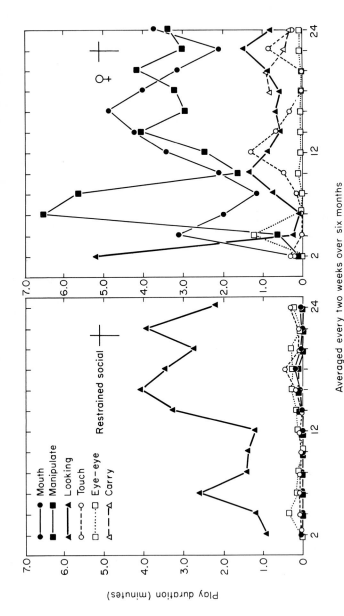

**Figure 1.** The toy-play behavior of two monkeys, a Restrained–Social (left) and a Restrained–Isolate Control (right). Durations of various response categories for the daily 10-min. sessions are averaged over two week intervals for the six-month period.

Figure 2. Psychopathological behavior of a Restrained–Social animal during toy session.

responded by huddling and rocking during all stranger and peer interactions. But the most drastic responses were given by the helpless, thwarted infants of the Social–Restraint pairs; they had never been unrestrained in the presence of another monkey. These monkeys were absolutely terrorized when first confronted with another animal in the dual cage tests. The female screeched, jumped, and convulsed so violently that we considered terminating the session. The male social restrainee froze, and when first touched by the other animal, tilted and fell like a solid concrete block, stirring only after the other monkey moved to another portion of the cage. After the first few social encounters with violent reactions, the formerly harassed Ss adapted slightly. The improvement, however, merely meant that they reverted to huddling, rocking, vocalizing, and, when the other animal drew close, convulsing.

The story was somewhat the same in the playroom tests. The Social Treatment Ss and the Ss which aggressed against the restrainee were the most mobile in exploring the environment. On a whole, however, the playroom was a

"Snake Pit." Figure 3 shows the typical playroom responses of a group of equivalent aged nonexperimental laboratory animals raised together. Harlow and Harlow (1962) describe the manner in which such monkeys cling, play, and explore. Peer or family-raised primates show few of the reactions of the experimental Ss shown in Figure 4. For most of these experimental participants, playtime involved no mutual interaction. The Ss moved only when touched or

Figure 3. A group of nonisolated infants, raised together, interacting in the playroom.

Figure 4. A typical playroom session for the first squad of six animals used in this experiment. Illustrated are three representative psychopathologic responses: hair pulling, huddle, and rocking.

approached by another monkey, and then it was more of a furtive scurry or a bellylike crawl. Figure 5 illustrates a response which was typical for our Isolated–Isolates and the aggressed-against social restrainees. Instead of play, these infants were pictures of despair. And with good reason. The former had no social contacts for the first six months of life; the latter were conditioned not to touch.

**Figure 5.** Typical behavior of Isolated–Isolates and the social restrainees during group playroom sessions.

Theoretically, the data can be interpreted in many ways. The learned helplessness hypothesis of Maier, Seligman, and Solomon (1969) is applicable, although explaining all of the pertinent data would be difficult. Berger's theory (1962) of human conditioning through vicarious instigation is also interesting in its use of classical and instrumental conditioning models to deal with empathy and sadism as determinants of interpersonal behavior. Brown's treatment of thwarting as a source of drive (1961) has appeal, but the explanation is very similar to that expressed by Dennis (1940b) in his critique of Watson's instinctive rage explanation of restraint effects. Of course, there are other ways of looking at the data. But regardless of the interpretation, it is obvious that physical restraint of sorts influences the development of bizarre psycho-pathological behaviors in a manner that differs from those found in isolated isolates, and that the concurrent measurement of generalization effects is vitally important as an experimental technique. If helpful or altruistic behaviors have an instinctive origin, the conditions of this experiment failed to show it. On the other hand, sadistictype aggressions were common and unlearned. Of course, there were other effects, but these will not be discussed here.

A final point: at the conclusion of this study, the first squad of animals was assigned to the depression-inducing pit described by Soumi and Harlow (1969). In spite of the mentally debilitating effect of this environment on most subjects, the formerly oppressed social restrainees showed a remarkable tolerance for frustration over the first four to six weeks of this experience. The more aggressive of our experimental *Ss* did not. Reports of these adjustments, however, will have to await the completion of further observations.

## REFERENCES

Ader, R. Gastric erosions in the rat: Effects of immobilization at different points in the activity cycle. *Science*, 1964, 145, 406-407.

Berger, S. M. Conditioning through vicarious instigation. *Psychological Review*, 1962, 69, 450-466.

Bexton, W. H., Heron, W., & Scott, T. H. Effects of decreased variation in the sensory environment. *Canadian Journal of Psychology*, 1954, 8, 70-76.

Brodie, D. A., & Hanson, H. M. A study of the factors involved in the production of gastric ulcers by the restraint technique. *Gastroenterology*, 1960, 38, 353-360.

Brown, J. S. *The motivation of behavior.* New York: McGraw-Hill, 1961.

Brown-Grant, K., Harris, G. W., & Reichlin, S. The effect of emotional and physical stress on thyroid activity in the rabbit. *Journal of Physiology*, 1954, 126, 29-40.

Campbell, D. T. *Ethnocentric and other altruistic motives. Nebraska Symposium on Motivation*, 1965, 13, 283-311.

Christian, J. J., & Ratcliffe, H. L. "Shock disease" in captive wild mammals. *American Journal of Pathology*, 1952, 28, 725-740.

Church, R. M. Emotional reactions of rats to the pain of others. *Journal of Comparative and Physiological Psychology*, 1959, 52, 132-134.

Dennis, W. Infant reaction to restraint: An evaluation of Watson's theory. *Transactions of the New York Academy of Science*, 1940a, 2 (No. 8), 202-218.

Dennis, W. The effect of cradling practices upon the onset of walking in Hopi children. *Journal of Genetic Psychology*, 1940b, 56, 77-86.

Harlow, H. F., & Griffin, G. Induced mental and social deficits in rhesus monkeys. In S. F. Osler and R. E. Cooke (Eds.), *The biosocial basis of mental retardation.* Baltimore: Johns Hopkins Press, 1965.

Harlow, H. F., & Harlow, M. K. Social deprivation in monkeys. *Scientific American*, 1962, 207 (5), 136-146.

248                                                                        JOSEPH B. SIDOWSKI

Hebb, D. O., & Thompson, W. R. The social significance of animal studies. In G. Lindzey (Ed.), *Handbook of social psychology. Vol. 1. Theory and method.* Cambridge: Addison-Wesley, 1954.
Holmes, S. J. The reproductive beginnings of altruism. *Psychological Review*, 1945, **52**, 109-112.
Kreb, D. L. Altruism—An examination of the concept and a review of the literature. *Psychological Bulletin*, 1970, **73**, 258-302.
Lavenda, N., Bartlett, R. G., & Kennedy, V. E. Leucocyte changes in rodents exposed to cold with and without restraint. *American Journal of Physiology*, 1956, **184**, 624-626.
Lavery, J. J., & Foley, P. J. Altruism or arousal in the rat? *Science*, 1963, **140**, 172-173.
Lorenz, K. *On aggression.* New York: Harcourt, Brace and World, 1966.
Maier, S. F., Seligman, M. E. P., & Solomon, R. L. Pavlovian fear conditioning and learned helplessness: Effects on escape and avoidance behavior of (a) the CS-US contingency and (b) the independence of the US and voluntary responding. In B. A. Campbell and R. M. Church (Eds.), *Punishment and aversive behavior.* New York: Appleton-Century-Crofts, 1969.
Mason, J. W. Psychological influences on the pituitary-adrenal cortical system. *Recent Progress in Hormone Research*, 1959, **15**, 345-378.
Mason, J. W., Wool, M. S., Wherry, F. E., Pennington, L. L., Brady, J. V., & Beer, B. Plasma growth hormone response to avoidance sessions in the monkey. *Psychosomatic Medicine*, 1968, **30**, 760-773.
Mendelson, J., & Foley, J. M. Abnormality of mental function affecting patients with poliomyelitis in a tank type respirator. *Transactions of the American Neurological Association*, 1956, **81**, 134-138.
Miller, R. E., Caul, W. F., & Mirsky, I. A. Communication of affects between feral and socially isolated monkeys. *Journal of Personality and Social Psychology*, 1967, **7**, 231-239.
Nissen, H. W., Chow, K. L., & Semmes, J. Effects of restricted opportunity for tactual, kinesthetic, and manipulative experience on the behavior of a chimpanzee. *American Journal of Psychology*, 1951, **64**, 485-507.
Prescott, J. W. The psychobiology of maternal-social deprivation and etiology of violent-aggressive behavior: A special case of sensory deprivation. Paper presented at San Diego State College, San Diego, California on July 18, 1967.
Rice, G. E., Jr. Aiding responses in rats: Not in guinea pigs. Paper presented at the meeting of the American Psychological Association, Chicago, September, 1965.
Sawrey, W. L., & Sawrey, J. M. UCS effects on ulceration following fear conditioning. *Psychonomic Science*, 1968, **10**, 85-86.
Sidowski, J. B. Reward and punishment in a minimal social situation. *Journal of Experimental Psychology*, 1957, **54**, 318-326.
Suomi, S. J., & Harlow, H. F. Apparatus conceptualization for psychopathological research. *Behavior Research Methods and Instrumentation*, 1969, **1**, 247-250.
Watson, J. B. *Behaviorism.* New York: Norton, 1924.

# Author Index

# Subject Index

## A

Abnormalities, chromosomal, 34
"Abulia," 82
Acquisition, 72, 74, 75, 76, 77, 89, 178
  fear, 178
Acquisition processes, 73, 74
Activity
  maladaptive, 42
  muscular, 38
Adaptation, 19
  natural, 166
Adaptive economy, 168
Adaptive inhibitory process, 169
Adaptive instrumental response, 167
Adaptive mechanisms, 177
Adaptive processes, 176, 177
Adaptiveness, 53
Addiction, 32
Adjustment
  adaptive, 169
  inhibitory 173
Adrenal medullary systems, 120
Adrenergic action, 165
Adventitious, 78, 178
Aggression, 22, 193, 196, 197
  shock-elicited, 84
Aggressive behavior, 215
Aggressive responses, 83, 84, 187
Aggressor, 240
Albumin, 127
Alcoholism, 73, 83
Alternatives, rewarding, 73
"Altruism," 22, 232
"Anal aggression," 16
Angiotonin, 45
Animal level, 72

Animal motivation, 183
Anthropomorphic, 19
Anthropomorphizing, 18
Antisocial behavior, 80
Anxiety, 38
Appetitive salivary conditioning, 169
Approach(es)
  behavioristic, 10
  comparative, 16
  dynamic psychobiological, 11
  two-stage, 2
Approach behavior, food-reinforced, 101
Arterial pressure, 148
Astrology, 1
Astronomy, 1
Attenuation of the CR, 173
Autism, 82
Autisticlike behaviors, 71
Autokinesis, 11, 42, 45
  negative, 43
  positive, 43
Autonomic changes, 120, 121, 123
Autonomic effects, 124
Autonomic–endocrine system, 142, 143
Autonomic nervous system, 10, 117, 172
Autonomic symptoms, exaggerated, 38
Autonomically mediated responses, 52, 121, 179
Aversive, 75
  consequences, 76, 85
  contingencies, 121, 135
  event, 55, 80
Avoidance, 75, 76, 89, 90, 96, 100, 123, 166, 169, 171, 172, 173, 190, 193, 197
  conditioning, 121, 172, 173, 185
  behavior, 80, 82, 83, 87